Y0-CBL-399

PRIVATE SCREENINGS, by JOHN SIMON

John Simon is well known to movie buffs for his pungent wit and his unique flair for flaying both picture and director. He has been called "at times hilarious," "right so maddeningly often," and "the man you love to hate." *Private Screenings* is a collection of his infamous views on the cinema, particularly from 1963 to 1966, during which time Mr. Simon viewed and reviewed all of the important and many of the supremely unimportant movies—among them, 8½, DR. ZHIVAGO, TOM JONES, DR. STRANGELOVE, ALFIE, BLOW-UP, VIRGINIA WOOLF, A MAN AND A WOMAN, MORGAN, SCORPIO RISING, THE CHELSEA GIRLS and LAWRENCE OF ARABIA.

"Particularly valuable account of 20-Century European film making and . . . an admirable addition to the literature of the cinema"

—*Library Journal*

"Simon is a major critic, and this is a major book, perhaps *the* book of this decade's films"

—*Film Fan Monthly*

"No movie critic writing today who can match him"

—*Baltimore Sun*

PRIVATE SCREENINGS

JOHN SIMON

A BERKLEY MEDALLION BOOK
PUBLISHED BY
BERKLEY PUBLISHING CORPORATION

Copyright © 1967 by John Simon

All rights reserved

Published by arrangement with The Macmillan Company

BERKLEY MEDALLION EDITION, FEBRUARY, 1971

THE AUTHOR wishes to thank the following publications and institutions for which some of this material was originally produced. Chapters 3 to 6 originally appeared in *The New Leader,* except for "Two From Below," which was delivered over WNDT, Channel 13, New York City. "Spotlight on the Nonwoman" appeared in *Holiday* Magazine. "A Critical Credo" was a lecture delivered to the Summer Institute of the National Film Board of Canada, and "Godard and the Godardians" was given as a lecture at Williams College, Williamstown, Massachusetts.

SBN 425-01951-9

*BERKLEY MEDALLION BOOKS are published by
Berkley Publishing Corporation
200 Madison Avenue
New York, N.Y. 10016*

BERKLEY MEDALLION BOOKS ® TM 757,375

Printed in the United States of America

CONTENTS

For Patricia

and

in memory of Joan Drooker

(1932-1960)

ONE

A CRITICAL CREDO

The most important thing to remember about film criticism is that it is not fundamentally different from any other kind of criticism. But because criticism itself remains such a largely misunderstood and therefore feared and hated concept, it may be well to posit one's general critical credo before proceeding to film criticism proper. Now if there is anything the public avoids more than criticism, it is discussions and theories of criticism; yet these, consumed in moderation, could serve as useful energizers of both criticism and the audience, leading, I hesitate to say to better art, but at least to better conditions for art, which is not so very different a thing.

Matthew Arnold called poetry the criticism of life; it is not impossible to invert the formula and call criticism the poetry of life. For if I understand Arnold correctly, he means that poetry, by setting before man an ideal existence with thought and feeling performing to the utmost of their capacities, urges him to recognize the insufficiencies of the routine he calls living and directs him toward the heights. If this is so, then true criticism, which renders explicit the achievements and shortcomings of art—man's noblest aspiration—is in fact a kind of poetry, a poetry of hate for what is ugly or false, and of love for what is beautiful and true. I realize that it has become un-fashionable in life—let alone in criticism—to use terms like "ugly" and "beautiful," but I accept the charge of being unfashionable with satisfaction and even, I confess, with pride.

The most common attacks on criticism (and especially on movie criticism, which, being as yet young and feeble, can least defend itself) are either that it is unconstructive or that it is unnecessary. Unnecessary, apparently, because the public can think for itself: if a book, a painting, a film is good, it will be accepted; if it is bad, it will fail. What need, then, for critics? The most obvious answer is that the world of art is full of works whose true worth or worthlessness took far too long to be comprehended, and that even if time does sit in just and inexorable judgment, its courts are apt to be as cruelly procrastinatory as those described by Dickens and Kafka. To the extent that criticism can accelerate the verdict of the ages, it can speed up the coming of pleasure and enlightenment, and, no less important, spare us the waste of what as mortals we have the least of—time.

Without criticism there would be no dialogue, and it is staggering to contemplate what would have been the history—if any—of government, education, philosophy, psychiatry, and any other important discipline of learning or aspect of life without dialectics, without the chance of both sides being heard and hearing each other. Without criticism, the artist receives no serious answer; we must, on solid empirical evidence, consider failure or success with the mass of one's contemporaries as nothing more than a snort from the crowd, to be interpreted however one pleases. It is not important that the critical answer be that of an infallible oracle—what oracle ever was that?—it matters merely that a critical answer be the best of which a sensitive, experienced, eloquent, and honest mind and sensibility are capable. Thereby a purposeful is-sue is joined: the keen yet bloodless struggle for human fulfillment, which it was once permissible to call the pur-suit of truth and beauty.

But what of "destructive" criticism, which is far and wide alleged to be bad? The terms "constructive" and "destructive," as applied to criticism, have no meaning whatever. There is only good and bad criticism. What indeed might "constructive" mean in reference to a critique? From the author in question, "Like me, don't knock me!" which is an absurd request. From the pedagogue, "Show him or her where and how the thing could be improved!" But any genuine artist would resent the critic's offering to remake his work; only school compositions can so be treated by teachers, and it may be that even they should not. I cannot write someone else's book, play, or scenario for him; I can only point out where and why he lost me—and that, I suppose, would already be called "destructive" criticism. To the casual layman, "constructive" criticism would be, "Go easy on him, he is doing his best." But this is the worst fallacy of all: it assumes that art does not really matter. If a surgeon's patients die on him, one after the other, does one excuse him by saying he did his best? Can a statesman's, a military commander's, an educator's errors be excused so cheaply? No; because those things *matter*. Whereas art, it would seem, does not.

But to the critic to whom art is important, sacred, and, ultimately, coextensive with life itself, to produce bad art and finally drive out the good—are the two most heinously dangerous sins imaginable. And the most destructive. Still the temperate person will say, "All right, forget about 'destructive' and 'constructive'—but couldn't you just be more moderate in your dislikes?" Different evils need different modes of attack: from Swiftian *saeva indignatio* to subtle puncturing, from "more in sorrow than in anger" to *reductio ad absurdum,* one chooses whichever method is most suitable; or, if one is less versatile, whichever method one is best suited to. The critic's words are his tools, or weapons, and he would be foolish and incompetent if he did not use them to the utmost of his, and their, ability. If the critic is mistaken or too harsh, time eventually proves him wrong—much more quickly than it

would a bad artist, because here it can rely on the enthusiastic help of the critic's colleagues. The genuine artist
cannot be destroyed by words: It is not the *Quarterly,*
"savage and tartarly," but consumption that killed John
Keats. And the man who slings mud pies at the Venus de
Milo hits only himself.

Good criticism and bad criticism, then; but what constitutes good criticism? Perhaps it is easiest to begin by
defining the commonest kind of bad criticism, which is not
criticism at all but reviewing. Reviewing is something that
newspaper editors have invented: it stems from the notion
that the critic is someone who must see with the eyes of
the Average Man or Typical Reader (whoever that is)
and predict for his fellows what their reaction will be. To
this end, the newspapers carefully screen their reviewers to
be representative common men, say, former obituary
writers or mail-room clerks, anything but trained spe-
cialists. To accept such a reviewer as critic and guide is
like expecting school children to reach one another, or patients in a hospital ward to undertake one another's cure.
A critic excites the public's curiosity, wonder, suspicion,
rage, and enthusiasm; a reviewer elicits mostly one of
two reactions: "Good! That's another one I don't have to
see!" or "Great! I like it already." Both reactions stifle
thought instead of encouraging the audience and, with
luck, even the artist to grow.

Now the good critic is, first and foremost, a teacher.
One problem, among many, with our education is that it
ends. After a certain number of years, always too few, the
last textbook is shut, the door closes on the last
classroom, and we are free—free not only to desist from
all further learning, but also to forget what we have
learned so far. How many of us can pass up such a golden
opportunity? This is where the critic comes in. With
cogency, suasion, passion, charm he induces us to think,
to widen our horizons, to open yet another book, to recon-
sider a snap judgment, to see something from a loftier
vantage point, in historic perspective, and using more and
truer touchstones. Good criticism of any kind—of movies,

ballet, architecture, or whatever—makes us think, feel, respond; if we then agree or disagree is less important than the fact that our faculties have been engaged and stretched. Good criticism informs, interprets, and raises the ultimate questions, the unanswerable ones that everyone must try to answer none the less. This is teaching of the highest order.

Secondly, the true critic is an artist. "Criticism is a good thing, but poetry is a better," wrote Richard Le Gallienne. As a poet, he had every reason to preconize poetry; as a bad one, every reason to patronize criticism. But even the most enthusiastic practitioner of criticism, if he is not Oscar Wilde, would refrain from placing it above poetry; it would, however, be wrong to deny that a good piece of criticism must be as well written and shaped as, *mutatis mutandis,* a poem, a story, or a personal essay. It is, therefore, in its own way a work of art. As that remarkable but still under-rated German playwright, poet, and novelist Frank Wedekind put it, "Without doubt, the systematic execution of a critique written with a sense of responsibility is a more difficult, worthy, and, even for art, more valuable task than the writing of mediocre plays." And he went on, "Critic and author are . . . different stages of development of the same calling. The two are collaborators on the same project." The critic, as that enlightened poet Pierre Reverdy saw him, *"fait, avec plus de liberté, l'office du melleur ami."* But the artist will accept the friendship of the critic only if he recognizes in him a fellow-artist: why should friendship become misalliance? In his occasionally *outré* but generally highly perceptive essay. "The Critic as Artist," Wilde observed, "the critic is he who exhibits to us a work of art in a form different from that of the work itself, and the employment of a new material is a critical as well as a creative element." Wilde called criticism "a creation within a creation" and so the purest form of creativity, and indeed the piece of criticism that cannot be read by a civilized and concerned person without knowledge of the work or artist discussed is not a true critique. And that which can be so

read is more than a review; it is a work of the con-
templative imagination, a work of art. So we can read
Longinus or Lessing, Sainte-Beuve or Hazlitt, without more than a general awareness of the writers that
were their points of departure. And in reading a drama review of Shaw or Beerbohm it is scarcely necessary
to have seen the production in question to savor the matter and the manner of the review as literature. Of which
one of our film critics is this true? How many people now
writing about movies are worth reading even when the
particular film is still fresh in our memories, and our
desire to discuss it still sovereign?

Thirdly, the critic is or should be a thinker. In an age
when philosophy has removed itself into theology or
science or even, of all places, literary criticism, it becomes
incumbent on the critic to turn philosopher. To quote
Wilde's essay once more, "the highest Criticism . . . is the
record of one's own soul." In other words, the critic must
have a world view, which, however one may wish to
disguise it, is a moral position. Nothing is more suspect in
criticism nowadays than a moral position, and yet there
can be no criticism without one. The moment something
appears to us better or worse than something else, we are
being moralists—for aesthetics is the morality of art, just
as morality is the aesthetics of living. But if criticism cannot do without morality, it can easily remain unaware of
its underlying morality, and the penalty for such
unawareness if inferior criticism. What form this morality
will take is comparatively unimportant; it may be—and I
myself would wish it to be—neither an established system
nor the systematization of a yet unestablished one. It
should be, as nearly as I can describe it, a relevance to
human life, an elegance of spirit, a generosity and
adventuresomeness of outlook, and above all, a concept or
intimation of what the ideal solution to an artistic problem
would be, and the dogged insistence on measuring every
performance against the envisioned model. It should never
judge something, as is commonly done, on how well it fulfills its own aims, for by that standard, if it sets out to be

only junk, junk will have to be found excellent. Essential too is an awareness of reconciled opposites: of the joy inherent in tragedy and of the pathos no true comedy can be without.

But I am not trying to develop a whole critical philosophy here. I am merely pleading for, or insisting on, the necessity of a realized philosophy translated into artistic expression as the irreducible minimum of the true critic's equipment. And it will be useful to bear always in mind the statement of the great sixteenth-century Spanish Jesuit Baltasar Gracián: "Not only in words, but also in works is lying practiced, and the latter form of lying is much the more dangerous."

With these general remarks out of the way, we may pass to considerations pertaining specifically to film criticism. The problem here is acute: Whereas the other arts seem to be blessed with more or less the critics they deserve—with modern music, painting, and sculpture receiving, as their just deserts, the most inept kind of criticism—film, which may well be the salient and vital art form of our day is getting hardly less imcompetent criticism as a gratuitous insult. The main trouble is that most intellectuals, even if willing to concede that film is an art, would not consider criticizing it an art or even a serious occupation, perhaps because there are not enough serious film critics, or indeed serious films, around to get a meaningful dialogue started. A case in point is Kenneth Tynan, whose drama criticism was, whatever particulars one might cavil with, manifestly serious (and let me make clear, once and for all, that by serious I do not mean long-faced), but whose film criticism, however much one may enjoy it, is patently frivolous. The fundamental problem, I suppose, is that film is being taken, ultimately, as an "entertainment" as opposed to a work of art, as if art and entertainment were mutually exclusive or, at least, separate entities, as form and content or meaning and style were once thought to be. While no one today would dare to think of form and content as separate or, except for purposes of classroom demonstration, separable, it still seems the most natural thing to erect a fence between the few films that "have something to say" and the many that are "merely amusements," and, apparently, come up with roughly equal endorsement for films in both groups, albeit by a double standard involving different scales.

Now I submit that the first responsibility of the film critic is to recognize that there is, to be sure, a superficial difference between comedy and tragedy, and a profound one between good and bad, but that to view and review *all* films as anything but an art is at best trivial and at worst stupid—always bearing in mind that I am talking of the serious critic. Suppose that I were speaking here as a literary critic, seriously and literarily (as opposed to banteringly or sociologically), and discussed the works of Herman Wouk or Leon Uris or James Michener. I should justly be considered, *ipso facto,* critically, if not indeed mentally, incompetent. But if, as a film critic, I were to present a rapturous tribute to the films of a Blake Edwards or Otto Preminger, or if I were to disgorge high-sounding effusions about the work of Godard or Chabrol (and, who knows, perhaps even that of Stan Brakhage or Jack Smith), I would be listened to with earnestness and deference, as if I were not dealing with men who are, in one case, hacks and charlatans, in the other, pretentious flounderers—and this despite the fact that one or the other of them may have stumbled on something useful, may have a certain facility, and may have even, *mirabile dictu,* turned out a passable film.

The point is that the critic—as distinguished from the historian, the sociologist, the collector, the faddist—has no business considering entertainment as an end in itself, any more than he may consider art, in film or elsewhere, as something dreary and unentertaining. This does not mean, of course, that the critic should refuse to review a so-called entertainment film: we do not as yet have enough films that are art, or even aspiring to that condition, yet serious criticism must go on. To adapt a saying of Clémenceau's, the reviewing of films, such as they may be, is much too serious a matter to be left in the hands of mere reviewers. And it is crucial to remember that there is no genuine entertainment without artistry, just as there can be no art that is unabsorbing, i.e., boring. There is, however this proviso: Artistry is not quite on the same level as art.*

A distinguished Polish film-maker and teacher remarked to me not long ago that we talk so much about film as art, yet there have been in the whole history of the cinema thus far no more than, at best, two works of indubitable art. I think that the number is higher, though not very much higher; I must also, in principle, agree. Hardly anyone writing about film today would maintain, for example, that D. W. Griffith was not an artist; yet, to me, he is the epitome of the nonartist, no matter how much he may have contributed to the *technique* of the film. I would say that Griffith is to the art of cinema what Achilles Tatius was to the art of the novel. Or that Griffith did for film what Sackville and Norton, the authors of *Gorboduc,* did for the English drama. And this, clearly, not because a film like *Birth of a Nation* is morally objectionable, but because it is artistically and intellectually insufficient.

This might begin to sound like support for all those potentially qualified film critics who prefer to abstain because of the grim prospect of bringing superior equipment to bear on nothing or next to nothing. It might be suggested here that Aristotle was able to write extraordinarily fine dramatic criticism at a time when there were only a half dozen dramatists worth considering. But the position of the film critic today is truely anomalous: It is to be confronted with an art that, even though it has done remarkably well in the short span of six decades, has not had anywhere near enough time to develop fully; and to

---

* Allowances must, I suppose, be made for such a category as "failed art." *Paradise Regained,* or most of Blake's prophetic books, for example, are art in intention, and do not make the compromises of pseudoart. But works which intelligent readers (except, perhaps, contemporaries struck by their timeliness) will read only under duress might as well be considered failed or nonart.

confront it with a critical discipline that, even if only in related fields, has acquired a vast tradition and imposing expertise and sophistication. The main thing the critic can do while waiting for the day when it will be possible to limit oneself to writing serious criticism about serious films for serious publications is, with every means at his command, to help bring about that day.

The age is eminently ripe for film to become a true art. For this is only possible when something newer and more profitable exists to syphon off the most irresponsible, inartistic, greedy elements from an older art. "It is unimaginable," wrote Friedrich Dürrenmatt, "what would have to be played on the stage nowadays if film had not been invented and the screenwriters were turning out stage plays." This statement can now be revised: It is inconceivable what trash would be put on film these days if television had not been invented, and the TV writers were functioning as scenarists. As it is, far too many of them are.

The next responsibility of the critic is to recognize the difficulties inherent in the form of film. There are simple and complex arts. Fiction, for example, is a simple art, based on the word. So too is painting, based—until recently, anyway—on the image. Conversely, ballet, opera, film are complex arts. Although this is not a value judgment, implying that complex arts are superior to simple ones, or vice versa, writing good criticism of a complex art presents a multiplicity of problems. Now, to make thing a little easier for the critic, one aspect of a complex art usually far surpasses the others in importance. Ballet is perfectly possible without costumes and sets, and even music has been dropped in some recent experiments. Opera could do without words, using nonsense syllables, which most librettos quite successfully approximate already. Modern composers, like Stravinsky, have tended to use the voice purely as an instrument; and even the best texts are likely to be of little avail: What the elaborate orchestration does not swallow, the singer's diction certainly will.

But film is the one complex art in which two main components are equally important: text and cinematography, that is, word and image. The youthful critic, contemptuous of words and proud, like the young filmmaker, of "thinking in film"—which means, I suppose, perceiving the whole work as images—should beware: Words are no less important than pictures. But the old-school critic should also be wary: Pictures are no less important than words. A film that is all image and poor words is like a beautiful woman who, the moment she opens her mouth, offends us. We cannot love her. But neither can we love a brilliantly eloquent woman who is ugly as sin. In any case, the relation between image and word is much more intimate than some people realize: Even in silent or near-silent films the mind tends to translate seen actions into words—so that the word, excluded, creeps in by the back door.

Now because film is such a complex—perhaps, indeed, a total—art, the ideal film critic would have to be conversant with cinematography, literature, acting techniques, painting and sculpture (form and composition), music, dance (film musicals), and in view of the generally poor subtitles, as many foreign languages as possible. Can one encompass all this? I dare say that when T. S. Eliot gave as *the* requirement for a critic that he be "very intelligent," he was not thinking of the film critic. Otherwise, I suspect, he would have had to say "very, very intelligent." But ironically, as we shall see, it is precisely some of the least intelligent people who wander into film criticism.

We have now reached the point where it is appropriate to indicate some of the things a film critic should not be. Film criticism, like film-making, is a field that attracts the anti-intellectual—whether he be an intellectual turned sour, or a bona fide anti-intellectual of long standing. Now, whereas film-making does not require a rational basis, film criticism does. Yet it is all too readily conceived of as some kind of game, if not, indeed a con-game, or even a form of public defiance—something withal that enjoys enough of a vogue to make it look like work. Thus, for example, the people who evolved and practice the *auteur* theory were playing a faddist in-game, which does not begin to hold up under rational scrutiny, yet they were able to corner a large part of the critical market. (I use the unsavory metaphor advisedly.) But film criticism, again like film, has particular appeal for an even worse crowd, the lunatic fringe, because it offers a perfect substitute world. The fact that film, of all arts, comes closest to looking both like life and like dreams, both like palpable reality and like wish-fulfillments made manifest, makes it the preferred medium for escape: it has neither the arrant artifices and inescapable limitations of the theatre, nor the crippling self-censorship and disintoxicating commercials of television to cope with. Thus it invites us on a voyage where all is *luxe, calme et volupté,* or, if we would rather, *luxe, frénésie et volupté,* and the seekers of artificial paradises flock right in. Consider the so-called Underground Cinema with its party fun and games that become films, and its film screenings that turn into fun and game parties in an uninterrupted daisy chain, non-world without end. And, in due time, the lunatic fringe evolves its own critics, even while it gradually wears down the resistance of those reviewers initially opposed to it.

And even when it is not the fanatical movie buff who turns critic, the temptation is great for the critic to become a movie buff, which is the exact opposite of being a critic. Because the history of the film is short and because film comes at one automatically, the way a book, for instance, does not, the critic may be seduced into trying to see as nearly every film as possible. Only, though the history of film may indeed be short, it is also extremely wide: the output is tremendous. What self-respecting literary critic would try to keep up with every novel, or even every slightly better novel, that comes along, to say nothing of all the other literary genres? That way lies madness. So, if our man is not already a madman when he becomes a film critic, he stands an excellent chance of ending up as one.

Yet, heaven knows, the film critic needs every bit of

lucidity and resoucefulness to do justice to a job in which
mountains of difficulty insist on mistaking him for
Mohammed. It is part of the critic's responsiblity to be
unremittingly aware of the almost insuperable problems
that face him the moment he wishes to be more than the
reviewer of a specific film that happens to come his way,
or, given that situation, to write something that will have
widespread and lasting value.

A book can be read slowly and reread. The painting
usually, though nowadays not always, stands still; it is also
available in reproduction. Music places score, text (if
there is one), and recordings into one's hands. Even the
ballet critic has the advantage of viewing and reviewing
certain ballets over and over again, and thus knowing at
least some of the staples of the repertoire practically by
heart. In film, even where a printed script is obtainable,
the critic depends on a few notes—often, because they
have to be scribbled in haste and darkness, illegible—and
on his evanescent memory of a fleeting experience.

And even if a cinematheque is at the critic's disposal—but how many of us are so privileged?—he still
cannot take the film home with him and ponder it at
leisure. True, some film lending libraries are beginning to
be heard of, but they are as yet only little more than a tan-
talizing promise, a drop in the bucket, and the problems
surrounding lending libraries being what they are, it is
doubtful that this bucket will ever quench anyone's thirst.
To be sure, new inventions may come along, but I am not
trying to practice Utopian criticism here. In any case, the
critic will eventually need to have his own film library,
just as today's literary critic and scholar has his own
essential books. But even that is not the end of our problems. However much access the critic may have to films,
his readers will most likely not have it. In this way it
becomes, in the large number of cases, hard or impossible
for the reader to verify the critic's contentions. But, worst
of all, there is no way of accurately *quoting* film: Still
photographs can barely do justice to stationary objects of
art; dialogue conveys only a fragment of what happens in

a film. Verbal evocation also has a hard time of it: If you use technical terminology to explain shots and camera movements, you may very well lose your reader, and will certainly end up boring him; if you use impressionistic, imaged prose, unless you are very skillful indeed, you may wander far afield. Thus a genuine understanding, let alone a dialogue, between critic and reader is almost impossible.

As if all this were not enough, the film critic is also up against a space problem, though, unlike greater powers with such problems, he is not asking for the moon, merely for enough space in a paper or magazine to develop his ideas and impressions. But the space accorded him is usually quite insufficient, precisely because film, as we said before, has so many components. Consequently it is the rarest thing to find a review that can begin to do justice to the manifold achievements and lacks of the film it deals with.

And there is apt to be yet a further obstacle. Because film represents such a large financial investment for the producers, the honestly outspoken critic, if he is working for an influential publication, becomes a threat to Hollywood. As a result, many are the tales of critics losing their jobs, or not even getting them, because of pressure—direct or indirect, actual or merely anticipated—from the big film companies.

If one contemplates the obstacles I have just enumerated, one might well consider undertaking to write film criticism an act of singular, if not suicidal, desperation. And yet, more than ever, good film criticism is needed. For, even though film production is more massive, far-flung, and ambitious than ever, the average quality has not substantially progressed since the time when Pablo Neruda's solitary gentleman took his newly seduced girl out for an evening,

> *y la lleva a los miserables cinematógrafos*
> *donde los héroes son potros y príncipes apasionados*
>   . . .

(and he takes her to the wretched movies where the heroes are horses or passionate princes), and, I might add, there is usually not that much difference between the two. The first and last responsibility of the film critic, then, is—prepare yourselves for a thundering truism—to raise the standard of motion pictures.

Unfortunately this is not nearly so self-evident as it might be to one segment of the population: the movie reviewers. To be sure, they will all tell you that they are in love with excellence; meanwhile, however, they are perfectly happy in their sordid concubinage with the second-rate. How depressingly they will latch on to this scene or that brief moment, gush over some very funny bit performer or a few clever little directorial touches. Now I am myself pathetically grateful for the slightest bit of genuine quality or inventiveness, in whichever corner of a movie I can track it down, but that does not mean that I am willing to forgo my appetite for the best in the work as a whole, or that I will bend over backward to justify that whole by one or two tolerable parts. It is not enough to love the good, it is also necessary to hate the bad; indeed, I submit that he who does not hate the bad cannot truly love the good. *Qui bene amat, bene castigat*: there is no rodless way of bringing up the movie industry, a big, fat, and extraordinarily corrupt baby. Of course, one is not infallible, but one must believe that one is: Nothing is less interesting to a reader than lack of conviction, usless it be lack of wit or poetry.

Yes, those two are the chief gifts the gods can bestow on a film critic: a poetic style to evoke the lovelinesses, the subtleties, the excitement of film; and a coruscating wit, whose edge is sharp enough—I draw the image from C. D. De Mille's *The Crusades*—to cut a falling feather in two. If you have those two qualities, you do not need anything else—except, needless to say, a point of view; but it is unlikely that a critic who is a poet and a wit would lack a point of view.

If you are a true film critic (or, for that matter, a true critic of any art form), there are three questions that are bound to haunt you wherever you go. They are, in fact, the same question manifesting itself in three guises, rather like Robert Graves's Triple Goddess. Its most commonplace form is, "Have you liked *anything* lately?" If this question embarrasses you, because, indeed, you haven't liked anything lately, you might just as well turn in your critic's hat immediately. If this question does not embarrass you, because you've liked quite a few things recently, you might also just as well turn in your hat. If, however, you are a real critic, you simply stare brazenly at the questioner and say, "There were a good many films I would have liked to like." Or, "It is press agents who are in the business of liking films."

Now for the second form of the haunting question, usually uttered with a patronizing sneer, "Do you *like* movies?" The obvious answer to this would be, "Yes, more than you; otherwise I would not accept so many substitutes." But politeness may be preferable, in which case it is good to have to hand a memorized list of favorite films; it does not matter how old they are, the mere quantity and rapid-fire comeback will silence the interrogator. My own favorite dozen, my all-time greats, in no particular order, is as follows: Ingmar Bergman's *The Naked Night* and *Smiles of a Summer Night,* Federico Fellini's *The White Sheik* and *I Vitelloni,* Antonioni's *L'Avventura,* Kurosawa's *The Seven Samurai,* Orson Welles's *Citizen Kane,* Jean Renoir's *The Rules of the Game,* René Clément's *Forbidden Games,* Marcel Carné's *The Children of Paradise,* Andrzej Wajda's *Kanal,* and one film of Chaplin's, which, I confess, refuses to remain the same one but varies according to which of three—*The Gold Rush, City Lights,* or *Modern Times*—I have seen last.

But sometimes the question arises in its third, most formidably pseudolearned avatar. "Why do you insist on judging the film according to some hypothetical notion of what ought to be there, rather than on what is actually there?" The answer to that may be simple: "Because there is nothing there." Yet, in some cases, that may be putting it too strongly: Something may be there, albeit scarcely worth serious discussion. Of course, sometimes it is these very somethings that give rise to the most heated discussions, and impassioned partisanship—in which case, one may have to take a stand. But whatever you do, never abandon that image of perfection at the back of your head, on which the film, superimposed, must fit like identical triangles; unless, that is, the film is better than your image of perfection, in which case drop the image.

And however bad the general state of film criticism may be, there have been and always will be critics from whom our hypostatized ideal critic might learn something. To speak only of American criticism, with which I am most familiar, I should like an ideal critic to acquire the passionate scrupulousness, the constantly self-searching enthusiasm of James Agee, the modesty and social awareness of Robert Warshow, the background information and scrappiness of Pauline Kael, the gentlemanly dignity of Stanley Kauffmann, and the idiosyncratic raciness of Dwight Macdonald. If all these virtues cannot be used simultaneously, let him practice them by turns, applying each where it is most called for, as a painter does his colors. And by all means let him have some virtues no other critic has, virtues that none of us has even dreamt of. The very worst thing such an ideal critic might do is to be wrong. And even that is not fatal, if we believe Henry de Montherlant: "Je suis convaincu que les oeuvres qui durent ne durent que par des malentendus, par toute la littérature dont la posterité les entoure, littéraure où les intentions venitables des auteurs finissent par être noyées du tout et perdues de vue." But, for all that, it is preferable to aim, to the utmost of one's emotional sensitivity and intellectual power, at being right.

TWO

FAVORITES

To remember one's favorite films is double pleasure. Not only does one recall hours well spent—experiences that, if art can do such a thing, refined and ennobled one—but also one is in a position to realize how various are the modes of excellence in this young art. Concerning film, almost everyone has some Procrustean axe to grind: It is merely an entertainment, it must be purely filmic, it has got to be avant-garde, it cannot depend on words, it must not resemble theatre, it cannot come out of a major studio, it must be the product of a single creative mind, it should not be merely an entertainment, and so on. The fact is that some of the best films have defied any or all rules that have ever been set down for them, and even the safest of generalizations, that nothing of real value has come out of Hollywood in the last five, ten, or X years, dows not entirely stand up under scrutiny.

How often, for example, are we told that a movie cannot be theatre on film. And it is true that filmed stage productions invariably suggest a museum with nothing but walls, and give us, rather than the sense of whatever imperishable performance is being enshrined, a feeling of claustrophobia, of being squeezed right into the idol's narrow niche. But consider a film like Ingmar Bergman's *Smiles of a Summer Night*. Granted there are elements in it that belong quite properly on film. A middle-aged lover pursues a former mistress and falls into a puddle (it is much more wistfully charming than it sounds); a lusty coachman explains to a chambermaid whose lover he has just become the three smiles of a Swedish summer night, as the light subtly changes and dawn gingerly negotiates those northern latitudes. But even this could be done in the theatre, with a revolving stage, good scenic design, and imaginative lighting.

The great scenes of the film, however, are all essentially theatrical: a faintly ominous, baroque dinner party presided over by an eccentric, wealthy crone, with saturnine liveried servants hovering in the background while the conversation in the foreground is almost enough to precipitate a revolution; a man and his virgin wife watching his ex-mistress, experienced and opulently feminine, performing in a play that unnervingly comments on their real-life situation; a preposterous game of Russian roulette during which drama and comedy play pattycake with each other; a subduedly sinister target-shooting scene between a philandering Count and his jealous wife, each plying gloved claws on the other; a battle of wits between a clever actress and her perhaps even cleverer, cynical old mother; a trick bed that comes right through a wall and accidentally unites the young lovers—all these could be equally effective on stage. But the important fact is that they are brilliantly transposed from the theatrical to the filmic. For example, the almost unbearably ornate cut-glass goblets in the dinner scene (photographed by Gunnar Fischer with a kind of voluptuous sharpness), by their aspect and their positioning in the image, convey the oppressive luxuriousness of the diners' lives in purely and uniquely filmic terms. Composition, lighting, photographic texture, editing translate a scene into cinematic idiom so perfectly that it matters little whether it was originally conceived in theatrical, novelistic, or painterly terms. Indeed, to be perfectly cinematic, a scene may have to register in all three of those, as well as in musical terms.

But it is possible for a film to succeed when it is yet more theatrical, to the point where montage is far more conventional than in Bergman's pictures—recall only the superb cutting in scenes such as the two first ones of *The Naked Night*. A film, in fact, may be directed no more than competently from the point of view of exploiting filmic values and still be a masterpiece. I am thinking here of *The Children of Paradise*. Made during the last phase of World War II, on very little money, the film can boast in Marcel Carné of a devoted, workmanlike director, but by no means of an innovator, or even a man of intense feeling for cinema. Yet I think that hardly anyone who has seen the uncut version (and I stress the *uncut*) fails to be deeply moved by this work, in which just about the only completely filmic elements are the occasional tracking shots through the Paris crowds. But what the film does have is, first of all, a magnificent scenario by the poet Jacques Prévert. Prévert is an artist who can make the sentimental ring chaste, the trivial assume romantically vast proportions, and the most outrageous romanticism appear homey and unassuming. He is as adept with wit as with poignancy, and he is a master shifter of gears between the two. The Prévert scenario is literature, and proud of it: let the camera do what it wants or can with it, literature it will remain.

And then there are the performances. The *demimondaine* and semiactress of Arletty; the all-soul and all all-suffering pantomimist of Jean-Louis Barrault; the witty, dazzling, arrogant, untrustworthy, and surprisingly generous actor—the quintessence of all actors—of Pierre Brasseur; the evil ragman of Pierre Renoir, as romantically hateful as a fairytale sorcerer; the unloved wife of Maria Casarès who treads the dizzying borderline between pathos and hysteria; the inhumanly fastidious aristocrat of Louis Salou; the pseudoblind, unsentimentally jolly beggar

of Gaston Modot; the assassin of genius of Marcel Herrand, macabrely exquisite, a fine artist in crime—the heart
rejoices to name them. I don't believe there was a finer
group of actors ever assembled on film; each, under the
Occupation, giving his best, as if France were to be
liberated by his or her performance. I could almost believe
that it was. A scenarist and a cast—hardly anything
more—and a masterpiece is born.

Novel into film? François Boyer adapted his own book
and out came another masterwork—though it may be
significant that it was not a great, only a good, small
novel. I am speaking of *Forbidden Games*. René Clément's
film is as fine as any I know, though I should be surprised
if it appeared on many, or any, of the lists of all-time
favorites. Yet this is a truly imposing achievement of
blending several seemingly unrelated elements into a
totally meaningful whole. It is, first, a war film, in which
the horror of war is conveyed in the opening minutes with
an economy and simplicity that cannot be surpassed in
harrowingness by the most elaborate full-scale antiwar
films. A chaotic column of refugees bound southward
from Paris is strafed by a German plane, and a
five-year-old girl, Paulette, loses both her parents and
her dog. The staging and acting are impeccable. The
bullets from the Stuka punctuate the road with little jets of
sand, except where they hit, and visibly penetrate, flesh.
The dead parents have been reduced to motionlessness
with monstrous speed; the dog, in his death spasm, quivers
in Paulette's arms. She cries and simply does not understand. She is told that the dog is of no further use, being
dead—a word she does not know the meaning of. The pet
is thrown into a near-by river; instead of continuing with
the refugee caravan, the tiny sniffling girl follows the white
corpse as it bobs downstream.

Thus she comes across a peasant family who finally
take her in. The peasants' venality and stupidity is set
forth with grotesque, raffish humor that disturbs as much
as it amuses us. Only the youngest, Michel, a boy of

eleven, is decent and becomes a true friend to Paulette.
Together, they make a game out of the death that rages
around them without their being able to grasp it. This consists of collecting dead animals and burying them in a
hayloft—even killing some of them, if they happen to be
beetles and such—and making funerary monuments for
them. Finally the kids steal the very crosses out of the
churchyard for their game—even that of Michel's just deceased elder brother, whom the family have allowed to die
out of sheer avarice and stupidity. As the children play,
they fall in deep childish love with each other.

The film now proceeds to juggle three elements with
consummate tact: war and its brutalities; the comic
brutishness of the peasants—two feuding families who
conduct a parody of war; and the children's elegiac morbidity that is yet a kind of loving. Each element, instead
of clashing with, complements the others, as a novelistic
constellation of plot, subplot, and overplot (the children's
games, the feuding, the war) is flawlessly transposed to
the screen. Indeed, the ending of the film, though less
gruesome than that of the novel, is, if anything, more
moving. The acting of even the smallest part is let-
ter-perfect—the peasant types pitched midway between
Breughel and Rabelais—and that of Paulette, by Brigitte
Fossey, incomparable. She is by turns a lost little girl, a
coquettish young lady aware of her finer breeding than
that of the peasants (even of Michel, one of nature's
gentlemen, acted with charming straightforwardness by
Georges Poujouly), and finally, a great, tragic lover even
though she is only five! René Clément's direction never
fails, through all the complex shifts of tone, to avoid the
mawkish, the sensational, or the arty.

But a film can be great even with a minimum of variety,
with an obsessive singleness of tone. Such a work is Andrzej Wajda's *Kanal*. In his other films thus far, Wajda
has erred either on the side of pretentiousness (as in *Ashes
and Diamonds*) or on that of triviality (as in *The Innocent Sorcerers*). But *Kanal* seems to me, except for one

minor flaw, as perfect an antiwar film as was ever made. It deals with an incident in that gallant and tragic Warsaw Uprising during World War II when the Russians were already close by, but did not, perhaps on purpose, come close enough. A small unit of men under its fine commanding officer is seen desperately fighting off the Germans, and these aboveground moments of bitter skirmishing have the casual, offhand horror that the more elaborate American war films, for example, do not achieve. The unit—it also includes a woman in love with a wounded young officer—retreats into the sewers of Warsaw, in the hope of coming up somewhere behind the Germans, whence it could join up with the Russians.

The wretched troop sloshes about waist-deep in muck, in abysmal darkness, and totally unsure of their way and of what will await them above, if they ever make it. Their sufferings, loyalties, weaknesses, quarrels, heroism, and hopes begotten on despair would suggest little fluctuation from the prevailing note of catastrope. Yet Wajda is able to evoke such a range of human reactions to this overarching doom, he can show such various shadings of courage, such nuances of discouragement and grief, that we can all locate ourselves on this scale of human responses to disaster; and we are given both a foretaste of our individual dying and an overwhelming taste of our common mortality.

The one false note is struck by an artist and intellectual in the band who goes mad and blindly wanders about reciting passages from Dante's *Inferno*. This is redundant—carrying symbolism to the second power; within a concrete image of hell, we do not need an abstraction of it. But otherwise the film is utterly spare and chaste, and the inevitable tragedies, all different, all manage to surprise, shock, and, without any diminishing returns, shattter us. Contrary to the layman's belief, there are several shades of black, and *Kanal* explores and exemplifies them all. A typically magnificent scene is the one in which the girl and her dying lover, after incredible effort, arrive at the exit of the sewer, only to find that the Germans have put bars on it. The young man is so close to death that he can no longer see; the girl holds him in her arms. Aware that she herself probably lacks the strength and will to go back and try for another egress, she envelops her lover in her embrace and in marvelous lies about the liberty which is so near to hand—which, indeed, lies only a few, untraversable inches away. And this is only one such episode among many. *Kanal* comes as close as any work of art can to breaking the heart; if any films can prevent us, even temporarily, from shirking our humanity, this, surely, is one of them.

Even so fundamental a rule as "Thou shalt not change tone at the end of a film!" need not be binding on genius. Jean Renoir's *The Rules of the Game* breaks that rule, at any rate. What begins and develops as high comedy ends tragically. To be sure, Renoir's keen perception points to both the farcical and the threatening overtones in the comedy, so that when tragedy does occur, it is more of a grim absurdity of which, later on, we can say, "Ah well, no wonder!" Thus the switch, though not exactly prepared for is at least cushioned. Yet this jarring ending fulfills a purpose: it connects the petty bickering and transgressions of the rich folk with similar immoralities of their servants. The Marquis's jealous gamekeeper thinks he is shooting his own wife's, the chambermaid's, lover, when in fact, he is killing the lover of his master's wife. In a case of mistaken identity, a romantic lover is killed in place of a burlesque one. The moral imposes itself: When a society is shot through with infidelities and jealousies, the relatively noble are apt to pay the price for the ignoble; what is more, class distinctions cease to matter—at night, all cats are grey, and all poachers targets. The chivalric aviator who wants to save Christine, the neglected wife, from drying up, may be a sympathetic character, but in a world where mischief and violence are rampant, he becomes a likely victim. Perhaps, moreover, as a member of a corrupt society, he too is guilty.

But it may also be that the ending of this enormously

witty satirical film is to read differently: that in a
disorganized and corroded society the only justice is
Chance, and that Chance is totally unreliable and absurd.
What is clear, in any case, is that however much masters
and servants may belong to separate worlds, in their
weaknesses they are alike and, however disastrously,
united. A neat symbolism identifies low adultery with
poaching, higher love for an unhappily married woman
with gallant but risky transoceanic flying, and jealous en-
forcing of conjugal rights with gamekeeping—an attack,
perhaps, on the excesses in the concept of private property.

Yet it is not as if *La Règle du jeu* were interesting only
through its ending. It was, in 1939, very possibly the first
film of serious artistic stature in which improvisation by
the author-director as the filming progressed played an
important role. If finding ancestors or forerunners for the
New Wave were not so otiose, inasmuch as the *nouvelle
vague* was so loose and ephemeral a coalition, one might
recognize in Renoir's film a precursor, perhaps even a pro-
genitor, of that movement. There is such an air of non-
chalant grotesquerie about the work, but also such pointed
preposterousness, that one is reminded simultaneously of
the *commedia dell'arte* and the comedy of manners, and
of both at their high points. In the cast, Jean Renoir himself, Mila Parély as the Marquis's mistress, and the
spendid Marcel Dalio as the Marquis distinguish themselves among the masters; among the servants, Paulette
Dubost as the chambermaid and Julien Carette as the
poacher who pursues her are especially noteworthy. It is,
in fact, a case of masterly ensemble acting by a large cast,
in which only Roland Toutain as the aviator and Nora
Gregor as the Marquise are less interesting than they might
be.

If the corruption of a whole society, however subtly
conveyed, is still an incendiary subject, what could be
more ordinary and, presumably, unmemorable than the
themes and stories of Fellini's early masterpieces, *The
White Sheik* and *I Vitelloni*? (His later work declined:
first slowly, than vertiginously.) To consider the lesser of

the two first: *The White Sheik* seems to me a model of a
comédie larmoyante in which laughter and tears are
blended in perfect proportions with the expertise of a
master bartender, or, better yet, an artist. It is the story of
a little provincial couple on their honeymoon in Rome. He
is a petty bureaucratic dictator, she a naïve little romantic
who has secretly adored "the White Sheik," the hero of
one of those popular Italian photographed comic strips,
the *fumetti*. Scarcely arrived at the hotel, Wanda, the
bride, sneaks away from a schedule of sight-seeing and
meeting relatives, and ends up, by a chain of hilarious circumstances, participating as an extra in the photographing
of an episode of her beloved serial on a beach outside
Rome. Her hero, the dashing White Sheik, turns out to be
an amiable, overweight, small-time Casanova, who half
believes in his exotic pseudoidentity and half exploits it to
get away from his huge and garish wife, whom he, nevertheless, quakingly reveres. Wanda slowly, very slowly,
awakens from her dream and realizes that her Prince
Charming is but a pathetic poltroon and that the Oriental
derring-do of the photo-romance is only a flimsy cover
for a grubby and cynical enterprise. But never has the
transition from naïveté and illusion to reality and a just
barely hung-onto innocence been conveyed through a
more engaging set of episodes: funny, absurd, and yet horribly ordinary. The scenes are always shot in a kind of
mental double exposure: You are continually aware both
of how Wanda sees the events and how they really happen. Thus her first glimpse of the rotund Sheik, perched
on an exaggeratedly high swing between trees of a seaside
grove, and trying to look at her both casually and seduc-
tively, manages to be at once glamorously exalted and
thoroughly ridiculous.

These sequences are crosscut with the agonized yet
ludicrous search of Leopoldo, the bedeviled husband, for
his missing bride. Obliged to keep his more and more im-
portunate relatives at bay with ever more desperate lies
and stratagems, embarrassed out of his wits by the condescendingly callous questionings of the police to whose

help he reluctantly resorts, and above all, hurt and frightened by his wife's mysterious disappearance, Leopoldo learns, through a series of comic yet sad misadventures, humility and forgivingness.

When, after an amateurish attempt at suicide, Wanda is finally reunited with Leopoldo, a whole sequence of awkward little gestures and utterances expresses her mingled confusion and penitence; his gruffness, in turn, masks insecurity and need. The last scene lives on untarnishably in the memory. Wanda and Leopoldo, in their Sunday best, have scurried like small, demented black beetles across the immense whiteness of St. Peter's Square to catch up with their relatives in the nick of time for an audience with the Pope. As the large group of people, including the ogling relatives, is being hustled in on the double for their glimpse of the Pontiff, the newlyweds get a chance to exchange one relieved but still nervous look. Brunella Bovo, the exquisitely right Wanda—with her just short of pretty face, benighted, small-townish, yet in possession now of a hard-won awareness—lifts her almost too round eyes at her homely little husband, the admirable Leopoldo Trieste, of whose former swagger only an unconvincingly knotted brow and a topheavy mustache are left. In a tremulous but, for the first time, womanly voice, she says: *"You* are my White Sheik!"

It is distressing to find such a relatively alert critic as John Russell Taylor (in *Cinema Eye, Cinema Ear*) remarking that these words, "after all she has supposedly learnt," prove that Wanda is "certainly incorrigible." On the contrary, this is, on a humble level to be sure, the beginning of true wisdom. Leopoldo, for all his conventionality and authoritarianism, has forgiven her. The White Sheik (a flamboyant caricature, which the gifted Alberto Sordi nevertheless prodigally invests with flesh and blood) was, after all, a phoney. So Wanda has learned that in a world where illusions crumble into reality, the only happiness is to raise reality to the level of illusion by seeing it with loving, forgiving eyes, grateful that it is at least as much as it is. White Sheiks do not fall

into our laps ready-made; we must fashion them patiently and fondly out of the brown or grey ones life provides.

With equally quotidian ingredients, Federico Fellini
made his next, and most beautiful film, *I Vitelloni*. The
vitelloni are fatted calves: overgrown, indolent youths living in a provincial town in which there seems to be no
place for them. There is Fausto, the dapper leader of the
gang, whose consuming interest is women; Alberto, a
comic version of Fausto, who lives in a dream of easy
money, leisure, travel, women; Leopoldo, who yearns to be
a great poetic playwright; Riccardo, who toys with the notion of becoming a singer; and Moraldo, the sensitive, shy
young man, whose main pleasure is friendship with the
other four. These five, along with several other people—like Sandra, Moraldo's sister, whom Fausto im-
pregnates, reluctantly marries, and promptly neglects—are
brought before us as well-defined individuals, the character and adventures of each amply developed both apart
from and in conjunction with the group. Indeed, in the
very first scene, during a seaside beauty contest interrupted by a downpour, all the main characters reveal
themselves with the utmost economy and with that slightly discomfiting, because uncompromisingly frank, humor
that suffuses the entire picture.

One of the most brilliant features of the film is the
musical score by the true *maestro,* Nino Rota. It consists
of only two themes. The first is a soaring, romantic
melody that can be made to express nostalgia, love, and
the pathos of existence. The other is a marchlike, merry
tune, carefree and irresponsible; slowed down, with emphasis on the cellos and basses (as in the episode of
Fausto's infidelity), it becomes lugubrious; with eerie
figurations in the woodwinds (in Leopoldo's nocturnal
adventure with the old homosexual actor, it turns
sinister. The quick-silver switches in the music ably support the changing moods of the story. Mercurially, from
one scene to the next, or with a sudden flip-over within a
scene, we are prodded from raucous jollity into a delicate

sadness, or inversely, or even into a unique, intimate blend
of pathos and absurd humor. For example, the fatted
calves will be horsing around a beach, relieving their
boredom with somewhat melancholy jokes and clowning,
when, suddenly, they discover Alberto's sister in a
desperate, furtive tryst with her married lover: The very
jaw of that scene seems to be left hanging in surprise,
sheepishness, and hurt. Or Leopoldo will follow a once-
great actor out into a windy night by the seashore; he is full
of touchingly preposterous hopes born of the aged actor's
praise for his unpublished play. The nocturnal promenade
is brashly funny until, of a sudden, the actor becomes a
hideous, wizened, coquettish travesty of a "gay" Lothario
trying to seduce our playwright. Leopoldo takes to his
heels in a scene that partakes equally of the risible, the
macabre, and the pitiful.

Around these five youths and their families, friends,
employers, and women, the film weaves its two main
themes: dry rot and the longing to escape. Everyone in the
small town with its bourgeois pieties and limited cultural
and recreational opportunities feels in danger of stifling.
Yet the modes of escape are different. Some, like Fausto's
employer and his wife, find solace in married love and
work; others dream of various fictitious escapes while
playing billiards, watching movies, or chasing after skirts;
still others, like Alberto's sister and, at the end, even
Moraldo, screw up their courage to depart into a wider
world. The variations on this theme are cunningly in-
tertwined, each complementing, commenting on, or undercutting the other. The story progresses through a series
of minor or major ironic twists: The smallest narrative
unit is, usually, a stroke of bittersweet irony. Thus, when
Fausto comes home very late after a bit of adultery, San-
drina could forgive him yet again. But he smiles fatuously
in his sleep, and that smile makes her pick up the baby
and leave. The ironies are so delicate that they can perch
comfortably on the razor's edge between laughter and
tears. Sandra and Fausto go to the movies; in the dark, he
flirts with the woman on the other side of him and,

mumbling a pretext to his wife, runs out after the stranger
when she leaves. Returning after an equivocal escapade,
Fausto finds a tearful Sandra waiting outside the closed
theatre. "How did the picture end?" he asks cheerfully.
"Did she die?" "No, she didn't die," Sandra replies getting
sadder by the moment. "They were married."

Even more masterly is the temporal and spatial
development in *I Vitelloni*. Both time and space are
elastic and highly subjectively treated. During the carnival
ball, time seems to rush by in a whirl of potentialities;
when Sandra disappears, time hurtles along as the *vitelloni*
ineptly race about looking for her. But during all those
night-time ambles through the sleep-drugged town and
the day-time moseyings around the beach, time seems to
have rusted in its very tracks. And space too changes
before our eyes. Out of the oppressive confinement of the
sleeping town, Moraldo and the little boy Guido look up
into the stars and suddenly confront the universe. From
the narrow streets one moves out onto the beach to face a
boundless sea. The dance hall, after the ball, has changed
in size: Emptiness has, paradoxically, made it smaller,
even as the music has shrunk to a lingering, solitary
trumpet. Thus the alternating rhythm of the film proceeds
parallelly on the temporal, spatial, and existential planes:
from shuffling about to rushing, from constriction to
spaciousness, from sadness to joy—and back again. Then,
once more, *da capo*.

Otello Martelli's camera joins in the imaginative movement. Perhaps the most stunning effect comes at the end.
Moraldo catches a dawn train for the big city. Guido, the
little railroad boy, is the only one there to bid him adieu.
And now, while we hear the clatter of wheels, the camera
moves through the various rooms of the sleeping *vitelloni*
as if it were the train. They sleep in characteristic
postures, constrained or abandoned, their expressions
typically smug or unsure, and as the camera (or Moraldo's
train, or train of thought) moves on, they drop helplessly
out of sight. Meanwhile it is becoming lighter. The music,
which was the march theme inverted into a dirge, now

shifts to a major key. We see, from the back, Guido, in his oversize railroad man's cap, whaling precariously along one rail. He keeps falling off. But, each time, he gets back on again. A symbol, yes; but an ever so gentle and uninsistent one.

How different from Fellini's sometimes farcical, sometimes touching boredom is the fierce *ennui* of Antonioni. One would think that a film like *L'Avventura* could not exist. It is about the disappearance of a girl that remains unexplained: From a beginning that is all weariness, we progress to an extraordinary, unsettling middle, only to lapse into a final weariness again—no one even thinks about the vanished girl any more. To put it another way, we go from a world of loveless, routine sex to a brief spurt of genuine passion, then back to failed love again. A gesture of forgiveness at the end, to be sure, but can it redeem a world of cynicism, indifference, and mechanical sex? A film, then, with a distinct middle, but no beginning, and no end. Yet what a marvelously absorbing portrayal—thanks, in part, to this very odd structure—of the condition hardest to convey without becoming boring: boredom.

Michelangelo Antonioni's way of making boredom interesting is to create sumptuous images and sounds, adult dialogue, and characters rich in money, good looks, intelligence—sometimes even in talent, sensitivity, and a kind of aristocracy—and then draining the middle of this luscious construct absolutely empty, like an egg that has been sucked out through the tiniest, almost invisible, hole. Moreover, in *L'Avventura,* unlike in some of his later films, Antonioni has a valid plot device that keeps our involvement going: the quest for a missing person, for the solution of the enigma, for truth. I have written at length about this film elsewhere (in *Acid Test* [New York: Stein & Day, 1963,] pp. 17-21), but I cannot sufficiently praise some of Antonioni's extraordinary gifts. Thus his way of composing individual frames, especially those of two heads either side by side or with one in close-up and the other somewhere off in a corner, has revolutionized

the use of space in films. (It must be said, though, that in
this respect Cocteau, especially in *Les Parents terribles,*
was somewhat of a precursor.) I have recently seen a
Hungarian film, *The Round-up,* whose composition of
images and dramatically white backgrounds are sheer Antonioni—just as I have come across Polish, Yugoslav,
Spanish, Japanese, and even American films that have had
the sense to assimilate some useful Antonionian devices.

But more than that, the manner in which people move
into and out of Antonioni's medium shots, the whole
grouping and maneuvering of actors, is always wonderfully elegant and harmonious, without, however,
calling such undue attention to itself as to seem artificial.
Consider the search for Anna on the little island: it is a
piece of inspired choreography. From all sides, including
from above and below, characters enter the frame, and
their comings and goings, overlappings and crisscrossings,
their occasional mistaking of someone else for Anna (a
delusion into which Antonioni is able, momentarily, to
suck even the viewer), are not only expressive of the prevailing confusion, but also conjure up the sinister beauty
that inheres even in the saddest aspects of life, making
them more beautiful and sadder yet.

There were other things new in *L'Avventura.* There
was, for instance, that succulent richness of whites and
blacks that made a film appear for the first time truly "in
black and white," rather than in a variety of lackluster
greys. (Fellini, in 8½, was to push this device even further,
perhaps too far.) And those coloristic extremes, thickly
sensuous in themselves, also became the bearers of symbolic values in the film: Claudia's golden hair, for example, which photographed white, became a symbol of purity
and faith among a bevy of brunettes, all cynical,
world-weary, or corrupt. Again, for the first time we saw
geography and topography tampered with, and liberties
taken with the landscape of Sicily. So routes were shown
to lead to places to which, in reality, they don't; famous
palaces were converted into hotels or police stations;

devices to produce estrangement, by subverting reality, and, by the same token, to increase the symbolic, universal value. Music was used with a sparingness previously found only in some of Ingmar Bergman's films, and sound effects assumed a revolutionary significance: As lovers embrace outdoors, a distant train is heard rattling closer and breathing becomes heavier on the soundtrack—we have an adequate auditory equivalent for the sexual experience. Such a device as showing a painting of the *Caritas Romana* (a daughter offering her breasts to her starving father through the bars of his prison) to comment ironically on a context of luxurious self-indulgence and ungivingness may well underlie the wholesale use of posters and street signs for similar purposes in the films of Godard, Varda, and other New Wave film-makers. But let it not be said that *L'Avventura* has only technical or historic interest. It is, in fact, a film in which human problems are insistently, though somewhat mutedly, present amid the tedium of upper-middle-class existence.

At the opposite end of the scale from *L'Avventura* lies Akira Kurosawa's *The Seven Samurai*. This, on the surface, is a work of relentless, unmitigated action, as epic as any film ever made, and, again on the surface, sheer entertainment. Yet it is also an unquestionable triumph of art. Certainly the film is almost continuous motion, excitement, fighting. It begins with a large gang of bandits singling out a village for future despoliation and destruction; a frightened villager overhears their plan to attack as soon as the barley is harvested. The terrified village elders proceed to recruit some of those disbanded, errant samurai who alone might save them, but the trouble is that the villagers can offer the wandering warriors precious little remuneration. The manner in which the samurai are enlisted, or rather, enlist one another, on the basis of their swordsmanship and resourcefulness, is exciting as well as amusing, but there is also pathos in the fact that these noble swordsmen must now sell their services—their very lives, perhaps—for a handful of rice.

The village can, finally, afford only six, plus a spurious, comic seventh who, though clearly an impostor, seems tough enough and hell-bent on earning samurai honors.

The rest of the film (and long as it is, it is considerably shorter than the uncut version shown in Japan) concerns the samurai's cogent organizing and training of the peasants, the attack of the bandits, the brutal and protracted fighting, a counterraid on the bandits' mountain homes by three samurai led by a villager, a love affair between a young samurai and a peasant girl, and the ultimate triumph of the chief samurai's strategy and wisdom. But this does not occur until some of his fellows and many of the villagers have perished. One thinks throughout that one is watching a dazzling epic, with the traditional blend of folkloristic and romantic elements along with bouncy dialogue, juicy humor, and apt psychological insights. Suddenly, at the very end, the full significance of the film dawns on us. After the moving burial scene, the remaining samurai depart. "We have won once again," one of them exclaims proudly. The leader corrects him, "We have lost once again," and explains that the farmers are the victors, Bandits and samurai pass; only those who live close to the earth remain, possessors of the land, sustained by it forever.

We realize the profound verity the film has painstakingly built up to: Warrior castes, whether noble or ignoble, are declining, slowly exterminating one another. There remain the timid and weak but canny peasants, who, for a fraction of their humble earnings, can buy the lives of noble champions and death for the outlaws. And when the samurai, too, have died of bandits, inanition, or uselessness, the world will become peaceable, industrious, uneventful. Will that make it better? This heroic epic is also a social problem film.

Kurosawa's "repertory company" ranks with that of Ingmar Bergman as the best in films and has for its anchor man Toshiro Mifune (by now an international star) who here portrays immaculately the pseudosamurai that turns out to be a capital fellow. As for Kurosawa, he manages to make every new test of a samurai, every new fight sequence, vividly differentiated and imbued with its own emotional flavor—in view of the quantity, no mean accomplishment. Minor characters come to life in the briefest flash, and landscapes are fitted, pictorially and psychologically, into the proceedings with refined but self-effacing artistry. The music does not always sound felicitous to our ears, and the photography, though always workmanlike, is only occasionally outstanding. But what truly distinguishes the film is that we care about its many charcters, indeed, about the whole village. There is a certain intimacy with which these heroes are viewed—their very poverty endears them to us; as for the villagers, their ineptitude and eagerness to surmount it, their cunning, as it were, Brechtian will to survive is engrossing if not endearing. Kurosawa, moreover, achieves true suspense from the very beginning: Will they get enough samurai? Will the few they get be equal to the task? Will peasants become soldiers in time? The preparations are shown skillfully on a daily basis: on such and such a day, this much training was imparted; by such and such a date, this much of the fortifications was built. Documentary technique makes the race against time utterly gripping.

As we watch these preparations, we apprehend another one of the film's points. Efficiency, the traditional education of a class for skilled fighting, is even more valuable than individual prowess, important as that is. This emerges amid some of the most faithful depictions of close combat I have ever seen: We get a deadly sense of chaos, of how hard it is to tell where the foe is, or even which one he is. Supremely beautiful, too, is the growing respect between samurai and peasants. The samurai begin by viewing the villagers as so much intractable material out of which to hew something resembling soldiers—material, moreover, that is hardly worth saving. To the peasants, the samurai are, at first, arrogant and incomprehensible beings whom they can barely afford to feed, and who may

not even be able to protect them, so that handing themselves over to them may scarcely be different from succumbing to the bandits. But by slow, delicate, touching
steps, these two widely different orders of men come to
need each other and value each other more. Then comes
the final irony: Once the peasants have been saved, they
start ignoring their saviors. Common humanity is, after
all, an insufficient link.

I once observed about Japanese films that the
remarkable thing about them is that they all have a beginning, a middle, and five ends. So, too, *The Seven Samurai*
has seemed overlong to some. Not to me. As the patient
and steadfast Kurosawa, like a careful chronicler, records
the progress of the matter day by merciless day, I grow
wiser, wearier, and older with his characters. In the end, I
feel as I do upon concluding my reading of some vast
roman fleuve: having rejoiced, suffered, and learned with
these characters for so long, it will be hard to go on living
without them.

An "action film," then—something that in most minds
immediately spells "mere entertainment"—can also be
art; and so, too, can be even a movie released by a major
Hollywood studio. It was R.K.O. that released *Citizen
Kane,* and there have been a few similar miracles since.
Penelope Houston has properly noted that seeing *Kane*
"for the first time . . . one got a first conviction that if
cinema could really do that, it could do almost anything."
And after listing some of the ingenious devices used, "the
deep focus, developed with . . . Gregg Toland [the
cameraman] . . . the overlapping conversations, the heavy
contrasts of light and shadow, with faces emerging, white
and isolated, from a chiaroscuro," she rightly adds that
the film has a style of its own that transcends these components. Nothing could be wider of the mark than Pauline
Kael's classifying this film, however condoningly, as *kitsch,*
though, of course, I realize that for her this is a term of supreme praise. In fact, Welles has found his own, highly sophisticated way of rendering isolation and estrangement,
and it is not for nothing that the later film-makers whose

work reminds one most of *Kane* are precisely those masters of alienation, Bergman and Antonioni. I am referring, of course, to alienation in its tragic, or tragicomic, sense; not to the fashionable but generally unfunny joke made out of it by certain New Wave film-makers and their imitators.

What places *Citizen Kane* spectacularly ahead of its time, as well as making it a contribution for all time, is the very aspect attacked by John Howard Lawson in *Film: The Creative Process*. This Marxist ideologue has to be read against the grain: "Photography in depth is a major contribution to cinematic art. But depth in the scene does not necessarily afford depth in psychological penetration. In *Citizen Kane,* the equal clarity with which people in a group are observed avoids the intimacy of the closeup; it does not emphasize the relationship between the people but almost invariably stresses the separateness of their existence. The brilliant manipulation of light and darkness strengthens the impression that they are cut from meaningful experience; when we catch a moment of anguish, the obtuseness of other persons or the play of shadows distract [sic] our attention." And Lawson further complains of the depersonalization in the telling of the agony of Kane's second wife: "When she fails in her theater appearance, the event is seen from the viewpoint of a workman high above the stage. When she has taken poison, her agony is observed through the medicine bottle on the night table." Though this may not be the realism that a Marxian critic is looking for, though the estrangement may be conveyed through certain "formalist" devices and images, the fact remains that it is superlatively conveyed. Seeing the unconcern of others simultaneously with someone's anguish, or seeing that anguish from a surreal or nightmare perspective, makes *Kane* more consciously aesthetic, more fantastic, more baroque, even; but one must be drearily obtuse to carp at a film for failing to achieve the diametrical opposite of what it wants to do and does very nicely.

I am not saying that the script of *Citizen Kane* is any

great work of art; it is, indeed, in many respects naïve and simplistic. But that does not make it *kitsch:* By its mannerist lushness enveloping a bleak vision; by its ability to make the protagonist a demonic figure deserving of contempt, compassion, and above all, awe; by its very larger-than-life dimensions, *Kane* is an imposing piece of expressionism, descended from *Caligari* and pointing toward *L'Avventura* and *The Naked Night*, and, even more perhaps, toward such painful but striking near-misses of genius as *The Magician* and *Eclipse*. But what may distinguish *Citizen Kane* most of all is its extracting the mythic from under the humdrum surface of the American experience, and doing this not in the area of the western or the gangster picture, where it comes with a spurious ease, but in the realm of big business and politics, where the movies had previously feared to tread.

It is with *The Naked Night* that I wish to end this cycle of happy reminiscences, and thus amplify my previous brief comments on it (in *Acid Test*, pp. 29-30). This, to me, is one of the extremely rare instances of a film's elements all blending perfectly. There is the discreet and concise music of Karl-Birger Blomdohl. There is the superbly controlled photography of Hilding Bladh and Sven Nykvist—the latter, one of the few cinematographers whose camera cannot touch on anything without making it art—by turns gloomily opulent (backstage at the theatre) or dazzlingly garish (in the overexposed flashback); amiably trivial (in Agda's shop and apartment: all muted tones) or moody and ominous (the night shots of circus wagons rolling). The direction carefully balances atmosphere or ambience with individual reactions to it, capturing every tremor in the drama of the interaction between person and setting. How strongly one is made to feel the not-belonging of the traveling circus owner in his ex-wife's settled bourgeois quarters; how acutely one senses the awe of Anne the bareback rider as she confronts the legitimate theatre, provincial and pinchbeck as it is in this instance. How deeply etched the differences in milieus become: theatre, circus, small town, each with its petty triumphs and consuming limitations.

And how is one to do justice in brief to the incomparable performances? Every one of them is right to the last detail, though, unjust as this may be, I would single out the pitiable yet eerie, brave but ineffectual clown of Anders Ek, and the ruthless, brittle, perverse actor-seducer of Hasse Ekman as *primi inter pares*. And there is the story: Simplicity itself, yet infinitely rich in suggestive overtones. Thanks to the literate but by no means fancy dialogue, characters and relationships emerge swiftly, in sharp focus down to their minutest ambiguities. The themes are Bergman's favorites: the artist and society, humiliation and loss of illusion as eye-openers and painful prerequisites for living; the growth of understanding between man and woman after each learns the worst of the other. But these themes, partly out of Strindberg, partly out of a very sharp eye for the nature of neurosis, partly out of faith in the artist's and human being's ability to bear the unbearable and even squeeze some sort of satisfaction out of it, emerge beautifully integrated and rounded off; they strike me as Bergman's own, whatever their exact provenience.

To communicate some of the excitement that Bergman's language itself carries with it, let me quote the speech of Sjuberg, the arrogant theatre manager, to the circus owner and his mistress, when they come humbly asking for the loan of some costumes: "Why shouldn't I insult you? You put up with it, you don't punch me in the jaw. We despise you because you live in wagons and we in dirty hotel rooms; we produce art, and you offer stunts and tricks. The plainest and least gifted of us can spit on the best of you. Why? Because you stake your lives and we our vanity. I think you look silly and patched, sir, and your little lady would surely be much more fun without her gaudy rags. If you only dared, you would realize that we look even more foolish with our fake elegance, our made-up faces, our studied accents. Why shouldn't I insult you?" The speech is a mine of psychological subtlety: the mixture of hostility and self-mockery, the cynicism

that draws sustenance from aggression, the marvelous ambiguity of "Because you stake your lives and we stake our
vanity." Does that mean that vanity, the ego, is more important than life? That art is vanity, *vanitas vanitaium,*
so the opposite of life? That values, particularly highbrow
values, are perverted? That those who commit themselves
less can lord it over those who give all? Yet this dense
statement is casually tossed off by Bergman; no Hollywood screenwriter I can think of could work himself up to
its like, were he to huff and puff away for months.
Moreover, Sjuberg's attitude toward the circus director
leads straightway into the affair of Frans, the actor, with
Anne, the circus director's "little lady," characterized as it
is by the same sado-masochistic ambivalence of tone.

In a way, *The Naked Night* is the perfect counterpart to
I Vitelloni. Whereas in Bergman's film everyone is guilty
but, for all that, not to be condemned; in Fellini's, almost
everyone has an animal innocence that yet causes suffering of one kind or another. This is the greatness of
Bergman's and Fellini's visions: That each in its own way
sees the complex interpenetration of good and evil, purity
and corruption: the tears in all things and the huge joke of
it all. There is in these visions an adultness, a seriousness,
a sense of tragedy but also of mirth that great films, great
works of art, have, though they go about achieving it in
various and heterodox ways. Would there were more films
like them!

THREE

1963

IMAGES: IMAGINATIVE AND OTHERWISE

The New Wave is wavering. Having, with a few notable exceptions, waived sense for the sake of scintillation, and pushed this to the limits of available technical resources, it seems now to have nowhere to go but up into narrative and (I write the word with trepidation) *human* significance. This is not redundancy: In *Sundays and Cybèle* the hero is neither the "significant" echolalia of a Marguerite Duras, nor the "significant" obsession with objects of an Alain Robbe-Grillet, nor the dromomaniac cameras and megalomaniac montages of several young directors. The hero is a human being, flanked by other human beings, about whom we can actually care.

This does not mean that Serge Bourguignon's first feature film disregards modernistically daring, often even ostentatious, technical devices, but it does mean that it generally subordinates them to concern with non-cardboard people in a noncelluloid world. The chief interest of the film lies in its earnest striving to reconcile the new demonstrative technical expertise with aesthetic and ethical considerations, an amalgam with hitherto only

François Truffaut could carry off, and even he only intermittently.

For it is obviously easier to achieve filmic bravura when literary and moral values are negligible. If the words, ideas or humanity of a film came fully to the fore, the technical effects would become, if not ancillary, at least challenged in their supremacy, which to any true-blue New Waver they must not be. Hence the preference for various forms of *alittérature* and amorality and inferior scenarios.

Not that the writing in *Sundays and Cybèle* is particularly good, or the technical brilliance wholly un-self-conscious. Still the film is one of the best seen hereabouts in some time, boasting in Bourguignon a director of superior achievement and superlative promise, and in Patricia Gozzi an adolescent actress whose performance will stand as a touchstone. What Brigitte Fossey did for a tiny girl in *Forbidden Games,* Mlle. Gozzi does for a little woman here.

Sundays and Cybèle is the story of an amnesiac war pilot, Pierre, whose memory is frozen by the guilt of having strafed to death a young Oriental girl. He is now living in Ville d'Avray, a suburb of Paris, with an attractive nurse who helped him back to partial sanity and who cares for him rather more possessively than therapeutically. He becomes dimly but strongly drawn to Cybèle, a *gamine* of not quite twelve, abandoned by her family at an orphanage, who responds to him first with the desperate eagerness of a lonely child, then with all the passion of a precociously feminine little girl. The nurse, finding out about it, is racked with jealousy, but comes to see that Pierre's affection is predominantly that of a now childlike being seeking commensurate companionship, and partly that of the involuntary child-killer obscurely trying to expiate a repressed sin. But the world malevolently refuses to understand; even Madeleine, the nurse, is shaken in her faith in the purity of the relationship and sets in motion the final, futile tragedy.

The story has many weaknesses. The motivation of the

characters is often left rather cavalierly nebulous; as if to compensate for the marvelous greys of the photography, people are rather too black and white; the preachment has a way of becoming too insistent; Pierre's cure is dubious—either too pat, or, perhaps, no cure at all. For the film never clarifies for us the relationship of Pierre and Cybèle, and leaves us with the uncomfortable feeling that the ultimate dissolution by arbitrary death is there to take the place of resolution by artistic insight. There are even some hints of adventitious parallels with Christian and Greek mythology, but these can be mercifully ignored.

What cannot be ignored is the ingeniousness and beauty of Bourguignon's cinematography. Alexandre Astruc coined the phrase *"caméra-stylo"* which most New Wave directors subscribed to, only to turn their cameras not into fountain pens but hypodermic syringes full of heroin. Now, Bourguignon's camera is a brush: sometimes that of a painter, sometimes that of a Chinese calligrapher tracing ideograms, whose loveliness is in the combination of shape, meaning, and the grace of movement that begets them.

Here is a camera almost always on the go, but whose rhythms are as manifold and controlled as those of a ballet. Here are transitions of the most seamless sort: Cybèle's brag that she will become a doctor and cure Pierre leads into a nurse's tray and Madeleine hatching the scheme which will turn into everyone's undoing; a shot of a real horse disappearing is followed by that of a wooden horse on a carrousel—and, ironically, the toy horse becomes part of the world of infantile adults, while the real horse is part of the sylvan paradise in which a child, charging ahead of years, envelops the man she loves. Again, an elevator rises toward the acrophobic hero's face and blots it out—the contraption is black and reminiscent of the airplane in which the malady befell him. Next, a bright rear-view mirror races along a roadway and picks up Pierre's excited face as he hurried toward the orphanage in innocently horizontal motion.

Clearly such transitions are not based on mere formal

and verbal echoes, but provide ideological commentary. If we go from nuns' and their pupils' hands folded in compulsory prayer to similarly but voluntarily folded hands of a sculptor joyfully modeling his clay, there is more in these meeting images than meets the formalist eye.

There are also superb long shots which often connect two distant but veiledly related people or places with the same frame. There are spine-tingling little discords, as when the dialogue ever so slightly lags behind or lurches ahead of the images, or when an aerial shot of walking figures is coupled with their words and footsteps heard from nearby—to suggest the soaring importance of these diminutive but contented creatures. But there are excesses, too, as when Pierre is suddenly viewed through the tiny peephole in a metal blind blatantly rolled down over a ticket window: This should create a natural iris effect, but because no one remains there watching Pierre, the device becomes more artificial than any conventional technique.

Bourguignon deserves further credit for getting incomparable photographic effects from Henri Decaé, who has worked admirably for directors as different as Truffaut, Claude Chabrol, and René Clément, but who here achieves masterpieces. We are transported now into the world of Corot, now into that of Monet or Seurat; desolate nocturnal cityscapes, enchanted woods of Ville d'Avray, a solitary gull skimming the waters of a pond while the small girl's voice pours out its great yearning, a romantic horseman taking almost forever to vanish down the corridors of trees, a minuscule pavilion emerging in the landscape so very far away that it hardly has the right to be there—yet it is here that the final disaster will take place.

From Maurice Jarre, Bourguignon has elicited a model musical score, infinitely various (Albinoni, Händel, Charpentier, Tibetan gongs, and Jarre's own edgy modernism) yet spare and unassuming. The performances, too, are fine and finely dovetailed: Besides that of Mlle. Gozzi, so lovely that it almost hurts even in its happiest moments, there is Hardy Krüger's Pierre, a little too Brandoesque at times but cogently balanced between naïveté and neurosis; Nicole Courcel's uneasy nurse, the best piece of work this fetching actress has done to date; and a handsome bit by Daniel Ivernel, hitherto known for his villains or weaklings, as a strong and kindly friend.

Sundays and Cybèle must be viewed in two ways: as a film, uneven but highly meritorious, and as a *first* film, auguring an extraordinary future for its gifted maker and juvenile star. It is also a near-triumph of the intelligently—and I stress the *intelligently*—mobile camera.

With Sideny Lumet's *Long Day's Journey Into Night* we are buffeted to the other end of the spectrum. Here a very great play has been not translated to the screen but reverently put behind glass—it matters little whether the plate glass around the stuffed fauna of museums or the glass of lenses encasing live theatre in inanimate images.

It is not that Lumet has done anything capriciously wrong—although a shot of Long Island Sound with anachronistic motorboats and yachts is disturbing, and a scene in which two men make drawing-room conversation while working on a car in the garage (Lumet's attempt to extend his range) without once referring to the work at hand is absurd. The problem is that a stage masterpiece can be put on the screen only if the author or some scenarist of genius recreates it in cinematic terms. Here, out of monumental but pedestrian veneration, we have characters and camera pacing restlessly around a small enclosure like so many caged panthers, or, in the case of Ralph Richardson, polar bears. This is stifling in its own right and quickly preempts the sense of confinement and frustration that should belong to the lives of the unhappy foursome.

When, at the very end, Lumet permits himself some fancy, though old-fashioned, camera movements, his endlessly receding camera, besides making the Tyrone family look like David Susskind's guests at the close of

Open End, merely draws attention to unresolved incompatibilities between two art forms. The acting is adequate—in the case of Jason Robards, excellent—and André Previn's music trashy. But neither peripheral pluses nor minuses can much affect the respectful leadenness at the center.

ACROSS THE SANDS AND INTO THE PSYCHE

The Riddle of Lawrence (if riddle there be) is certainly not solved in *Lawrence of Arabia.* But what is made abundantly clear is how one man could accomplish all those superhuman feats: Lawrence did it, very simply, by being Peter O'Toole.

O'Toole is everything a leading man—in or out of movies—should be: young, handsome, sensitive, talented, manly, and charming. Charming not merely in the Cary Grant or James Dean way; this is a mysterious, deep-rooted, magically compelling emanation which can move men, women, mountains—even four-hour movies. He is the unwobbling pivot of *Lawrence of Arabia;* its pillar of strength and, for all I know, pillar of wisdom.

And *Lawrence* is, for all its enormous and somewhat excessive length, and despite the unanswered question at its core, a major film and a magnificent one. It is by far the best of that opprobrious genre known by such names as "spectacle" or "superproduction"; in fact, and this is the supreme tribute, one is never aware of its size, and almost never of its length. Not the least reason for this is that, unlike other such films, it does not have an impossible scenario with either typical Hollywood or typical Christopher Fry dialogue. It is neither holier nor sillier than thou, does not have Kirk Douglas making noble speeches from a cross, and "The Christ," in Lew Wallace's phrase, does not appear in it either in effigy or in person. When God is mentioned in Robert Bolt's sinewy and thoughtful dialogue, he is mentioned to good purpose.

The second hero of the film is the desert. Under David Lean's direction and Fred Young's photography, it performs as never before. I suppose this is because it is not a hammy California desert accustomed to showing off to tourists and film crews; not even one of the better known African deserts, jaded by the admiration of travelers and blasé about cameras; and certainly no studio sandlot. This is a desert its few Bedouins don't bother to look at, and few Westerners after Lawrence have had a chance to look at. It is a virgin desert, and it unfolds its loveliness shyly, dune by dune, vale by vale: white oyster or red in the daytime, seagreen before dawn, sheer silver and quicksilver during a simoom.

When a distant rider approaches through the heat-waves, your eyes ache as they try to keep his figure from deliquescing, as they try to distinguish between mirage and reality. Sometimes the desert yields to rock formations which look like prehistoric temples of savage magenta or sacerdotal mauve. Naked feet of men and camels struggle and fray themselves across these sands and rocks; twisters blow columns of sand over the landscape, pillars of fire that lead nowhere. You feel the temperature rising unendurably at the back of your brain and you are parched down to the pit of your stomach. You have not merely been transported to the desert; the desert has been inculcated in you.

The third hero of *Lawrence of Arabia* is David Lean, the director. Whatever film Lean directs turns to gold, or as much to gold as a director can make it. Films that have the makings of ordinariness about them, like *Brief Encounter* or *Breaking the Sound Barrier,* become extraordinary; films that ought to be no more than gripping or engrossing, like *In Which We Serve* or *Great Expectations,* achieve a simple, incomprehensible perfection, a classic completeness, the possibility for the mind to see them in

the round, as one views a statue. *Lawrence of Arabia* does
not close that perfectly upon itself, but some of its parts
are worth many another good film whole.

There is, for instance, Lawrence's solitary return into
the desert to find a straggler; the episode combines pictorial beauty, suspenseful cutting, profound emotion, extreme restraint to achieve a mounting tension and its
release in a series of climaxes—one of the two or three
greatest bits of movie architectonics ever.

The last climax: Sherif Ali, the haughty Arab who was
hitherto more rival to than collaborator with Lawrence, is
utterly awed by Lawrence's impossible achievement. Ali,
on foot, is bringing his gourd—like a wreath to a con-
queror—to Lawrence who has refused other water, and is
barely able to keep on his camel. With jubilant veneration,
Ali and his Bedouins reach Lawrence. Another director
would now give us a close-up of Lawrence's happy smile
signifying, "I have won—by winning over Ali and his
men, I have conquered Arabia." But there is no
close-up, not till much later. The triumph of Lawrence is
conveyed by a medium-to-long shot: a slight straighten-
ing of the exhausted body, the least bending of the head
toward Ali. We can only guess at the expression of that
far, burnoose-shadowed face, but the guess is more suggestive than any sight.

Or take the poetry which Lean disengages from mere
objects. A nocturnal colloquy is interrupted for a shot of
the desert sky full of overripe stars, a shot held for what
seems like an unconscionable length of time. At first we
feel that nothing the men are saying matters in the
presence of these huge, near, untransient stars; but then
we know better: that the most trivial thing said under the
aspect of these stars becomes ratified by eternity.

Or again, much later, a crazed Lawrence with his
bodyguard of assassins is about to butcher a Turkish company that surrenders to him. As Lawrence's Arabs
marched through the night, we had an occasional shot of
two large ladles hanging from the bottom of a mule-drawn

field canteen. The ladles are continually banging against each other, and their honest, ingenuous clatter has about it a canine fidelity to the riders. "No prisoners!" yells a revenge-maddened Lawrence, and as his column swoops down murderously on the Turks, we are suddenly moved by the sight of the two big, foolish ladles clanging away, uncomprehending, into a massacre.

Lean's camera plots are marvelous—as when we see Lawrence skipping along the tops of Turkish railway cars he has just derailed: David dancing before the Ark, while a horde of ecstatic Bedouin looters follow him in the sand below. Next, we see only Lawrence's boots at the top of the screen and his enormous shadow scurrying across the sand at the bottom; the Bedouins, drunk with victory, follow only a shadow. And Lean elicits superb performances from a large, fine cast—down to the very camels whose every whinnying and snorting becomes meaningful and endearing.

The film has its flaws, to be sure, like leaving certain key actions hardly motivated. It does not examine Lawrence's psychological complexity deeply, does not come to grips with the Deraa episode, shies away from any hint of homosexuality. Some of the last climaxes pall on us. The excellent composer, Maurice Jarre (*Sundays and Cybèle*), was not allowed to follow through on the terse drumbeats that enliven the best scenes—obviously the producer could not see a lot of drumming as a best-selling "original soundtrack album." So periodically we get jolted by stereophonic pseudo-Tchaikovsky. No matter: *Lawrence* remains one of those rare films that cannot be merely watched but have to be lived through.

Lawrence's conquests swept across the plane of vision and are thus eminently photogenic. Sigmund Freud's was a conquest of depth, a dimension not readily accessible to the camera, especially when the deep is that of the human psyche. That is the first strike against John Huston's *Freud*. The second is that psychoanalysis does not conform to dramatic or filmic necessity but lasts for years, flounders, goes around in circles, follows false scents, progresses by tiny and tedious steps. In the film, patients are hypnotized at the first wave of a pencil or cigar; a question is fired at them and pop! out comes a trauma, and pop! in goes a therapeutic suggestion; they wake up and lo! they are appreciably better.

"I'm clearly an analyst and feel that synthesis presents no problems once you've got the analysis," Freud wrote in a letter. But in the film foreshortening becomes—perhaps unavoidably—so great that analysis begins to look like a quick preliminary to a vast synthesis. The transition from neurosis to cure becomes almost as accelerated as those life cycles of flowers or insects in nature documentaries. The effect is, in more than one sense, synthetic.

Still, John Huston and his scenarists have made conscientious efforts in the direction of integrity. They did regrettably, feel obliged to show Martha Freud as a wife at first jealous of the pretty patients, yet later, when her "Sigi" is ready to quit discouraged, nobly urging him on. But they did try to stick to facts, albeit rearranged: attempting to show Freud occasionally bogged down or stumped or too upset to treat someone who then goes mad and dies; presenting some of the parochial Jewishness of the Freud family, though little or no hint of the anti-Semitism Sigmund had to contend with. They even show Freud's own neurosis, possibly overdoing it a little to accommodate Montgomery Clift's mad stare, which is rather more suited to Cagliostro or Dr. Miracle than to Sigmund Freud.

The casting is altogether peculiar. A hoofer like Larry Parks plays Dr. Breuer, while a brilliant actor like Alan Cuthbertson has (like some other notables) a five-second, nonspeaking part. When the bewhiskered Parks and the bearded Clift jointly treat Susannah York by laying her psyche bare, she so far outacts them both that the scene seems like a retelling of Susanna and the Elders. As for the dream sequences, photographed mostly in negative

or overexposure, they belong not on the couch of Dr.
Freud but in the Cabinet of Dr. Caligari.

Even so, the film is respectful and, Lord knows, serious.
And elementary though its analyses are, it had a supposedly sophisticated New York preview audience ex-
citedly Probing Along With Sigi. If it does alert the unini-
tiated to the existence and importance of Freud's work, it
will not have been made in vain.

FASHIONS IN FAILURE

If I were asked to name some of the things the film has not
been able to do, and perhaps cannot do, the successful
conveying of utter bordom, of psychiatric cures, and of
Greek tragedy would rank high on my list. The makers of
Eclipse, David and Lisa, and *Electra* should, therefore, be
treated with forebearance; but one might wonder why they
bothered to try.

That boredom can give substance to a film has been
proved by Michelangelo Antonioni himself in *L'Avventura,* the first part of the trilogy whose conclusion is
Eclipse. But *L'Avventura* had three additional things. It
had a character who was outside and above the general
ennui: a heroine in whom hope, faith of a kind, and
charity of all kinds refused to run dry. It had a plot which,
though a shaggy dog story, kept one's curiosity alert
enough to respond to the parenthetic statements which
were Antonioni's real point. And there was the pullulating
atmosphere of Sicily.

In *Eclipse,* none of this. A girl, vaguely searching for
spiritual fulfillment but not far removed from emotional
catatonia, and a boy, cheerfully but unjoyously thriving on
the meaningless materialistic bustle of his existence, try to
find happiness in a love affair. They fail; and life, to call it

that for lack of a more horrible word, goes on. Of the
boy's existence we know only that he works on the stock
exchange and occasionally consorts with whores. But as
he says—in a line which the subtitles cautiously do not
translate for us—he is too much of a hustler himself to go
with hustlers. Of the girl, we know only that she lives
quite comfortably off some minor literary work and, more
likely, her nouveau riche mother. Piero cannot make anything out of Victoria's non-materialistic yearnings, she
cannot settle for a man she should love much more or not
at all. They part.

To suit the barrenness of the tale, Antonioni has tried
to tell it almost without incidents, and make what incidents there are, with one exception, insignificant. Conversations are sporadic, inchoate, lackluster. Often we
hear the human voice as a brash, amorphous hullabaloo.
At other times, people are at a distance from us; their lips
move, but we hear only an indistinct buzz. And much of
the time there are just street noises, vulgar and arrogant,
or silence. But this is a damaged silence, soiled by the
whirr of a soulless electric fan, the whoosh of jet planes
smudging the sky, the eerie knocking together of tall,
spindly flagpoles—skeletons dancing in the wind, more
macabre than in any old engraving because these bones
never knew flesh.

Eclipse is a metaphor made up of many smaller
metaphors. Man is in eclipse because he has lost belief,
without which he becomes an object. And not content
with making himself into a thing, man must also debase
things, remove them further from reality or purpose. But
things will have their vengeance; they may, in fact, sup-
plant us.

Take the first shot of the film. A nondescript white object lies on top of a row of books. The books are in sharp
focus, the object is only a blob. Presently it moves, and is
revealed to be a man's white-sleeved elbow. Later on,
the heroine remarks, "There are days when a chair, a
table, a book, or a man are all the same thing to me." Our

first glimpse of Vittoria shows her framing some objects with an empty frame, to make them back out of reality into a pseudopicture. And the walls are covered with action paintings in which both man and objects are traduced to the absurd.

Throughout the film, Antonioni exhibits his customary brilliance in handling details. There is the moment when Vittoria decides to go to Piero's apartment and give herself to him, only to be struck motionless in the middle of the street as she watches another young man, handsome in a very different way, walk by. "He has a beautiful face!" she exclaims with the wistfulness of a sudden, aching insight into a world where one is free to make choices, but condemned to choose. Or the moment when Piero tells Vittoria that he will kiss her on the other side of the street: the roadway is ribbed with thick white lines to denote a crossing, but these flat lines, beyond which lurks decision, become at once a steep, exhausting stairway. In the middle, Vittoria observes, "We are halfway across," reminding us, surely not accidentally, of Dante's first line.

Particularly imaginative is the last sequence of the film, from which the hero and heroine have faded away. The movie began with the end of a previous love affair, and now we realize that in its beginning was its end—that what seemed merely a point of departure was, in truth, a giant flash-forward hanging over the rest of the film and the rest of Vittoria's life. So we see now, for the last time, Vittoria and Piero embracing in his office. Suddenly, both look into the camera: his eyes show discomfiture and the need to escape to something else; hers, fear and despair. They make brave promises for the future. But the objects now take over. Piero is promptly surrounded by stock-exchange reports flapping in the breeze from the window, pencils hedging him in, and a whole orchestra of telephones from bass to piccolo clamoring for his attention. He yields almost contentedly. Vittoria wanders away alongside of curious parapets and fences isolating her anguished face from the world.

Forthwith we are at the place where these lovers used to meet. The customary objects and sounds are all there as before, living their ineluctable, unswerving and therefore real life; but the people are different, unknown to us, meaningless. A sports car we associate with the hero, the sliver of wood which the heroine dropped into a water container, the chattering burlap and straw covering on an unfinished building, the jet planes which strange eyes are watching, the white lines of the crossing which is nobody's *gradus ad Parnassum* now. Close-ups of an embittered old man and a worn-looking woman: The hero and heroine as they will be?

The last and most awe-inspiring image of all: an ultra-modern street light goes on; in blinding close-up, it takes over the screen; and the movie ends. Is this radiant end an eclipse? It is: the brilliance of artificial suns, the splendor of objects, and the long, neon-streaked night of the soul.

Why should so many superb details add up to an unsatisfactory film? Because we cannot care for people who will not even put up a fight against boredom, because we are not allowed to go inside the characters, because no possible alternative to defeat is offered. A young woman from Kenya arouses Vittoria's longing for Africa; but even in that unovercivilized land we hear of anxiety and bloody turmoil. There, too, life is becoming objectified—what was once an elephant's foot is now the leg of a coffee table; and objects overshadow the living—Kenya is at its best in the inanimate photographs in an album and on walls. *Eclipse* is a luminous failure.

In *David and Lisa,* we can overlook the deficiencies caused by inadequate financing (the bane of independent film-makers in America), such as wobbly sound recording, pedestrian photography, scenes that seem stagey and insufficiently rehearsed. What cannot be excused is the inferior writing, at least partly the consequence of the psychiatric theme.

David and Lisa are adolescents in a school for disturbed children. A gradually developing mutual affection and enlightened psychiatric care enable them to give up their destructive delusions and head for apparent salvation. I do not know who is more to blame: Dr. T. I. Rubin, for his book, or Eleanor Perry, for her screenplay. Both tried to keep the technical matter of psychiatry down to a minimum and see the boy, his unhappy parents, the torn little girl and the kindly psychiatrist in properly human terms. But it's no go. The view is still that of a doctor, and a well-meaning social worker, not the artistically valid one of the poet.

The psychiatric sessions seem merely sheepish in their effort to be humane and unscientific, and the rest of the plot does not escape the shorthand of clichés about domineering mothers, weak fathers and fellow-inmates who are stock little homosexuals and nymphomaniacs in the making. David and Lisa's talk, however accurate it may be, is only the language of dementia or pathos, never that of poetry. Lisa, in fact, maniacally talks in abominable doggerel; but even the prose of the other characters is no closer to the language of insight.

Frank Perry's direction escapes few of the pitfalls for beginners: hysterical cutting, not showing the main character in a scene for the longest time, the obvious crane shot at the end. Yet he has imaginatively cast the little-known but greatly talented Keir Dullea and Janet Margolin as David and Lisa, and obtained performances which triumph even over Marc Lawrence's blatantly graceless score.

Michael Cacoyannis' *Electra* is not a tragedy, merely a disaster. The writer-director, who previously proved himself a true artist with present-day subjects, comes a cropper with Euripides. He was clearly trying to steer a middle course between the vulgar pretentiousness of modernizations like Jules Dassin's *Phaedra* and the uncinematographic stodginess of leteral transcriptions like

George Tzavellas's *Antigone*. But instead of avoiding Scylla and Charybdis, he falls between two chairs.

The poetry and much of the psychological profundity of Euripides are cut, and what remains of dialogue and acting that continually jerk us twenty-five centuries forward and back. How is one to reconcile a stilted, grand-style Clytemnestra with a neo-realist Electra, modern to her very hair-do? A chorus that shuttles between ordinary women shuffling and skipping, and hooded Parcae filing and dancing in stately unison? Walter Lassally's photography of the Greek landscape is majestic, and the film has won numerous prizes at the Salonika festival. Patriotism, at any rate, is not yet dead in Greece.

LOVE AT TWENTY

DESPAIR AT FORTY

Love at Twenty is like a dusty, bumpy, twisting country road: not easy to drive along, leading nowhere in particular, but sometimes charming or scenic. As a film, it has no specific importance, but it does raise two general questions that merit attention.

First, the question of subtitles. No doubt about it, the worst subtitles are still preferable to dubbing, but must we really have the worst subtitles? *Love at Twenty* consists of five episodes—French, Italian, German, Japanese, and Polish—related only insofar as in each a young writer-director from the respective country has a look at some aspect of youthful love. Since the film is in five languages, it gives the subtitle writers a splendid chance to show off their incompetence in no less than six languages, English, as usual, included. (I cannot vouch for the Japanese part, but the very paucity of subtitles seems indicative.)

There is, to begin with, the matter of sheer ignorance. In the French episode, the young people are music and hi-fi enthusiasts. The narrator observes at one point, "*Ils se parlaient stéréophonie,*" which, of course, means, "They talked about stereo." But to the subtitle writer it is, "They talked stereophonically," which if it had any meaning, might imply that they blared at each other from every nook and cranny. Not only is this inaccurate but, worse, it suggests a pretentiousness of diction wholly alien to the gifted François Truffaut.

Such mistranslation can reach alarming proportions. I remember with especial horror a subtitle in Clouzot's *The Truth,* in which the accused Brigitte Bardot is told by the judge that already as a little girl she stole her sister's doll. The word used for "steal"—a deliberately somewhat grandiloquent one to poke fun at bureaucracy—was *dérober,* and, sure enough, in the fractured French subtitle this come out as "already as a little girl you would take the clothes off your sister's dolls," implying that, instead of being merely selfish and childishly amoral, the unhappy girl was a lesbian fetishist and incestuous voyeur.

More dangerous, because more frequent, is the insensitivity to detail, to the tone or overtones of a statement, to its originality and literary value. Thus, in the German episode, the young journalist who flies back from Singapore to see his illegitimate child, born a week before, tells its mother how brave she has been. The legitimate husband of the woman in the adjoining hospital bed comments ironically, "*Ach so haben, Sie's auch gemerkt?*"—"Ah, so you've noticed it, too?" But the subtitle reads, "So you realized, too?"

Now "realized" is exactly the wrong word here. If the young man were, in fact, realizing anything even at this late stage, the irony would be uncalled for. But something has only just begun to dawn on him; hence the well-deserved sarcastic barb of "noticed," which the "realized" blunts to nothingness. Later on, the hero tries to justify himself to the girl for not marrying her. She is a terrible little *bourgeoise,* he tells her; she should have gone to Switzerland for an abortion: "If we here in Europe were to have kids right away, *würden wir uns gegenseitig auf den Füssen herumtrampeln*"—"we would be stamping around on one another's feet." But the subtitle has it, "there wouldn't be room any more." Mood and character are thus falsified.

No less sinister are the omissions of bits of dialogue that seem unimportant to the translators, a needless diversion of the viewer's attention from the images. In the Polish episode, made by the highly talented Andrzej Wajda (whose *Kanal* is a masterpiece, and whose other films all have moments of brilliance), a young man rescues a child from the polar bears' pit at the zoo. This so impresses an impetuous young girl that she takes him to her home and bed. When the girl notices that her hero has scratched his hand during the rescue, she proceeds to put iodine on the wound. "I'm scared it's going to sting," protests the brave fellow, and we have the first hint of the irony which informs this little parable.

But the subtitulists blithely ignore the statement. It is typical, however, that in the Italian episode, which is as trashy in its dialogue as in everything else, great care was taken to translate almost every insipid platitude. Which goes to show that there is less concern here for the audience's ability to keep up than indomitable bad taste and poor judgment on the part of the translators.

Lastly, there is the inevitable bad English, which strikes one as even more offensive in the subtitles of a film like Michael Cacoyannis' *Electra*. There the heroes of Greek tragedy—that high point of linguistic beauty and purity—emerged as purveyors of solecisms such as "I cannot help but stop," or illiteracies like "Who can a man turn to?" Again, in a new film version by the Comédie Française of *Figaro's Marriage,* Beaumarchais' elegant and witty prose is translated into the basest basic English, whereas the songs are taken from Jacques Barzun's printed translation. The result suggests that Beaumarchais was a poetic albatross ineffectually dragging his wings when forced down into prose—whereas, if anything, the opposite is the case.

The argument for the defense, of course, is that you can't keep people reading when they should be watching, and that too much print obliterates the pictures. Granted these are valid considerations, but I am convinced that more intelligent compromises could be found. And I have no doubt that our graduate schools and the ranks of our less established and pecunious *littérateurs* could be made to yield translators of greater competence. Better subtitles could produce better—if not bigger—audiences.

The second question raised by *Love at Twenty* is that of the episodic film: Can a collection of short stories be effective on screen? Only, I think, if the impact is cumulative, and if there is thematic development. For the film, unlike writing, exists in time more than in space, and so resembles music rather than literature. Five unrelated short films—even if each deals with the vaguely unifying topic of young love—tend to create the effect of several movements of *different* symphonies played consecutively. Symphonies of the same period, if you like, but by different composers. It is the sort of thing one inaugurates Lincoln Center with, but it is not music.

What *Love at Twenty* does demonstrate is that Truffaut, though always competent, has exhausted the reminiscent, quasi-autobiographical vein of *The 400 Blows* (by the way, what a mistranslation that title is!) and must move on to other themes; and that Wajda even in his minor efforts bears watching and thinking about. Clever as it is, though, I regret his archly stylized treatment of sexual intercourse in a sequence that otherwise subsists happily on imaginatively heightened realism.

Love at Twenty, further, indicates that Marcel Ophüls, the son of Max, may in time become a director of note, though at the moment, like his late father, he tends toward sentimental trivialities. Renzo Rossellini, who made the Italian installment, takes over exactly where his father left off—grandiosely wallowing in vacuity. But Roberto, with a little help from the late war, made a genuine contribution to the film, which now enables two Rossellinis to have one brilliant future behind them. The Japanese sequence, by Shintaro Ishihara, a name which it is too early to start struggling to remember, is distinguished only by derivative montage and gratuitous violence.

Speaking of futures in the past, I know of no more terrifying example than that of Judy Garland. Two new films, *I Could Go on Singing* and *A Child Is Waiting*, should make it abundantly clear to any but the most rabid Judiolatrists that the old Judy is no more, and that the new Judy never was. In the first of these films, Miss Garland plays herself, which is horrifying; in the second, someone else, which is impossible.

I shall pass over the fact that her face has become that of a wizened child—rather like what Mae West used to call Shirley Temple, "a 5-year-old-midget"—and that her figure resembles the giant economy-size tube of tooth paste in girls' bathrooms: squeezed intemperately at all points, it acquires a shape that defies definition by the most resourceful solid geometrician. Nor shall I dwell on Miss Garland's acting, which surpasses that of any *doyenne* of the Actors Studio for unrelieved substitution of hysterics for histrionics, so that the reading of a line is punctuated not by pauses for breathing but by spasms of the larynx. The truly deploable thing to consider is the effect premature stardom is apt to have on a Hollywood personality. In Miss Garland we now have someone whose physical and psychic development has been arrested, who has neither youth nor age, but as it were a senescent infantilism belonging only in the paintings of Botero, and not even there.

I Could Go on Singing is, despite the able Ronald Neame (who gave us *Tunes of Glory*), merely standard fare in an age without standards. In *A Child Is Waiting,* the avant-gardist John Cassavetes demonstrates that, given the chance, he makes as good a commercial director as the next fellow, but not much more. I have, however, serious doubts whether the garish spectacle of retarded children makes a suitable background for a story that is only a short cut above the standard Hollywood "drama," complete with child star who, though supposedly retarded, seems intelligent and attractive enough for Groton. I doubt also whether Abby Mann's attempted mingling of documentary and fictional techniques in the screenplay helps either mode, and whether the protracted exposure to so many authentically deformed, jabbering little creatures will produce on the audience the desired effect and not its opposite, as it did on me.

TRIAL AND ERROR

The sad thing about Orson Welles is that he has consistently put his very real talent to the task of glorifying his imaginary genius. Now one of the few definable traits of a genius is that no matter how much he loves himself, he loves something beyond himself more. There is nothing about the work of Orson Welles to convince us that he has ever felt humility of love anywhere except in front of a mirror. The success of *Citizen Kane,* Welles's only unassailable achievement, stems in large part from the fact that the protagonist elicits mingled contempt and envy, feelings that Welles is perfectly equipped to dispense. The sentimental note in *Kane,* the quest for Rosebud, is much more of a useful narrative device than a convincing expression of fellow feeling.

But if Welles's solipsism vitiates his bid for genius, his colossal lack of taste tends to mar even his talent. True, when he adapts or concocts entertainments such as *Journey into Fear, The Lady from Shanghai,* or *Touch of Evil,* or when he broadcasts an invasion from Mars, there is little or nothing for his proliferating showmanship to smother, but in such cases the audience cannot be quite sure that a really good three-ring circus wouldn't be closer to art. In his attempts at great works, however—and he is fatally drawn to them—Welles's tastelessness becomes a nagging pain in the discriminating spectator's stomach. *Macbeth, Lear, Othello, Moby Dick, Danton's Death*—all these were approached by Welles as though they were no different from something by Jules Verne or Eric Ambler, and, by the time Welles got through with them, they weren't.

What characterizes Welles's work is the continual subordination or rejection of the idea for the sake of the trick. This, to be sure, may be understandable coming from someone who is obviously strong on tricks and weak on ideas. But, let it be said once more, *tout comprendre* is not *tout pardonner*. The closing sequence of *The Lady from Shanghai,* in which two characters try to shoot each other in a maze of mirrors and cannot tell the person from his reflection is emblematic of Welles's work (with the exception of *Citizen Kane* and perhaps *The Magnificent Ambersons*): always perceiving reality distorted by a cabal of mirrors, Welles repeatedly misses the mark.

For his newest film, Welles has picked Kafka's *The Trial,* and if ever two temperaments were polar opposites, they are the delicately devious Kafka, whose meanings seem one great iridescent elusiveness, and the assertive Welles, who loves the stridently grandiose, the unmistakable effect. The only trait shared by them is irony, but where Kafka's irony hovers in disturbing suspension over ego and universe, Welles's crashes down so heavily on a specific, and sometimes questionable, target that it tends to annihilate itself along with its object.

There are so many things wrong with *The Trial* that I shall have to limit myself to a few principal objections. The gravest of these is that Kafka's work has to be perceived on at least three levels—psychological, political, religious—whereas Welles, with typical oversimplification, makes it purely political. No less improper is the turning of the protagonist K. into someone who is manifestly free of guilt and never doubts his blamelessness;

as W. H. Auden points out in *The Dyer's Hand,* "If the K. of *The Trial* were innocent, he would cease to be K. and become nameless . . ." Concomitantly Kafka's world is irrational, pettifogging, dilatory, unsympathetic, ugly, and worst of all, incomprehensible. But it is not, like the world in the film, grossly vicious and, in its lack of shading, dull.

Again, there is no crude and obvious trickery in the novel; the logic of time and space is not deliberately jumbled. The film, however, is continually tampering with sequential and topographical consistency. This, no doubt, is largely owing to Welles's determination to simplify matters, even to the point of stating in the narration, right at the beginning, that *The Trial* has the illogic of dreams, and underlining this by focusing on K.'s sleeping face. For once you have implied that the whole thing is one big nightmare, anything goes.

Unfortunately all urgency goes, too. The audience is only too happy to shrug off the whole thing as mere phantasmagoria. Yet Kafka's impact derives precisely from the fact that everything is nearly ordinary, nearly classifiable, nearly our own experience, so that we, like the hero, are perpetually jumping for solutions dangled just above us, and cannot settle into easy disbelief or, what is worse, easy belief in some obvious answer. If Kafka, the artist, errs, it is because he himself does not know the answers (which, in art, is as likely to be a virtue); if Welles, the nonartist, errs, it is because he knows all the answers, and they strike us as wrong.

Here are a few examples: The office in which Kafka's K. works is a perfectly everyday office, which makes it a more likely scene of rivalries, anxieties, humiliations, and failure than the office in the film, where identical desks over which bend identical ciphers stretch literally as far as the eye can see. The effect achieved would suit the works of expressionists like Kaiser and Toller; but expressionism was concerned with universal symbols and social issues, whereas Kafka's primary concern was with burrowing into the individual psyche.

If the lawyer's quarters in the novel are lit by candles—with disquieting implications of stinginess, backwardness or a guilty fear of light—Welles seizes on this as an excuse for plastering every inch of the set with candles: enough candles to outfit all the churches in Spain. The effect is baroque and bizarre—striking but meaningless.

Kafka ends his novel with K. being butchered with a knife even as in a distant window someone waves at him. This has psychological value (failure—death—in the proximity of possible help; or, perhaps, misguided optimism to the very last), religious significance (we are the human sacrifice on the altar of an inscrutable divinity), and political meaning (the state, or society, disposes of us obscurely, brutally, efficiently). In the film, K.—played by Tony Perkins as Jack Armstrong Behind the Iron Curtain—is dumped into a pit by his cowardly executioners who do not dare stab him but toss in after him what looks like a firecracker. He picks it up, makes a speech full of bravado and platitudes, and hurls, or almost hurls, the firecracker back at his tormentors, whereupon (I swear I'm not making this up) an atom bomb explodes. Welles has degraded the ending to an absurd piece of didacticism.

There is something to be said for the sets and locations and for some of the visual effects, however reductive they are of Kafka's purpose, and for Arnoldo Foa's police inspector and Akim Tamiroff's Bloch. But Welles the actor is unsubtle as the defense attorney; Welles the director cannot get a decent performance from even as gifted an actress as Jeanne Moreau; and Welles the scenarist goes in for wit like "What's this pornograph?" (about a phonograph), profundities such as "Even the saints have temptations," felicities such as "I'm just sick with guilt," and many a bit of aphoristic satire like "A computer—one of those electronic gimmicks that give you the answer to everything you see." Even if it did not go at Kafka's expense, this would be quite bad enough. To quote Auden's essay on Kafka again, "He [who] tries to interpret a parable . . . will only reveal himself." Welles goes this one better and reveals himself with horrifying success without half trying to interpret the parable.

Another new film, the Italian *Mondo Cane* ("A Bestial World"), on the other hand, successfully reveals whatever is horrifying about human nature. Under the guise of a plain documentary, a reportage of quaint folkways around the world, it manages to be the most devastating travelogue in 236 years—or since the appearance of *Gulliver's Travels*. It documents wittily, ruthlessly, and beautifully man's inhumanity to men, animals, nature, and himself. The indictment of our inconsistency, vanity, meanness, and stupidity is made fiercely effective by consummate photography and economically mordant narration. The particular brilliance, however, is in the film's structure: it progresses from madness to complementary madness, and the seeming contrasts between aborigines and ourselves turn out to be parallels.

Thus a sequence in a Pasadena pet cemetery where Pharaonic funeral pomp and orgies of grief accompany the demise of Fido is followed by a scene in a Formosan restaurant where terrified caged puppies, awaiting the same fate, watch their fellows being devoured by lip-smacking gastronomes of Taipae. Or, in an idiotic mass ceremony, hordes of Australian Girl Lifesaver "rescue" male victims of a mock drowning by applying mouth-to-mouth respiration—redundantly bringing life to the living amidst foolish sexual games. But not far away, on Bikini, the bomb has crazed the animal world: birds lead ghastly underground lives, fish climb trees, and sea turtles, their sense of orientation destroyed, painfully die deep inland.

Not since Brecht's *Seven Deadly Sins* has there been such a Philippic against both extremes and such skeptical doubt of any *via media*. And what middle road is there? If one old woman among the grim crones toiling away to beautify themselves at Vic Tanny's seems happy, it is only because a rubber belt massaging her behind elicits a garishly sexual smile in front. Dread irony is everywhere. The sea turtle baking to death thinks it is in the water and dies in a fearful parody of swimming. In Macao, a rich man's funeral entails burning large quantities of his money; tersely the narrator comments: "The heirs watch the solemn ceremony in tears." Between two scenes in which the natives of New Guinea are at their Stone Age best, we see them piously embracing Christian ritual. *Mondo Cane* does simply and efficaciously what the Theatre of the Absurd accomplishes usually only with much huffing and puffing. True, some of the alleged facts of *Mondo Cane* are, most likely, fiction; but I feel that this is a case of artistically fictionalizing truths, rather than crudely falisifying them.

SCRAMBLED EGGS

For this Easter season, the cinema has been laying eggs plentifully. Grimly as I pursued my nonegg hunt, I could find no films free from the curse of the ovoid. "I don't care for the cinema any more," remarked t'.e mother in *A Taste of Honey,* "it's getting more and more like the theater." If so—take it from one who reviews the drama, too—we've had it.

Consider, first, two American films set in exotic places: *Nine Hours to Rama,* which deals with India and the assassination of Gandhi; and *The Ugly American,* concerning Sarkhan (a pseudonymous Vietnam) and its political and military turmoil. Both films are based on subliterary novels, but whereas *Rama* sticks close to the original, *American* does not. Both scenarios, however, are equally execrable. They are, in fact, insults to the gravity of the events treated, and are, in turn, made ridiculous by the nobility of the backgrounds.

Against the ancient splendors of India's architecture and scenery, dilapidated commonplaces like "Are you afraid of me?—Then I wouldn't be here.—Of yourself,

perhaps?" followed by decomposing platitudes like
"Opposites attract!" produce a peculiarly ludicrous and
depressing effect. "I tried, but I couldn't get you out of my
mind," says the hero, a young fanatic who kills Gandhi
largely because his married girl friend cannot run away
with him instantaneously. For a banality such as "Your
hair is darker and more beautiful than the night," which
Amaru or Bhartrihari would have discarded a dozen or
more centuries ago, he is rewarded not with "Are you an
elephant boy?" or "Are you an engineer?" but with, of all
things, "Are you a poet?"

And it is surely a bitter affront to Gandhi's majesty,
humility, and above all, originality, to have someone say
of him: "He sits there, a lonely, tired, anguished man." Is
there no greatness that Hollywood, the great leveler, cannot flatten into a pancake? Pancake make-up, by the
way, is also working overtime, and all the main Indian
characters (except the Mahatma—after all, film crews
could get lynched) are played by Americans, Britishers,
Canadians, and Horst Buchholz. The only interesting line
in the whole movie is the thick brown one visible on the
inside of every white collar.

Mark Robson has directed *Nine Hours to Rama* with a
remarkable lack of imagination and suspense, and the cast
walk through their parts, with the exception of Buchholz,
who waltzes through his. But José Ferrer, as the chief of
police, is unexpectedly authentic and even touching, and J.
S. Casshyap's Gandhi is satisfactory, And, in Arthur Ib-
betson's photography, India itself almost justifies seeing
the film, especially if one can turn it inside out or, more
precisely, backgroundside forward.

In *The Ugly American*, the superb backgrounds shot in
and around Bangkok have to contend with the additional
sins of pretentiousness and a wavering point of view. This
is not to say that plain bad dialogue isn't abundant, as
when Harrison Carter MacWhite (Marlon Brando),
our ambassador to Sarkhan, addresses the local nationalist
leader, his wartime buddy, with, "What happened to us,
Deong?"—a line making its triumphal transit from the

bedroom of domestic drama to the arena of the political spectacular.

Similarly, MacWhite, whom we are to view as an honest, intelligent, strong but humanly fallible American diplomat, keeps uttering encomia like "This sort of thing is worth a million dollars in foreign aid!" (about a small hospital run by Americans) and "You know, this is so like Deong to do something like this!" (about a piece of sculpture sent him and his wife as a present). And what of Ambassador MacWhite's saying to Deong, as they informally eat and get drunk together while, quite informally, settling the future of Sarkhan: "What you got here? Kosher pickle?"

MacWhite's character makes little sense. He is one part surly, slow-spoken but profound, Brandoish prima donna; one part taciturn, tough yet occasionally boyishly exuberant, Brandoish matinee idol; one part demigod; one part bumbler; and the remaining 96 parts Marlon Brando. Everything he says or does is preceded by an almost audible Cape Canaveral-like countdown, and one has the feeling that between his cue and answer there is always time for the pro-Western forces to lose at least one blitzkrieg. "If you're just absolutely sure, darling," Brando tells his wife (played uninterestingly by Sandra Church), "to keep your mouth shut at all times, you'll be all right." He himself has no such luck with mouth either shut or open.

The other principals are conceived with equal ambivalence. The nationalist Deong (played mediocrely by Eiji Okada) is, by turns, a decent, lovable, ordinary guy, as Americanly wholesome beneath his mispronounced l's as any Rodgers-and-Hammerstein hero; then a mouther of every Communist slogan, who quite rightly cannot be told apart from the Communists; then, again, an honest, noble dupe, taken in and murdered by his own trusted second-in-command. The Premier of Sarkhan (beautifully played by Kukrit Pramoj) is first represented as a sleekly sneaky Oriental, against whom Deong was right to fulminate and rebel; next as a wise, courageous, generously upright man who alone can avert all-out war; lastly as one who has to admit that he did play a game of reactionary nepotism. And the only American who is represented as being authentically and heartily ugly is a very minor figure who gets his just deserts in no time flat.

George Englund's direction, however, has its moments, especially in a riot scene at the airport when the Ambassador arrives; and there are two times when even the screenplay comes to life: during a Senate investigation at the beginning, and again, at the very end where the first ingenious, psychologically and cinematographically effective point is made. But it comes a bit late.

While the American films concern themselves with men of—however misplaced—good will, the European ones are preoccupied with rascality—however metaphysically contemplated. But wickedness can be made as dreary as sacrosanctness. There is, first, Claude Chabrol's and Françoise Sagan's collaboration, *Landru*. To try to outdo even such minor Chaplin as *Monsieur Verdoux* requires some arrogance, but in that area both Chabrol and Sagan are amply endowed. Since his relatively modest start with *Le Beau Serge*, Chabrol has bombarded us with such grandiloquent trash as *The Cousins* and such indescribably boring pieces of inhumanity as *Leda*. Mille. Sagan's career of infamy needs no rehearsing here, but Georges Schlocker's comment on her current Parisian play, *La Robe mauve de Valentine*, is relevant: "By way of bait for her superficial following, Miss Sagan conducts a fashion show with dresses by Dior. Truly, the gowns have it, for the people are hollow."

Much the same happens in *Landru*, Jacques Saulnier has designed almost painfully heady settings, Maurice Albray has created witty and spectacular costumes, and Jean Rabier has photographed them in pastel shades worthy of Renoir *père* at his lushly stifling best. But we cannot, and are not meant to, consider as people the phantasms caught in this trap of color, deliberately dehumanized whether they be murderers or victims, wives or mistresses,

policemen or their quarry, and placed on sets often made
to resemble the stage of a puppet theater.

We recongnize no human beings, only thefts from more
humane film-makers: Chaplin, Truffaut, the Keystone
Kops. But whereas the war scenes in *Jules et Jim* add a
dimension to the plot, in *Landru* they are merely garishly
tinted ornamentation; whereas a gag in *Monsieur Verdoux*
is used economically, in *Landru* it is milked besides being
stolen. And typically, Landru's character is sheer manipulation. He is a walking anthology of French poetry
from Lamartine to Baudelaire, a sophisticated amateur of
opera and *bel canto,* who, when apprehended, bids good-
bye to his mistress and love nest with Manon's farewell,
"Adieu, notre petite table!" (which the subtitles meaninglessly turn into "Adieu to our little *tableau!*"), but who
must presently become inconsistently ignorant and speak
of "that painter—Manot or Manet or Monot."

Is there, perhaps, an idea behind this? Apropos of
Baudelaire, Landru comments, "They always call geniuses
monsters," and explains that he is saying this "for the sake
of posterity." But Landru is not shown as anything nearer
to a genius than a wisecracker, nor as anything more
charming than Macheath as he might be played at the
Théâtre National Populaire, and it is only the other people
who are exceedingly slow-witted. If, however, the point
is to ridicule humanity, there must be better ways of doing
it than this.

A Spanish import, *Lazarillo,* based on that marvelously
hardheaded, proletarian, and picaresque novel of the
1550s, *Lazarillo de Tormes,* proves only that an
amateurish film-maker is no match for Franco's censorship. When I saw the motto with which Cesar Ardavin
prefaces his film—a quotation from St. Augustine—I
knew the jig was up. Sure enough, none of the novel's
robustness, and very little of its irony, survives. Where the
book contrasts the greed of the clergy and folly of the gen-
try with the great physical hunger of the poor which forces
them to become rogues to survive, and ends with the poor
hero's absurd *embourgeoisement,* the movie gives us a

nice Horatio Alger story in which blows knock out no
teeth, the hero is a Murillo cherub rather than a shrewd
starveling, priests and monks become sextons and actors
impersonating monks, and vices are poorly impersonated
by peccadilloes.

The risible incompetence of the subtitles provides the
only relief from boredom; we get everything from pidgin
English to pig Latin. What this extraordinary story needed
was the presence of a Buñuel and the absence of a Franco.

GODLESSNESS AND GODAWFULNESS

Like the great artist he is, Ingmar Bergman is striving for
that limitation, that circumscription, in which the master,
as Goethe says, reveals himself. The human foursome,
two related pairs of lovers corresponding to the string
quartet, has attracted him before (notably in *Dreams*),
but he never before hewed to it so closely as in the new
Winter Light. And in the restraint of this film—carried to
fanatical extremes even in such things as camera angles
and cutting—the master truly reveals himself. But, sad to
say, the film-maker's mastery alone does not guarantee
a great film. *Winter Light* is scarcely even a good one.

It concerns a dour, middle-aged village pastor still in
love with his dead wife but having an affair with an
amiably dowdy yet helplessly passionate schoolmarm. The
pastor smarts under what he calls "God's silence"; the
schoolmarm is an unbeliever but, with characteristically
Bergmanesque irony, has had "evidences" of God such as
the pastor cannot have. He wants to end the relationship,
while she hangs on all the more desperately. The same
stark Swedish village and same arid northern winter are
shared by another couple: a fisherman and his wife with
three children and a fourth coming. The fisherman's anxieties over the atom bomb, which, he reads somewhere,

the Chinese will use indiscrimately, are driving him to suicide. His wife, a simple soul, cannot cope with such problems. But neither can the pastor, to whom she sends him.

The fisherman, further appalled by the pastor's *accidia,* kills himself. The pastor breaks off and does not break off with the teacher. The fisherman's wife stiffens herself to carrying on alone. The pastor's mistress stiffens herself to carrying on somehow with the pastor, though without his love. And the pastor stiffens himself to carrying on with his ecclesiastic duties without the presence of God.

It is a stiff, barren film, in which situations are guessed at rather than explored, a suicide is received impassively by all concerned, and the human heart seems lost in the depths of a bottomless, hyperborean winter. The action, such as it is, takes place between matins in one church and vespers in another. Few people attend the first service, and only the atheistic school-mistress the other.

The film conveys its mood brilliantly. It could take for its motto two verses of the great Swedish poet, Gunnar Ekelöf: "You say you almost can no longer breathe/What of it? Who do you think can breathe?" Nobody in *Winter Light* can breathe freely. The faces, all the faces, register only more or less violent despair, more or less frustrated expectancy. There are outbursts of passionate desire and passionate loathing or self-loathing. But they are seen only as under glass—glass which really is not glass but ice, impenetrably thick and unbreakable.

The dialogue is, unfortunately, less than distinguished when grappling with the issue of God. This inadequacy we know from before: from *The Seventh Seal* and *Through a Glass Darkly*—the image of "the spider God," by the way, recurs here. We must face the fact, then, that Bergman is no St. John of the Cross. When, however, he deals with human beings rending one another, Bergman's dialogue is as pointed as ever. "I am fed up with you," says the pastor to his mistress, "your eczema, your periods, your chilblains," and he excoriates her in a scene all the more fierce for being set in an innocent country schoolroom where the boys' and girls' lavatory keys hang, neatly labeled, peaceably side by side. Finally he warns, "I'd better go now, before I say anything worse." "Is there anything worse?" asks the young woman, and, helped by Ingrid Thulin's masterly handling of these simple, penetrant words, Bergman achieves the grandeur of true pathos.

I have already mentioned the spareness of the film: no music, scarcely any long shots, minimal cutting. In one bravura scene, the pastor, played by Gunnar Björnstrand with his customary controlled intensity, begins to read a letter from his mistress. Presently the camera plants itself squarely before Miss Thulin, who now proceeds to speak the contents of the long, impassioned letter. She looks directly at us and tells her dismal little story under the unblinkingly merciless scrutiny of the camera: for minutes on end she meets her agony head on. It is like a screen test being administered to a performer, only much more ruthless. And it works.

Again, near the end, there is a shot of Miss Thulin alone in the dark church. Her head, in profile, is lowered and totally dark except for contours limned by the thinnest outline of light. The next shot is of Björnstrand's face, also in profile, but fully lit by the lamps of the sacristy. The two antithetical profiles correspond. The antipodes are not really antipodes; they are united by their suffering.

Sven Nykvist's photography performs its usual miracles, as when the pastor and the teacher are driving across a darkening snowy landscape, and their faces are shot behind a passing parade of wintry trees reflected in the car window through which we look in. But more important than any tricks, the photography faithfully yet economically conveys the bleakness of the weather, the atmosphere, and the *condition humaine*.

Here the acting also does wonders. Miss Thulin, as the school-mistress and mistress, impeccably blends frowziness—almost frumpishness—with the awesome ardor of the Rilkean beloved shooting up far above her lover's

pettiness. That a woman of such glorious loveliness and
femininity should consent to heap so many ashes on
the fire of her beauty does immense credit to Miss
Thulin's artistic integrity. The same goes for the darkly
ravishing Gunnel Lindblom, splendid in the tiny role of
the fisherman's wife. She is marvelously solicitous, bewildered, and tough, and as ready as Miss Thulin to forgo
all glamor. (American actresses, please note.) Max von
Sydow's fisherman in a sea of troubles is a beautifully understated performance. Only Björnstrand seems less suited
to this and other recent parts: he does not strike me as a
man who could cry. At least, he is not an actor who can.

For all its powerful sequences—let me mention also
a church service fraught with chilling undercurrents
—*Winter Light* is one of Bergman's rare disappointing
films. This may be because the absence of God can
touch us only if we are first made to feel his presence. Or
it may be that such starkness of plot, such spareness of incident, simply does not lend itself to filmic treatment. Or,
perhaps, Bergman, whatever his greatness, does not have
enough "ideas" for a film of ideas. Or, conceivably, God,
around whom the whole thing revolves, is not a very interesting character. In any case, *Winter Light* is inferior
Bergman. But it is Bergman, and, despite its limitations,
deserves to be seen. To quote Ekelöf again, "It is its
meaninglessness which gives life its meaning." As a sermon on this text, Pastor Bergman's film—especially in the
sumptuous irony of its last line—certainly does make its
point.

A sermon of a very different sort is *Black Fox*, a
documentary about the rise and fall of Adolf Hitler. Its
maker, Louis Clyde Stoumen, is a man of many talents: he
is a photographer, film-maker, writer, designer, and intellectual. Such manifold qualities are needed for a good
documentary, indeed for a good film of any kind. Nothing
in this world (with the possible exception of action painting and film criticism) has suffered more from the
one-sidedness of its practitioners.

Black Fox compares the rise of Hitler to that of Reynard the Fox in Goethe's retelling of the folk tale, and Stoumen crosscuts from the Teutonically oppressive, malefic illustrations by Kaulbach to the malefic, Teutonically oppressive history of the Third Reich. Stoumen also uses, judiciously and tastefully, the graphic art of George Grosz and of the film's staff artist, Byron Goto—to say nothing of Hitler's own unsuccessful paintings: *qualis artifex*! A little less judiciously, perhaps, we get the Doré illustrations for Dante's *Inferno*.

Writing and visualization are equally good in this commingling of history, art, hitherto unknown film clippings, the folk parable, knowing montage, and a just sense of how much horror is horrible without becoming unbearable. With the possible exception of Resnais' *Night and Fog*, this is by far the best antitribute to Nazism ever put on film. And Stoumen's artistry extends even to the acquisition of an imaginative musical score by a genuine composer, Ezra Laderman, a rare boon in movies, especially American ones. Even people who are sure that they could not care less for a film like *Black Fox* will, if they see it, care.

I must report also on two antitributes of another kind: masterpieces of injustice to their subjects. *Dylan Thomas,* by Jack Howells, attempts seriously to glorify the poet. But it comes out only as a showcase for Richard Burton, who mopes around with poetically windblown hair, recites Thomas' poetry unpoetically (when there are all those fine recordings by the poet himself!), and speaks the florid and bathetic commentary as if it were as profound as the best of Dylan Thomas. There is a jejune attempt to suggest the seamy side of Thomas' life, but it is almost more cowardly than no mention at all. The very quotations from Thomas manage to sound shabby out of context and surrounded by Howells' vapid interpolations. And, typically, for one or two brief shots of the dilapidated Thomas as photographed by Rollie McKenna, we get endless lingering over Augustus John's portrait of the angelic young Dylan.

Marilyn, on the other foot, is a full-length "tribute" to

Marilyn Monroe, consisting of clippings from all her Fox
films and sappy narration sappily spoken by Rock Hudson. There are no credits listed and none due. Miss
Monroe emerges not as a human being, but as a mere fig-
ment of Hollywood's imagination. And what a second-rate
imagination it is.

A GRAMMAR OF MODERN LIFE

Il Posto, absurdly retitled *The Sound of Trumpets*, is
about as slight as a film can be. Yet it contains enough
compassionate sensitivity, youthfully laughing wisdom,
and understated gallantry in the encounter with existence,
to make its thirty-two-year-old author-director, Ermanno Olmi, justly proud.

Olmi's first full-length story-film has about as much
plot as a *New Yorker* short story, but has all the freshly
baked crispness and honest aroma lost to that moribund
genre. A young boy from a poor suburb goes up to the
City to take his psychological and aptitude tests for a job
(*posto*) with a large company. He and his fellow-ap-
plicants—including a girl on whom he develops a
crush—are subjected to a series of ordeals more ludicrous
than stringent. The boy and girl wander about Milan between examinations. Both of them are hired, but end up in
parts of the organization far from each other. The youth
begins as a messenger boy, sees the girl only once or twice,
waits for her in vain at a grotesquely pathetic office New
Year's party. A tragi-comic clerk—always hunched over
and straight out of Gogol—dies; our hero gets his job. He
sits at the darkest desk at the rear of the office, but he has
a place (*posto*) in life, for life.

It is on this pun that the film is based: *posto*, a position
that pays and a place in life. Domenico, the hero, is no
Sunday child, despite his name. He is as ordinary as a
well-meaning, ill-educated, petty-bourgeois-just-up-from-
peasant Italian boy, with chickens still promenading

around his street, can be. Yet there is something extraordinary about his diffident longings, his good humor always brushing finger tips with melancholy. The things he needs most is that one firm position *inside* the world, which, together with the lever of his will, may suffice to move the heavens out of their callous indifference.

An anchorage inside life: for life to this adolescent is still as big, buzzing, blooming a muddle as to any newborn babe. It is this muddle that Olmi, with the sturdy support of Lamberto Caimi's camera work, records with devout yet droll fidelity. And the secret of the film lies in its shrewdly varied rhythms, in its sovereign sense of life as jumble of kinetic frenzy alternating with deadening doldrums.

There is, first, walking. I can think of no other film so full of manifold, promiscuous perambulation. From moseying around rooms to citywide meanderings, from traipsing down catacomb-like corridors to chilly canters after the morning train, the movie follows man along his intermittent marathon. The pace changes from dizzying dodgings of traffic in which the camera skitters along with the harassed walkers, through somnambulistic loping along sidewalks where siren shopwindows lure one off his course, to an unhinged New Year's dance, whose jigging and bounding couples are only slightly paroxystic pedestrians. And when people seem to get tired of moving, trains or trolleys are eager to take over for and with them, and the race continues: cross-country, cross-city, across life.

In between, there are islands of stasis. But not of rest. Though others, many of them, may share these islands, they are desert islands nonetheless. When Domenico, time and time again, sits waiting for something to happen, for someone to come and tell him what to do, the rest between movements becomes as aimless and hectic, as restless, as movement itself.

But as Domenico lolls, scurries, mopes and rides through his days, other people touch on his path: abut on it, cross it, parallel it, tangentially caress or ruffle it. These others, if you put them end to end, are the alphabet that

spells out humanity. At a neighboring café table, a middle-aged woman nervously drains a cup of coffee and
shoves it emphatically away; for the cup, emptied of coffee, has filled up with her weariness. No sooner has the inquiring Domenico been told at an information desk where
the examination will be held—the eighth floor—than a little old man has taken his place tenaciously demanding to
be told where it is they're giving out money to the poor.
The clerk behind the desk throws up his arms, and already
the camera (which is anything but a sentimental dawdler)
has leapt away: there are answers to some questions here;
others remain unanswered.

Sometimes the other people are no more than a girl who
trails the hero down a corridor for a moment, her face as
blank as the walls, then remembers she has to go the other
way, and vanishes as casually and unpredictably as she
popped up. Sometimes it is a mother on a train who points
out Domenico to her little son and says, "You see, that
boy is going to school," though, in fact, Domenico, from
his classroom untimely ripp'd, is already going to work.
Or it is a shopkeeper who, when Domenico bangs a candy
machine that refuses to spew up its chewing gum, berates
the youth for not having deposited a coin. He tells her he
has, whereupon, no longer concerned, she disappears like
the coin.

Add up these wonderfully offhand vignettes, these
wistful, uncaring, sardonic Others, and you get as full a
picture of the human show as the moving pictures have
tendered. These passers-by are each of them a passing
comment, cold or kind. Together, they are the casualism
that usurps the throne of causality.

As the boy and girl who barely meet, barely win, and
quietly lose each other, Sandro Panzeri and Loredana Det-
to are quietly perfect. I say "quietly" because everything
in this film is quiet—neither in joy nor in protest is a voice
raised above *mezzo forte*. Even the photography is a little
soft, just this side of sharp focus, as if we were watching
an improvisation or a newsreel—not a brilliant, loudly uttered, premeditated piece of fiction.

Near the beginning of the film, Domenico leaves for the City from a railway station which, though emblematic of every small railway station anywhere, reminded me particularly of the one from which, at the end of Fellini's *I Vitelloni*, the autobiographical hero entrains for the World. This is a happy and appropriate reminder. For Ermanno Olmi seems to me a worthy and by no means slavish disciple of Fellini. *Il Posto* has the knowing innocence, the bittersweet sagacity, the artless artistry of Fellini. In one respect it even surpasses him: in the handling of time and space. Cunningly hours shrink to minutes, instants refuse to end; places change quixotically. We see a group of office workers at their comically dreary tasks and, presently, as if in a long parenthesis, the camera hops about showing us in rapid succession what each of them does with his free evening hours. The film is full of such parentheses, ellipses, anacolutha, interjections, paragraphs in which languorous subordination yields to the staccato of parataxis. Olmi has brilliantly captured the syntax of our lives.

Compared to this, the firstling feature film of Jack O'Connel, *Greenwich Village, U.S.A.*, is less than striking. Yet it is a film that augurs well for its writer-director, and one that should be seen. It is a curious work: Nothing about it quite comes off, but there is so much honesty, intelligence, and budding cinematographic sense about it that one is ready to forgive the failings and enjoy the good points liberally scattered throughout.

It is a story of young lovers in the Village—a struggling novelist and a hopeful ballerina—their friends, their poverty, their brushes with conventions and the law, their entanglements with the tourists from uptown. Nothing that Murger could not have done if he were alive today—or come to think of it, that he did not do anyhow. But there is objectivity: the hipsters haven't got it made, and the squares aren't that bad. The writing is undistinguished but inoffensive; the sex, though unconvincing, tries to be frank and warm; the tragedy, when it comes, is somewhat contrived. Still, there are flavorsome scenes; the photography is often winning despite a limited budget and equipment; some of the performances, especially James Frawley's and John Avildsen's, are quite captivating; Hy Gubernick's music, mostly for solo recorder, is genuinely endearing.

Perhaps my main reservation concerns the principals, Melinda Plank and Robert Hogan. Americans would appear to be doomed in the roles of very young lovers. Unself-conscious grace and expressiveness such as the young couple of *Il Posto* have is foreign to them; and by the time they might learn how to act it, they are too old. There is something a bit stilted about these lovers: They are either too bland or too blatantly pushing. But the film has integrity and imagination. If by the time he makes his third film Jack O'Connell has not been sucked into Hollywood, that should be a movie worth waiting for.

My Life to Live, the latest film of Jean-Luc Godard, the maker of *Breathless,* is interesting only as a repository of every defect the New Wave at its worst can muster up: crass and pointless experimentation for its own sake, tiresomely indiscriminate revival of silent-film techniques, perverse disregard of the audience, pretentious dabbling with pseudoprofundities, deliberate trampling of psychology in the mud of wantonness. Possibly the best way of describing this piece of legalized abortion is to say that if the boys from *Cahiers du cinéma* and the kids from *Film Culture* were each of them to shoot five minutes worth of film, and the whole were spliced together in an order determined by dice, the result would be roughly comparable. And they'll probably get around to that one, too.

FELLINI'S 8½ ¢ FANCY

Things started going wrong with the Steiner episode in *La Dolce Vita.* Fellini was trying to show the problem of the modern intellectual, yet Steiner and his psyche were far from convincing. The devoutest Felliniites donned their most superior faces and informed us that, of course, Steiner was not meant to be the real thing, but an unsuccessful would-be intellectual—look at all those creeps at his party. True, the creeps were creeps all right; but Steiner—witness his trusting altruism, delightful musicianship, appreciation of good painting, modesty, borrowing of books on Sanskrit grammar, exquisite and loving wife and children—is clearly meant to be the genuine article. If he were not, he would be nowise different from Marcello, the hero, on whom he is meant to be a potentially salutary influence. But, here lies the tragedy, the potential savior goes berserk with fear of the future and kills his children and himself. Fellini could not make his motivation very believable, but, luckily, he did not try very hard.

Of his third of *Boccaccio 70*, Fellini made a much bigger hash, though the other two thirds were scarcely better. The episode was meant to be ideological—that censorship is a form of prurience, that puritanism is hypocrisy—but the ideas were either too old and obvious or too feebly expressed, and the only thing that registered fully was a more-than-life-size Anita Ekberg, of whom even life size is too much.

Now comes *8½*, and despite two or three good scenes, it is a disheartening fiasco. There are several reasons for this. First, it is extremely hard, virtually impossible, to make a good autobiography out of one's present. The present hurts too much. The past is the proper study of autobiography, for it allows of tranquil recollection, self-distancing and perspective. The story of Guido Anselmi, the famous director, successful yet criticized for his recent work, troubled by not knowing what kind of film to make next, torn between Catholicism and Marxism, devoted to his wife and dependent on her yet drawn to all other attractive women and involved with some, attempting to use his film as psychotherapy—all this is humanly understandable and even touching; unfortunately, it makes for bad, because confused, art: The tone is never sure, but falters between irony and self-pity, between shamefaced poeticism and tongue-tied self-mockery.

Confused, also, because ignorant. That is the second failure of *8½*: its ignorance. Art is made out of knowledge—intuitive, partial, prejudiced, illusory—and kind, but knowledge. *8½* is about floundering, and it is not the flounderer who can give floundering a concrete form. (Floundering, incidentally, should not be confused with doubt, which is the assertion of the self in a negative direction; rather, it is stumbling about in various directions all of which seem, successively or simultaneously, positive.) *8½* piles problem upon problem, which is permissible; but sheds no light, which is not. There is, indeed, a mock resolution tacked on at the end: a kind of dance of life begun by a group of clowns which includes the hero as a boy, and is eventually picked up by all the motley dramatis personae. Yet whereas such a *commedia dell'arte* ending may fit into the style and non-intellectual *Problematik* of a film like *Cabiria,* it is foreign to the matter of *8½*, and remains an inept *deus ex machina.*

Foreignness brings us to the third weakness of the film. In *8½*, Fellini, apparently afraid of becoming a self-repeater with diminishing returns as so many famous Italian directors have become, tries for something new: symbolism, metaphysics, solid intellectual content. Now the sad truth is that he and his fellow scenarists could not be more unsuited to this kind of art. What made Fellini's early films great—and they, too, tended to be quasi-autobiographical—was their almost total avoidance of intellectualizing, and reliance on character study, accurate local color, honest and controlled emotionalism, bittersweet humor, an occasional bit of satire, and a simple, lyrical view of the world through a camera that had an eye for the poetic but a stomach for the realistic.

Already in Fellini's masterpiece, *I Vitelloni,* the incident that did not quite ring true was the one involving the stolen statue of the angel, where the film was straining for symbolic value. Fellini, after all, is typically and gloriously

Italian, with all this implies of a kind of sensuous wisdom, of tragicomic profundity. That remarkable writer, all too little known here, Vitaliano Brancati, has been aptly called an *"umorista serio,"* and the title sits as well with his kindred spirit, Fellini. A serious humorist, that is what the creator of *The White Sheik, I Vitelloni, La Strada,* and *Cabiria* is; gravely metaphysical or esoterically symbolist films—*trobar clus*—he should leave to more rigorous or recondite minds, to Bergman or Buñuel or Antonioni. In Fellini's hands, this approach is rather like the attempt of a typical Italian composer to forsake *bel canto* for the symphonic; *8½* reminds me of those truly dreary orchestral works of a Respighi, a Casella, or a Malipiero.

Wherein does the symbolism consist? The film moves from reality through daydreams into dreams, and one of its main points is that all three states are of equal importance, indeed not readily distinguishable one from the other. Therefore, everything in the film should be equally relevant. But what, for instance, are we to make of the Cardinal's disquisition on the bird called Diomede, because when Diomedes died, these birds, ululating profusely, accompanied him to the grave? What does the satanic young man in the Cardinal's entourage represent? Why are so many of the priests at the seminary manifestly androgynous? Is there a parallel intended between the embalmed saint in a glass case at the seminary and an obviously fake sideshow fakir in a similar case at the thermal resort? And so on.

And the intellectual content? Somewhere or other Fellini must have heard that amiguity is, or is supposed to be, the hallmark of advanced art. And behold, all the principal characters of *8½* are sublimely dichotomous. There is the protagonist's wife, honest, neglected, touching, yet also a shrew. There is her bosom companion, Rossella, the intelligently muckraking voice of the film, yet she is the very one who goes in for spiritism. There is the sardonic scriptwriter, significantly called Daumier, intellectually and artistically intransigent, critical of Anselmi's weakness and compromises, but for all that a prating, negativistic bore. There is the Cardinal, humane yet dogmatic, gently repeating the horrible slogan: *"Extra ecclesiam, nulla-salus."*

The same goes for the hero's other women. La Saraghina, the woman-mountain, is a loathsome monolith of flesh, a whore, but also childlike and genuine. Carla, Anselmi's mistress, is nice yet imbecile, devoted wife and perfect slut. Claudia, the beautiful actress (played insipidly by Claudia Cardinale), remains completely bisected by the intellectual chiaroscuro. Only Guido Anselmi is a coherent type—but a type, precisely, not an individual. Though his foibles are recognizable enough, and his child-hood neuroses exemplarily Freudian, there is little about him that is specific, interesting, compelling enough to make us care.

The dialogue itself bulges with antinomies; here the in-tellectual cleavage is given yet more indecent exposure. Thus Daumier is continually citing Stendhal, Mallarmé, Suetonius, and what have you, appositely yet unenlighten-ingly. Claudia is repeatedly described as "young yet old," "a child, yet ancient"; Guido is always characterized in terms of seeking without finding, having nothing to say but wanting to say it anyway, wishing to bury the past but lacking the courage to bury anything.

Worst of all is the systematic undercutting of every ut-terance. The Cardinal quotes Origen with unassailable finality. But Origen mutilated himself for the sake of the heavenly kingdom. Are we to believe such a celestial *cas-trato?* An effete American journalist (played all too believably by Eugene Walter) mumbles critically, *"Le cinéma n'est pas né comme un jeu intellectuel,"* which would seem to give films like *8½* short shrift; yes, but this character is a ludicrous phoney. Ah, but it is from the mouths of phoneys that the truth comes: It is the absurd American girl, an intellectual flapper, who has written a dissertation on "The Solitude of Modern Man in the Con-temporary Theatre"—which Anselmi's life and work demonstrate with a vengeance, if they demonstrate anything at all.

Life is complex and even contradictory; but it is not so simplistically antithetical. Art has every right to subtle ambiguity; but premeditated ambivalence, splitting, hatchet-like, every character, every statement, every hair, is not art. The great masters of ambiguity—Pirandello, Brecht, Proust, Valéry, Eliot—however much they may undercut ideologies, do not chop up the ground on which they stand.

And what of Fellini's metaphysics? Is it better to create at all cost, or to admit one's sterility and refrain? Should Anselmi strive for the truth through autobiography or through a film about atomic destruction? Can one say Yea to life without apprehending its quiddity? To all these questions Fellini manages only the already mentioned corybantic answer: a stagey dance of life, even less convincing than the dance of death at the end of *The Seventh Seal,* which undoubtedly suggested it.

There are other obvious echoes—of *Wild Strawberries, Last Year at Marienbad,* Fellini's earlier films (the very score is a reworking of the *Dolce Vita* score), even a broad allusion to Dante's *Inferno* in the steam-bath scene—but the borrowings are not integrated and do not crystallize anything in *8½*. Fellini's intellectualizing is not even like dogs dancing: It is not done well, nor does it amaze us that it is done at all. It merely palls on us and, finally, appalls us.

THE LAST ASP

A nondaily reviewer inevitably finds it necessary to bypass discussion of certain films for the sake of others, but the film scene, no less inevitable, sooner or later gets

becalmed, enabling him to profit of the doldrums for a little corrective retrospection.

What, at this late date, has not yet been said against
Cleopatra? This perhaps: that it manages to be a *total*
disappointment. Whatever was interesting about it clearly
ended up somewhere else: on the cutting-room floor, in
various hotel rooms, in the newspaper columns. The range
of the film extends from the expensively vulgar to the expensively ordinary; it lacks not only the intelligent spectacle of a *Lawrence of Arabia* but even the spectacular
unintelligence of a C. B. DeMille product.

I shall be speaking of the four-hour-and-three-minute
egg, as previewed for the critics, though the same objections apply, I gather, even more strongly to the three-hour-
and-forty-minute one finally released. It has been noted
quite properly that no single film can encompass in sufficient detail both Caesar and Cleopatra and Antony and
Cleopatra. The attempt of Jonah to swallow the whale is
one initial difficulty here. Another is the scrupulous
avoidance of echoes from Shakespeare and Shaw, which,
on the face of it, is exactly as it should be. But there is obvious trouble when the absences become more manifest
than the presences. It is surely not lines like, "It's over—
Caesar and the dream that was murdered with him," or, in
a more amorous vein, "Was it a century ago, or was it last
night?" that are going to compete with anyone but
Kathleen Winsor or Rona Jaffe.

Yet what is so wrong with the screenplay of Joseph
Mankiewicz, Ranald MacDougall, and Sidney Buchman is
that it does not even manage to be consistently all that
bad. Only once does Cleopatra speak of Antony's having
been as happy as a little boy, or of her wanting "One
world, one nation, one people living in peace." For the
rest of the time, barring moments of grand passion ("Do
you want me to live with you? I will. Would you want me
to die with you? I will." Or: "You and I will make of
dying nothing more than one last embrace!"), the
dialogue is as earnest, self-regarding, and misguided as
the Ptolemaic view of the world. It is equally devoid of

imagination and, at least, involuntary humor. The only character whose lines have any flavor, *faisandé* as it may be, is Caesar, and Rex Harrison duly gives one of the film's two satisfactory performances, the other being Martin Landau's valiant Rufio.

Mankiewicz as writer or director, has no genuine flair for the action-crammed historic canvas; his gift, such as it is, is for brisk comedy, which is of small avail here, and for witty repartee, which will not be squeezed from stones like Elizabeth Taylor. Nor does Richard Burton offer much more than craggy grimaces and rocky mouthings.

But the three gravest lacunas of the film can be labeled Grandeur, Passion, and Sex. We actually have a scene, for example, of Burton and Taylor in bed, which for sheer excitement matches the juxtaposition of the two last remaining sardines in their tin. And the love-death arouses only one emotional response in us—relief, for when death is here, can THE END be far behind?

Of Miss Taylor's acting I can say only that it remains under-developed (her speech, moreover, is unpleasantly commonplace), while her looks have become rather overripe. All the same, she still has moments when she would look pretty if costumes, make-up, and hair-dos did not successfully conspire against her. And the desperate device of casting only unattractive females in the other parts acts only as a further depressant.

The remaining performances are mostly undistinguished (when they are not, like those of Kenneth Haigh and Hume Cronyn, downright poor), though in some cases it may be the Dranconic cutting of the film that cripples the characterizations. One absolutely inexcusable performance, however, is that of Roddy McDowall, whose Octavian is a screaming, peroxided queen, every bit as bad history as it is bad taste.

Taste of any kind is certainly not the strong point of the film, whether we consider the uninspired costuming, the trite and cheap choreography of Hermes Pan, the unmoving cinematography (imagine making the pedestrian Leon-Shamroy director of photography while the brilliant

Claude Renoir is relegated to second-unit work!), or the complete disregard for accents, which has the Egyptians sounding indiscriminately British, French, Austrian, and American.

Perhaps the one thing that can be said for *Cleopatra* is that it looks indubitably opulent. The sets and props are lovingly and munificently constructed: a mere tent could house the Roman Senate, and Cleopatra's barge could carry the Queen Elizabeth piggyback. There are sets whose dimensions run a close second to infinity, and there are imposing edifices lavished on three-minute sequences. A fairly good short-subject could have been made by showing us nothing but the sets and props in full detail unmolested by actors and action.

To sum up, I can merely seize upon the most notorious line of English blank verse and deflect it to another African queen: "O, Cleopatra! Cleopatra, O!" But even that sounds more scrumptious the way James Thomson wrote it: "O, Sophonisba! Sophonisba, O!"

Hud is an American movie of which we need not be ashamed, and that, nowadays, is saying a good deal. It is a simple—perhaps oversimplified—moral tale about a sensual opportunist who goes his more or less merry way, alienating everyone around him, until he ends up lonely but unbowed. The locale is Texas, but for no other reason than that it provides backgrounds closest to the bare stage of the morality play. Story and dialogue are unspectacular but adequate, Martin Ritt's direction is his best to date, James Wong Howe's photography is forceful and incisive. The acting of Paul Newman and Brandon de Wilde is only passable, but Melvyn Douglas is fine and Patricia Neal unsurpassable. What is best about the film is the mood, the atmosphere it creates; even if it has little to say and less that is new, it says it authentically and in adult terms, and the direction never fails to keep you at least interested if not involved. *Hud* may not be a major film, but it is a very useful signpost. It is also worth seeing.

This Sporting Life is the long-awaited first feature film of Lindsay Anderson, who has made some excellent shorts and written some provocative film criticism in *Sight and Sound*. Still another entry in the new British wave of social, and socialist, realism, it deals with the life and loves of a hulking professional footballer. When it most approaches the documentary, or concentrates on local color, it is neatly executed and effective; in these scenes, acting, photography and direction blend into a meaningful whole.

But the plot and characters refuse to work. The hero's unsuccessful love affair is not brought into clear focus: neither his own problems nor those of the young widow he lives with are fully realized. We never get to understand what went wrong with the woman's marriage or why she cannot truly respond to her lover, or how the hero's career interferes with his emotional fulfillment. To make matters worse, there are two separate homosexual subplots hinted at but left cravenly unanalyzed and unresolved.

As usual in these films, the performances are first-rate: Rachel Roberts' widow, Alan Badel's sinister president of a ball-club, and William Hartnell's pathetic old camp follower. As the hero, Richard Harris would be perfect if he did not ape Marlon Brando so sedulously; but if he lacks the charm Brando had at his best, he does have a genuinely beetling massiveness; the power which Brando could merely suggest—and that, for the most part, less than convincingly—is staggeringly real in Harris. Despite an unfocused and only sporadically compelling script, *This Sporting Life* offers some real though tangential rewards.

Much the same can be said of *Sparrows Can't Sing*. Here, too, we get a long-awaited directorial bow—it is Joan Littlewood's first film, and she has proved herself something of a genius in the theatre—here, too, the ambience is more absorbing than the story, and here, again, much cannot be understood, though the opacity is not in the writing but in the impenetrable Cockney spoken by most of the characters. (An attempt was made to supply "American" subtitles, but the experiment, apparently, did not prove successful.)

Miss Littlewood, unfortunately, allowed the minor characters and extras to proliferate to the point where the principals were very nearly swallowed up by them, and the plot seemed to her just an excuse to explore the numerous layers of London's lower classes. It is quite clear from Miss Littlewood's work for the stage that she is much more interested in society than in art. The stage, imposing its somewhat greater artificiality, disguises the imbalance felicitously; on the screen, with its greater freedom, the lopsidedness becomes aggressively apparent.

Nevertheless, the film is well photographed and zestfully acted—especially by James Booth and Barbara Windsor as the comically sparring couple, and by Roy Kinnear as the hero's ludicrously bestial brother-in-law. It is regrettable that it should have seemed necessary to get Lionel Bart to garnish the beginning of the film with one of those American-style extraneous title songs. Aside from the inappropriateness of it all, Bart, whose fame has ballooned on the slender achievement of his musical, *Oliver!*, can compose scarcely better than sparrows can sing.

31 HATH SEPTEMBER

As we entered Philharmonic Hall for the opening of the first New York Film Festival, a floating uneasiness hovered over our heads, exuded perhaps by the architecture, a fine specimen of the Late Midwestern Cafeteria style. Once inside that hall of or and azure, we were welcomed by William Schuman who then introduced the Chairman of the Sponsoring Committee, August Heckscher, as the President's Cultural Adviser (which he no longer is). Mr. Heckscher, who knows all about Culture and nothing about the arts, proceeded to inform us, with a true-blue smile and honey-golden voice perfectly matching the color scheme, that film has now become an art (which it has long been) and that we were about to witness "some films which are good and some which are very good." By now the atmosphere was truly ominous.

And sure enough, the first film, Buñuel's *The Exterminating Angel,* proved to be an unsound and unsightly mixture of spurious allegory and genuine craziness, whose human beings were uninteresting, story unconvincing, and cinematography mediocre. It is disheartening to find this in the wake of the imaginative and challenging *Viridiana,* but Buñuel has always been an unbalanced and fluctuating artist.

Before discussing the quality of the other films, let us consider their quantity. In ten days, 21 new films were screened at Lincoln Center, and 10 somewhat less new but hitherto unreleased films were shown at the Museum of Modern Art. That meant an average of three films a day, not counting numerous short subjects, and even though I saw only 26 of the 31 features, the experience proved both dizzying and enlightening.

Now for the quality. Of the story-films I did see, only three seemed to me unquestionably worthy of festival showing: *In the Midst of Life* by Robert Enrico (France), *Knife in the Water* by Roman Polanski (Poland), and *The Fiancés* by Ermanno Olmi (Italy). There were a few honorable misses or near-misses, of which more later, and, for the rest, some incredible junk. Let's start with that.

At Philharmonic Hall there was the Hungarian *Love in the Suburbs,* about as bad as a film can get. The Hungarians sent it to Cannes no doubt because they were proud of its "Western" themes: unhappy marriage, adultery, the emancipation of women. If you can imagine a high-school version of *Brief Encounter* grafted onto an Eskimo adaptation of *A Doll's House,* poorly photographed, leadenly acted, with dialogue (I happen to know

Hungarian) almost as bad as the subtitles—thus "Edited" in the credits emerged as "Compilated"!—you may have an inkling of something that would have made the crassest Socialist Realism seem interesting. (Not that the implicit propaganda wasn't there: A wife not allowed to continue her work as a weaver will weave a tangled web of adultery.)

Then there was *Elektra at Epidaurus* from Greece. That Greek tragedy is virtually impossible on our stage has become clear to all but the most desperate culture-mongers to whom art is all Greek anyhow; that it is impossible in the movies has been demonstrated by the recent *Antigone* and *Electra*. But to film the production of Sophocles' tragedy as staged at Epidaurus, that is, to compound impossiblities, could have occurred only to a pair of Greek-Americans who combine American culture-vulturism with Greek chauvinism.

From Argentina, there was *The Terrace*, Leopoldo Torre Nilsson is very likely the chief purveyor of pretentious artsy-craftsy sensationalism to artless art-film audiences. The schema is always identical: his wife, Beatriz Guido, writes a lurid scenario—something about sadism, sexual slavery, the corruption of adolescents—and then Torre Nilsson decks it out with fashionable chiaroscuro, arty camera angles, lots of turning door handles and opening doors (count them in *The Terrace*!), guarded liberalism, and musical scores that, in the best New Wave tradition, shuttle between cool jazz and Scarlatti. Of six of his films I have seen, only *The Fall* (characteristically not released here) has any merit; the others, and most particularly the recent *Hand in the Trap,* are so much claptrap with the film-maker's foot in it.

No less appalling was *Rogopag,* another of those doomed episodic group efforts. Rossellini contributed a feeble joke amateurishly filmed; Jean-Luc Godard more of his attitudinizing and maundering about the human crisis, with the same poverty of invention straining to be different that made his *My Life to Live* insufferable. Pier Paolo Pasolini's bit was a ponderous and tasteless pseudosatire on religious films and man's inhumanity to man, which was chiefly a pretext for dragging in various pederastic types and jokes in which Pasolini revels, and to show off Orson Welles in the depths of his degradation: a horrendous leviathan, beached and barely capable of moving its bulk, heavily sneering at everybody to over-compensate for its physical and spiritual paralysis. Only Gregoretti's episode had a little flavor.

Others ebbs were *The Sea,* a trickle of homosexualized Antonionification, well acted and studiously photographed in a style that out-Antonionis Antonioni, but perfectly pointless—except perhaps to inverts—and nasty and soporific to boot; *Magnet of Doom,* more than usually trashy Simenon turned into a slack would-be thriller, with Belmondo perpetuating his irresistible, smilingly evil, stereotyped self; *Le Joli Mai,* an interminable specimen of the genre *cinéma-vérité,* in which the candid camera in-terviews exhaustively random people in the streets who af-ter a couple of sentences become living tautologies—while the aim is to probe the pathos and callousness of man, the result merely displays his uninterestingness both as inter-viewer and interviewee.

Little good can be said about Bresson's catatonic *Trial of Joan of Arc* and less about Resnais' *Muriel,* a further stage in the disintegration of an impressive directorial talent. Here again is the technique of fragmentation, se-quential scrambling, dislocation of the aural and visual; but whereas in *Marienbad* the schematization, stylization, and oneirism gave the technique its spurious justification, here, forced onto a simple and trivial story, the method produces a dissociation of sensibility to make Eliot's mouth water and befog the viewer's brain. *"Au fond, cest une histoire banale—ça me rassure,"* says the heroine; but *Muriel,* alas, is banal without being reassuring.

One of the worst monstrosities was *Lola Montès,* the closing bill at the Museum, and the last film of the late Max Ophüls, who had the taste and mentality of a cham-bermaid along with a talent for *kitsch* barely equaled even by Vadim and Chabrol. This film that brazenly announces in an epigraph that it is a new departure in cinematography is nothing of the sort; it has much the same gimmicky frame as Ophüls's vulgar *La Ronde,* the same dime-store sentimentality as his *Earrings of Madame De . . .* and *Letter from an Unknown Woman,* plus lavish over-production whose stifling opulence merely underscores the exiguity of Cécil St.-Laurent's script and the blatant insufficiency of Martine Carol in the lead.

There were other bad films and shorts, but let me turn to the somewhat better ones. Kobayashi's *Harakiri,* after an unendurably static first half, inched its way to a splendid finale, whereas Joseph Losey's *The Servant* went from an extremely promising beginning to preposterousness and dreariness for dreariness' sake. Kanelopoulos' *The Sky* was by turns as touching and chastening as a war film can be, and vacuous and Mariendadized beyond the call of duty; the Brazilian *Barravento* was an amiable mixture of exoticism and rank amateurishness; Jacques Baratier's *Sweet and Sour* was sometimes tartily satirical but generally juvenile and aimless.

At the Museum, James Blue's *Olive Trees of Justice,* though hampered by a mediocre script, had a fresh and authentic way of dealing with experience whether quotidian or catastrophic; Kurosawa's *I Live in Fear* was often poignant though essentially routine; Herbert Vesely's *The Bread of Former Years,* based on Böll's novella, had some fetching touches, but the Marienbad technique, not even expertly handled, and crippling subtitles did not help matters; Gregoretti's *The New Angels* was an occasionally amusing trifle, at least unassuming. Space permits me no discussion of some interesting shorts and documentaries such as the excellent *Point of Order, The Chair,* and *Crisis*; on the three outstanding features I shall report at the time of their release.

A meager and generally tiresome festival, then, which brings us to the question of selection and organization. The films were picked by Richard Roud, a young

American living in England (if you can call going to the movies 10 to 15 times a week living) and, as organizer of the London Film Festival, shuttling between the world's festivals to choose films for London and now New York. (Most of the films here were gleaned from other festivals.) It has already been announced that next year's Festival will have the same format and the same Mr. Roud.

Neither, I submit, is satisfactory. This much unrelieved film viewing is stultifying, and Roud's taste is woefully inadequate. I doubt that some of these were the best movies available, but if they were, they should have cheerfully been left to rot wherever found. And if—as I definitely do not feel—one needs all this quantity, at least Roud should refrain from publicly proclaiming the high quality of all his films. Things like *Rogopag, Magnet of Doom, The Sea, Lola Montès,* you would hate yourself for spending fifty cents on a rainy day in Oshkosh. I would have serious *a priori* doubts about anyone who, like Roud, writes in a program note of "the divinely tinny music" in a film, and who quotes approvingly the Lincoln Center credo of providing "enrichment beyond understanding." Still, how anyone can tout *Love in the Suburbs, Muriel,* or *Le Joli Mai* is certainly beyond understanding.

KEEPING UP WITH JONES

The poet Andrew Young, in a bucolic lyric, speaks of losing a contest with the river Stour: "I knew I lost the race—/I could not keep so slow a pace." The person who could have beaten the Stour with unseemly ease is the Indian film-maker Satyajit Ray, Hailed prematurely and irresponsibly as a genius on the basis of his *Apu* (pronounced "Opu") trilogy, he should since have persuaded all but the Zen Masters and Mysterious-East worshipers in our midst that he is fast becoming the maker of the slowest movies in the world. If Newton could have seen *Devi, Two Daughters,* or *The Music Room,* how it would have facilitated his discovery of the principle of inertia!

To a large extent, Oriental philosophy is to blame. Where nirvana is the condition to aspire to, where quietism, denial of the self, submergence of the individual in eternity are the order of the day, the day becomes unimportant—to say nothing of the hour or the minute. But to the enlightened Westerner it is the moment that is of supreme importance; the problem, as Pater clearly saw, is "how shall we pass most swiftly from point to point, and be present always at the focus where the greatest number of vital forces unite in their purest energy?" Having scuttled eschatology and risen above resurrection, most Westerners have traded in a fictitious marriage to eternity for a passionate embrace of the moment, fleeting but real.

Unless a film is precisely an analysis of boredom, and a cogent one at that, we will not countenance dullness for a minute; we shall not forsake the integrity of narrative movement for endless minutes of cinematic naval-gazing. The most beautiful umbilical panorama (whether by Satyajit Ray or Alain Resnais) cannot make up for a single misspent moment of our film-going—or of our lives.

This does not mean, as we shall see, that a film should profligately hurtle ahead, debasing the currency of movement. But neither can it, as in *The Music Room,* embalm itself into an odoriferous stasis. I say odoriferous because the film has its moments of perfumed charm. But a touching moment here, a fetching effect there, do not constitute a film.

The story of a proud, old aristocrat who has wasted his money on musical soirees, who clings to cumbersome traditions and despises his neighbor, the rich, up-to-date parvenu, has possibilities. The hero's loss of wife and child and subsequent renunciation of music and the outside world, his final bid to outdo his neighbor with a grandiose musical evening at the cost of his last remnants of money, sanity, and life—all this has validity, especially as Chekhov might have written it in a short story.

But here the camera maunders and meanders while some quite able actors are allowed only one-dimensional portrayals and rudimentary dialogue. The photography, repudiating the *juste milieu*, manages to be almost always over- or underexposed. Acting areas are severely limited, other locations appear only as evanescent interpolations, and there is no fluidity of motion to unite them into topograhical reality. The highlights of the film are three well-nigh interminable musical numbers which consist chiefly of a lugubrious plunk-plonk-boing on the instruments (continuing with subliminal variations as the background music of the entire film) and a cross between bleating and croaking from the vocal cords. As for the dancing, to one who does not know a *mudra* from a *raga*, it offers little. The other scenes, too, have their built-in obsolescence.

Ah, you will tell me, I'm being parochial. Why can't I transport myself into another culture, another mentality? Because there is something artificial about espousing an outlook that cannot convince one of its validity. Our enthusiasm for Indian literature, for instance, seems at best *voulu*, and at worst phoney. A fable like *Shakuntala* is exquisite, but can any intelligent Westerner relish the vaporous effusions of a Rabindranath Tagore? Yet it is precisely Tagore who was Ray's mentor and the source of *Devi* and *Two Daughters*, which, despite an isolated felicity in the latter, are two of the dreariest films ever.

Pather Panchali, to be sure, had considerable poignancy, some fine photography, and sympathetically observed people in it; but one had the feeling that Ray was the filmic equivalent of the *homo unius libri* who has poured all of his gifts into one work that contains them snugly, with nothing left over. The latter parts of the *Apu* trilogy merely plucked the same string with diminishing returns. The later films can be characterized only as the world of oh, pooh!

There are a few small jewels in the big, sagging lotus of *The Music Room*. There is the moment when the old aristocrat, well played by Chabi Biswas, catches sight of his decaying self in the dusty, grimy mirror of his abandoned music room; or that other one, when he emerges after years of seclusion to look at the ancient elephant his dead son had loved. The elephant is facing away from the camera and is further diminished by distance, decrepitude, and the deteriorating lands around him. Presently a truck comes chugging down the road; in large, crude lettering, the vehicle is inscribed with the name of the old man's *bête noire,* the thriving, arriviste moneylender. As the old man watches, the dust cloud from the truck engulfs more than the elephant: a world of memories, a way of life. But such scenes are very few; soon we, too, are engulfed in the dusty stagnancy of the film.

Another way of assaulting the dignity of the moment is the opposite of letting it die of inanition. It is to stuff it full to bursting with every kind of kinesthesis, noise, trickery until it explodes in our faces. This is the way with much of *Tom Jones.*

Once in a while a movie comes along that makes poets of our reviewers, and their ballpoints in a fine frenzy rolling sprout pure rhymes like "brawling, sprawling" (Judith Crist), slant rhymes like "rowdy, bawdy" (Jesse Zunser), and even rhyming pairs like "roisterous, boisterous . . . uproarious and glorious" (Justin Gilbert). Obviously a film that elicits such lyric ejaculations from the reviewers cannot be all good.

The fact is, *Tom Jones* is fun. If entertainment is all you want from a film, it is there in plenty, though not unalloyed. What gets in the way of even simple somatic enjoyment is the furibund pace, often maintained at hysterical pitch with the most frenetic assortment of bustle, hubbub, camera movement and feverish cutting. One's eyes and ears frequently fall behind, yearning for a respite. Yet, oddly enough, some scenes go on too long and become wearying. There is a fox hunt, beautifully staged and photographed, that ends up being the animated equivalent of a mighty collection of eighteenth-century prints (as are a few other scenes), and a surfeit. A surfeit, too, is the already celebrated eating scene between Tom and Mrs. Waters in which, by means of suggestively shaped comestibles and their still more suggestive mode of consumption, a long night's journey into sex is acted out, going from temporary impotence through various stages to fellatio and cunnilingus. This is certainly obscene and even quite funny, but it is drawn out well beyond the point of the joke.

What adds to our exhaustion is the use of devices and more devices: imitation silent-movie sequences, stop shots, jump shots, acceleration—anything you can name, often used recurrently, with much the same effect as a fancy word appearing twice in the same paragraph. It is as if the camera had become a method actor; there are times when you wish you could buy, as on certain juke boxes, five minutes' silence. Tony Richardson, the director, has rightly been likened by Robert Brustein to an English Elia Kazan.

More serious, however, is the betrayal of the novel. John Osborne's script concentrates, first, on the salacious elements in Fielding, and, secondly, on the more obvious social satire. Lost, however, is all of that gracious irony, that magnanimous geniality, that vast expanse of verbiage which, so far from boring the reader, gives him ever the sense of being in the presence of a delightful, prolix, mischievous, humane man—the author. What was it, wonders the hero of Isak Dinesen's "The Poet," that "had made King Lear so exceptionally safe, so that even the storm on the heath, and even all the wickedness in the world, could not harm him in the least." And he concludes: "The old King had been in the hands, whatever happened to him, of the great English poet, of William Shakespeare." And that is the feeling of the reader of *Tom Jones*: I am in the hands of Henry Fielding, artist and gentleman, and I am, even in the cesspool, enchantedly, enchantingly safe.

And that is the great shortcoming of the film. Never mind that it is an adaptation of a great novel and cannot help losing much in the transposition; what we *must* mind is that we are not in the film qua film in the presence of a commanding intellect serving up vital truth in a subtle sauce of style. What Fielding wrote was "a comic epic poem in prose." The film is comic enough, and decidedly prose; only in Walter Lassally's marvelously downy, velvety, opalescent photography is it a poem, and in no way is it epic. It is, in fact, trivial. To give only one example: Thwackum and Square, far from being satires on distinct but equally reprehensible types of religious and moral attitudinizing, become interchangeable vaudeville villains.

With the exception of Susannah York's Sophia, a mere assortment of poses and *moues,* and the cruelly miscast David Tomlinson's Fellamar, the performances are funny, often excellent, down to the last extra. For this alone the movie is worth seeing. Still, I cannot but feel that we are witnessing the Revenge of the Richardsons. Two hundred and twenty-two years ago Fielding published his *Shamela,* a parody of Samuel Richardson's *Pamela.* Now, to avenge his putative forebear, Tony Richardson gives us this caricature of *Tom Jones.*

FICTION TO FILM: IS THIS TRIP NECESSARY?

Some time ago, apropos of theatre, I enunciated a theorem: "There is a simple law governing the dramatization of novels: if it is worth doing, it can't be done; if it can be done, it isn't worth it." Though I had no hopes of joining such eminent company as Boyle and Gresham, certain reviewers and readers—more of them in sorrow, but not a few in anger—did me the dubious honor of dubbing this Simon's Law.

As far as theatre is concerned, I shall stick by Simon's Law through sticks and stink-bombs; but does it, we may ask, apply also to film? Certain arguments would still seem to hold. If mere translation from one language into another tends to impoverish a work of art, transportation from one medium to another can be assumed to do graver violence. But is this so when the other medium is not the stage with its obvious limitations vis-à-vis the novel, but the screen with its potential as limitless as that of the page? Have not film-makers like Truffaut spoken of their cameras as fountain pens? Can we not, therefore, expect an efficacious transposition?

In theory, yes. Certainly when a mediocre novel falls into the hands of a brilliant cinematographer (as in the case of Stanley Kubrick's as yet unreleased masterpiece, *Dr. Strangelove,* made out of the potboiler, *Red Alert*), this is possible. But a great novel has yet to make a great film. We cannot accept substitutes, even good ones, for something we already cherish as our own—try switching perfectly good babies on a mother; no corporeal Emma Bovary or Daisy Miller can live up to the one we were made to imagine; favorite passages must inevitably be altered or omitted. Rarely, very rarely an estimable achievement comes along: *The Game of Love (Le Blé en herbe), Great Expectations,* Georges Lampin's version of *The Idiot, Outcast of the Islands, Devil in the Flesh, The Confessions of Felix Krull.* But always either the book or the film is less than absolutely first-rate.

The main difficulty concerns, I suspect, time and space even more than style, for which acceptable equivalents may be found. The passage of time in a film seldom becomes as real as in a masterly novel; space, on the other hand, can rarely become as subjective in a movie as in a book. A scarcely smaller problem is that of narration, almost inevitable in adaptations, yet harder and harder to sneak convincingly into our progressively more filmic films.

These thoughts are prompted by two current motion-picture adaptations, much the worse of which is *All the Way Home.* James Agee's Pulitzer Prize-winning *A Death in the Family* is not, properly speaking, a novel at all, but a series of prose poems, vignettes, short-short stories held together by nothing so much as Agee's enchanting humanity which his prose exudes just as a beloved body gives off its *odor di femina.* As such, it was bound to make a poor, unstageworthy play and get the Pulitzer Prize as a particularly heartwarming bit of Americana. Everything about the play, starting with the new, upbeat title, *All the Way Home,* was mellifluently mediocre. But two Pulitzers proudly displayed on a property's chest are irresistible—rather like one of those faculty wives who wears her husband's and her own Phi Beta Kappa keys as earrings—and David Susskind, never a fellow to say no to surefire culture, now gives us the movie version.

Philip Reisman Jr.'s scenario makes the big initial mistake of following Tad Mosel's feeble play much more than Agee's book. Plays, moreover, never work on the screen, for these two media are fundamentally antithetical. Furthermore, Reisman felt obligated to tone down even that play. Neither the foolish jokes and chatter with which a family tries to channel its bereavement, nor little Rufus's hysterical reveling in the fact that his father is dead, nor the brother-in-law's outburst against God, not even the religious friction between Catholics and Protestants in the family, survives in our fearless script. What on earth did Susskind think he had left?

Well, he had the title, straight from its prize-winning (but money-losing) Broadway engagement, and the prestige of Agee's novel and name. But whom is this lopsided, aimless, empty film to please? The elite audiences? Hardly. The large public? With no sex, no controversial star, no super-spectacle, no suspense—not even that *pis aller,* a plot—unlikely. The ads spoke of this "moving" film as being "almost unbearable"; for once, Susskind is being modest.

A more serious attempt at transmuting a novel into film is *Thérèse,* directed by Georges Franju, a man of some

talent, neither entirely New Wave, nor entirely con-
servative. This is an adaptation of François Mauriac's
beautiful *Thérèse Desqueyroux,* made by Mauriac *père*
and his novelist son, Claude, along with Franju. The
cinematography is by the outstanding Christian Matras,
the music by the extremely gifted Maurice Jarre, though it
is not one of his best scores. Moreover, the novel is
reasonably short, contains a goodly amount of evil, and is
totally absorbing. So one might expect it to become a good
film, particularly since the cast is altogether exemplary,
and a more bewitching and haunting Thérèse than Em-
manuèle Riva could not be found in the *Malleus
Maleficarum.*

Yet the sad truth is that *Thérèse* is a dull movie, because the essential flavor of the novel is not rendered.
What good are all those brilliantly subdued images of the
Landes—of pines, sand, and sea—if the film cannot quite
convey Thérèse's attitudes toward them? What avails it to
observe her sin, even to hear some of her animadversions,
when the camera, despite Mlle. Riva's wordless eloquence,
cannot reproduce the texture of her psyche? Least of all
can the film recreate Mauriac's fascination with evil: his
"tormented conscience," which provides, as Gide put it,
writings that "must be very welcome to those who, holding
sin in abhorrence, would be very disappointed if they
could no longer take an interest in it"? Well, this basic
ambivalence, which is not only the reader's but also the
author's, does not become the camera's.

More could have been done. There is one brief sequence in which Bernard, the husband, excellently played
by Phillippe Noiret, turns away from the dinner he finished almost without conversation, picks up his postpran-
dial pipe and newspaper, and swivels his chair around
toward the fireplace. We get a reverse shot now, and see
behind the cozily complacent face of Bernard the solitary
suffering one of Thérèse, more bewildered even than
reproachful, slowly hardening into despair. The very fuz-
ziness of Bernard's face, slightly out of focus, and the
sharpness of Thérèse's, on which the furrows deepen and

darken in the firelight, speak their pieces. Could not better film-making have achieved more of this?

Indeed, *Knife in the Water,* the first feature film by a highly talented young Polish director, Roman Polanski, has all the virtues of an intensely psychological, sardonically probing modern novel. It is the story of a husband and wife who, out for a weekend's sailing, pick up a young beatnik and take him along on a dare. The husband is a successful sports-writer approaching middle age, who bullies his young wife for fear of losing her. She retorts by a silent passivity that is a long, resentful pout. The youth is feckless and reckless, but not without a genuine animal warmth that the husband has lost in himself and all but extinguished in his wife.

During a day's sailing, there develops a quiet but deadly rivalry between the two men. The husband's chief weapon is a mocking condescension backed up by experience in sailing and living; the youth's inexperience in both is compensated for by his vital physicalness, his ingenuous impudence, his skill with a knife—his youth, in short. Without wishing it, the wife becomes the audience, the arbiter and, finally, the pawn of this contest.

Against the flowing loveliness of a sailboat expending itself on the water, we get the parched, landlocked pettiness of egos that can make contact with others only by clashing. It is a curious, covert, almost subcutaneous battle, only occasionally leading to violence, and ending in a climax unmatched for muted morbidity. Both men emerge defeated, but even the victorious female loses out. For what kind of happiness can she find in men who will be boys or boys who cannot be men?

Polanski and his two collaborators on the screenplay, Skolimowski and Goldberg, have fashioned a film remarkable for its ability to make dramatic gestures that are so delicate, words that are so revealingly oblique and fragmentary, silences that are so sullen and falsely pregnant, that we seem to be confronted not with three people but with three naked—forgive the awkward plural—subconsciouses. Contributing immeasureably to the film are an able cast, K. T. Komeda's incisive jazz score, Jerzy Lipman's ebullient photography, and Polanski's direction —sheer condensed spontaneity.

But, on further thought, *Knife in the Water* could probably not be the modest masterpiece it is (marred only by execrable subtitles), were it adapted from a novel. For the kind of creative freshness that has gone into every part of it can most likely exist only in the joy and freedom of creation, not in the comparative subservience of adaptation, translation, recreation—in the imitation of the imitation of an action. Render unto cinema that which is the cinema's, and unto fiction that which is fiction's.

TRIPLE BRASS

As our films strive toward maturity, they must triumph over that most dangerous temptation for a nascent art: pretentiousness. Here is Brocéliande, the enchanted forest of symbols, from which few come back alive. There is Malebolge, the pit of pseudoprofundity, into which it takes great intellectual balance not to fall. Yonder is the Slough of Despond, the chic gathering place for those afflicted with existential despair; hardly any ever rise again from the tables of this sad café. And over there is the Palace of Pleasure, with the labyrinthine gardens and hall of mirrors, from whose formal delights and technical marvels—and its calendar that stopped at last year—there is no return to reality.

We distinguish three main kinds of pretentiousness: intellectual, aesthetic, and sexual. The first kind tells you that here is a film of Ideas, fearlessly grappling with important issues of our day; the second trumpets its technical innovations, its new cinematic form—in short, Art; the third announces that it is shockingly adult, unblushing and uncensored. But the pretentious film delivers little of what it promises, and that little confused and smudged. Worse yet, it seldom sticks to just one category of pretension, but usually embraces all three, shockingly and unblushingly.

Otto Preminger's *The Cardinal* is very probably the last word in glossy dishonesty posturing as serious art—the word "art," by the way, is one of Mr. Preminger's favorites. Along with *Exodus,* this film may be part of a series, of which the next might well prove a glorification of Islam; its hero, a slightly fictionalized Nasser, to be played by the then presumably grown-up Sal Mineo. Well, this time round Preminger is glorifying Catholicism—for sound commercial reasons—and he is going to make it art, too, by showing us the unadulterated truth.

What kind of truths about Catholicism do we get? A priest orders that, even though this means the mother's death, a doctor must not crush the skull of her about-to-be-born baby; the mother is the priest's sister. The problem should be handled with searching intensity. But it is not even properly discussed, and (*a*) the mother has become a fallen woman and her life a ruin, anyhow; (*b*) the child grows up to be a lovely, wholesome girl, as much of a joy and support to her entire family as her mother was a nuisance, so that Grandma remarks, "Having her around has made it easier for me to accept God's will"; and (*c*) the same actress—if one may dignify the inept Carol Lynley with that appellation—plays both mother and daughter, implying that the same being, only purified and transfigured, lives on under the new guise and a different wig. At the end of the picture, moreover, we see her happily engaged to a nice Catholic youth.

Another example. The Nazis both German and Austrian, are taking over Vienna. The only protest is that of a group of young Catholics singing hymns on the steps of a church. If they were plain ordinary boys and girls, the scene might be moving, whether or not historically authentic. But they are, first of all, played by members of a professional choir; they are also, every one of them, clean-cut and good-looking; and they are led in the singing by that celebrated and handsome artist, Wilma Lipp. And the scene emerges stagey and factitious.

Historical facts are, however, brazenly tampered with when, for example, the Austrian Cardinal Innitzer, a known and egregious collaborator, is shown as swiftly realizing the error of his ways, and switching over, almost immediately after the *Anschluss,* from the side of the Nazis to that of the angels. But never mind history and dogma, problems of mere faith are treated infantilely. Thus the hero, on leave from his priesthood because of doubts, in love with a charming Viennese girl, rushes back to Mother Church for reasons that, if they be reasons at all, are certainly not decently explored.

To be sure, Preminger is no more dishonest in his approach to Catholicism than in his approach to film-making. The march of the Nazis on Innitzer's residence—the vandalism, fighting, and defenestrations—is directed with such geometrical neatness, photographed in such slick, toney colors, is altogether so elaborately literal-minded, that one can take it no more seriously than a well-staged panty raid.

The dialogue is commensurately pious and platitudinous, ranging from apothegms like "Priesthood isn't something you can put on and off like the cassock you wear," to this exchange between a dying parish priest, utterly incompetent but humble and saintly, and the stern cardinal who persistently demoted him: "Larry, would you do me one last favor? Would you give me extreme unction?" "I'd consider it a great honor, Ed." Far from exhilarating, this is merely hilarious.

The one pleasant surprise of the entire movie is the good English it displays. A blackboard in a Viennese English-language classroom boasts such fancy group terms as "a pride of lions"; we actually hear "different from" and not "than"; and Tom Tryon struggles rather touching not only with acting the principal part but also with placing the accent on the second syllable of "details."

Even here, though, truth will out: of all words, "impious" gets mispronounced.

Carl Foreman's *The Victors* has several things in common with *The Cardinal*. It, too, will take up three hours of your misspent time; it, too, contains an episode showing vicious racism among Americans (the inclusion of which ten years ago might have been a sign of courage); it, too, is pretentious, hollow, misdirected.

Foreman has stated his purpose: to make a total antiwar film "without employment of the pablum of romance and adventure." In the past, he feels, his films have been hurt by the "uneasy collaboration" with others. I think it was precisely the presence of directors like Carol Reed, David Lean, and J. Lee Thompson that made his previous films interesting. His current easy uncollaboration is unspeakably heavy-handed; John Coleman of the *New Statesman* has aptly defined *The Victors* as "doggerel epic."

The story trundles along episodically with a platoon of American soldiers from the invasion of Italy to the occupation of Berlin. The aim is to show the hellishness of war without even going into the fighting, which is "the pablum of romance and adventure." And so some of the boys lose their lives in peripheral foolishness, some lose their women, one loses a dog, some lose face either figuratively or literally, and some merely lose their innocence. If the substitute for the pablum of romance and adventure is a diet of boredom, Foreman has succeeded. There is nothing achieved by rehearsing once again the catalogue of clichés of dreariness: the honest wife forced into adultery by loneliness, the nice girl respected by the nice soldier and turned into a whore by the un-nice one, the young widow gone neurotic and the brutalized woman turning herself into a shark, the two young sisters supporting themselves and their family as concubines to the occupying armies. Unless, of course, you can be novel and compelling; Foreman is ponderously obvious.

A typical scene has the stunned widow of a wealthy,

cultivated French collaborationist spend a night of bombardment in a house with a well-meaning slob of an American sergeant. He is nonplussed when she quotes Valéry at him, and she is horrified when waking up in bed with him, she sees his garishly tattooed arm. If this sounds mildly preposterous in summary, it is absurd in drawn-out detail. The most "controversial" scene is the execution of an American deserter, squeezed for all the pathos in the world—including a beautiful cherub of a boy about to be shot—while the folks back home are seen having a good time and the soundtrack chirrups unceasingly a jungle called "Have Yourself a Merry Little Christmas." This lasts at least ten minutes, and in case you might miss the point, it is irony.

But the real irony is that Foreman does not succeed in divesting the film of romance and adventure. The cloddish viewer is left with plentiful images of gorgeous women possessed, enemy wine cellars uproariously depredated, stuffy officers played tricks on, abject civilians lorded over. I do not know how much pablum Foreman finds in Wajda's *Kanal* or Rossellini *Paisan,* but they are far more devastating antiwar statements. "War," said Heraclitus, "has revealed some as gods, others as men." It reveals Foreman as a pompous bore.

Ben Maddow is already guilty of the logorrheic *The Savage Eye* and of turning *The Balcony* into a travesty, but *An Affair of the Skin* tops both. From the opening moment when, against the shot of a wintry branch, an off-screen voice intones a proem in pose, we know the score: "In things—in ice, in water, in wood—there is a black harmony, a molecular music. But in people, in people in love, there is only the fine stretching of invisible wires." After this, it's no surprise to hear a girl say "Truth is sharp and delicate and funny" and be responded to with "You are a remarkable woman." And why not "I do believe in God—I don't know why—maybe it's because someone has to be blundering with that whole ridiculous mess up there—it can't be just chance."

This is an adult investigation of sex, which we recognize by the fact that a husband must practically rape his taunting wife on the floor and hiss "I hate you!" as he takes her. Later he tells his mistress about his marriage: "First we fight. Then, just once a month, the first day after her period . . ." The mistress interrupts, "I don't want to hear about it. It's too sad!" This same husband speaks of "the sad dance of ordinary life" for which a subsequent scene in which he empties the garbage to background music by Mozart may be an objective correlative. It certainly establishes that the film is artistic as well as adult. I could go on, but you don't want to hear about it. It's too sad!

INFANTILISM REVISITED

Possibly the one memorable sentence in *Life*'s double issue on the movies read, "When Doris Day puckers up,
Senegalese and Swedes feel the touch of her lips." As I am
neither Senegalese nor Swedish, the only thing I feel when
Doris Day puckers up—and we shall sooner see America's
Sweetheart without her clothes than without her pucker—is nausea. Against my better judgment, I again attempted to stomach one of her films, *Move Over, Darling*,
which, yet again, affected me as a cross between an all-day
sucker and a hand-painted necktie.

It should give us pause that Doris Day has been, for
years, the number one box-office attraction in the
American cinema; it should start us thinking that her
sickening films have been well received by the reviewers;
it should make us sit up that a reputable critic on a recent
TV show, after knocking some of her films, hastily added
that this was not meant to minimize her very real talent.
The only very real talent Miss Day possesses is that of
being absolutely sanitary: her personality untouched by

human emotions, her brow unclouded by human thought, her form unsmudged by the slightest evidence of femininity.

What, then, does it mean that this heavily sugarcoated, as well as sugarskinned and sugarboned, pill should coax the largest number of coins from the hands of American moviegoers, from the tiny, sweaty ones of our young to the daintily manicured or virilely hirsute ones of our adults—for only by the conjoint spending of all these hands is one anointed America's number one box-office attraction. Now the alleged virtues of Miss Day's persona are three: crisp wit, girlish radiance, and healthy sexuality. As anyone who scrutinizes even one of the Day movies will note, the wit is so crisp that, dropped on your head, it produces instant coma; the radiance is so girlish that it has to be shot through special screens to disguise a bad case of creeping pucker which has begun to ravage that once youthfully insipid face; and the healthy sexuality is a coy, protracted game of teases and *double-entendres* played between husbands and wives or couples well on the way to the altar, and with all ambient beds remaining prelapsarianly unsullied.

What, I repeat, does this endemic Day-worship mean? It means that two or three generations of Americans are basking in witlessness and calling it wit, in facelessness and calling it radiance, in sexlessness and calling it sex, in total darkness and calling it Day. It means that until this spun-sugar zombie melts from our screen, there is little chance of the American film's coming of age, whatever delicious shivers may course up and down the spines of Senegal and Sweden.

The subject of arrested development brings us quite naturally to Dore Schary. As producer, director, adapter and writer, Mr. Schary is responsible for more unmitigatedly awful plays and movies than any other dozen great Broadway and Hollywood names. Lacking the pen of Horatio Alger to do justice to Mr. Schary's staggering want of mind and taste, I can describe Schary only as a man whose few successes were even more distasteful than his many failures. Whether he reduced F.D.R. or *Miss Lonelyhearts* to his own micrometric size, whether he gave us the stale gefilte fish of *A Majority of One,* the cut-rate incense of *The Devil's Advocate,* or the grass-roots, pioneer platitudes of *The Unsinkable Molly Brown,* Mr. Schary has consistently maintained a level nothing short of subliminal. But with *Act One* he plumbs depths that one would have thought unattainable by a craft so much lighter than air.

Moss Hart's autobiography is every bit as shallow and trivial as one expects anything of Hart's to be, but, at least, it contains here and there an honest bit of asperity, a confession not doused in Joy, Cheer and (pink) Thrill. Schary's adaptation of *Act One,* written, produced and directed by himself, manages to be a vulgarization of a vulgarity. Acting and writing, direction and photography are on the level of the early Betty Grable movies about the glamor of show business: its little heartbreaks and big brainless triumphs. To see a crowd of bright-eyed youngsters stream across the screen toward a Y.M.H.A. stage on which they are about to perform a new play by the young Moss Hart—in a schmaltzy boom shot accompanied by the boom of Skitch Henderson's brashest pop-music score; to hear George Hamilton (who gives us a Hart inept and inane beyond the call of verisimilitude) say with a modest smile, after a reading of his first farce to a bunch of awe-struck amateurs, "It is not perfect yet, but neither was *Hamlet* at the first reading"—these are moments not easily forgotten, however much one might wish them to be.

What *Act One* exudes, besides amateurishness and clichés, is imbecile adulation of show business in its grimiest, sleaziest, and most ephemeral aspects: groveling before Theatre-as-Success which is automatically equated with Theatre-as-Greatness. This abject acclaim of mediocrity wearing Adler Elevators as the height of artistic achievement goes beyond mere bad film-making: It is benightedness so complete it deserves not even scorn, only pity.

Compared to this, *America America,* third-rate as it is, might seem genuinely second-rate. Elia Kazan is still another whose growth is arrested, or, more precisely, tripped up by his cleverness and crassness (two sides of the same coin, and I do mean coin) over which he keeps stumbling. Not even into a three-hour movie can one crowd so much incident, social and political history or pseudohistory, and sentimental moralizing posturing as hard-boiled realism, as Mr. Kazan crams into *America America.* The title itself is emblematic: Kazan would always rather say a thing doubly than singly, but, to find time for so much duplication, he must breathlessly hurtle over the decencies of punctuation. To aggravate matters, he sometimes overcompensates by slowing down the hectic hugger-mugger to a virtual standstill (as in the wooing scenes) and throwing the timing further out of joint. He is like a composer with four notations; fortissimo, pianissimo; prestissimo, lentissimo. And he is no writer, as his screenplay and his book on which it is based prove.

The result is a film often muddled or superficial. Not only is the three-way relationship of the Anatolian Turks, Armenians, and Greeks presented sketchily, but often one does not even know who is which. Characters do not become convincing; the young hero, who will do anything to get to America, does not develop. Even in the book, his ambiguous state of someone who sinks to considerable depravity to achieve a noble end was made clearer and more moving; in the film, he remains, despite everything, a lovably ingenuous young fellow. Nor is the bandit Abdul believable: He might play cat and mouse with his victim, but he would not abdicate the cat's cunning and invite the mouse to outwit him.

Things are not improved by the monotonous acting of Stathis Giallelis in the lead and inadequacies in other key performances: Elena Karam's mother (pure Brooklyn), Lou Antonio's bandit (pure Lou Antonio), and Harry Davis' father (pure nothing). On the other hand, Linda

Marsh, Paul Mann, Gregory Rozadis and a few others come through with excellent performances; the Turkish faces and locations look marvelous; and there are scenes, like the dumping of killed conspirators into the sea, that are powerful.

But the main problem that *America America* raises is whether there can be such a thing as epic cinema. Films like *The Bridge on the River Kwai* or *The Guns of Navarone* are possible, but they are not truly epic in that they concentrate on a single action involving mainly a few characters. The moment you try to tell the story of a whole nation, of a struggle involving vast numbers of people in a prominent way, or, as in *America America*, have an eponymous hero embodying all the strivings and hardships of all immigrants ever—the film no longer is a receptive medium. I am respectfully aware of Griffith and Eisenstein, and admire even *Lawrence of Arabia* (before the exhibitors chopped some twenty important minutes out of it). But even such rare successes were only partial: what the epic needs is much, much time in which cumulative effects can be obtained; the kind of attention span that can be accorded to listening or reading in installments; and words *without* pictures, so that Siegfried may truly be superhuman and not the current paunchy Metropolitan *Heldentenor*. In any case, *America America* takes after, not the *Odyssey,* but the *Kalevala.*

Ladybug Ladybug (more echolalia!) is not, as you might expect, about the daughters of President Johnson, but about a bunch of children caught in a supremely improbable atomic-attack scare. "You have done childhood an injustice," Rilke once wrote the novelist Friedrich Huch, and proceeded to explain that the children in Huch's novel were only miniature adults. The children in Frank and Eleanor Perry's film are not even that, they are diminutive symbols and have almost no reality at all. They also have very little talent, with the possible exception of Alice Playten. Though Frank Perry has picked such accomplished adult actors as William Daniels, Jane

Connell, Nancy Marchand, and several others, his direction is rudimentary, and his wife's script is, if possible, even worse to the adults.

If one wants to see what can be done with children in the movies, there is a delightful example in *The War of the Buttons*. This, though the scenario is again by François Boyer, is no *Forbidden Games*; but Yves Robert, the director, himself a very funny comedian, succeeds in making his children childlike, spontaneous, and human. Toward the end, the film becomes tendentious; until then, it gives free vent to the innocent toughness that is the essence of childhood and its inexhaustible charm.

THE STRUGGLE FOR HOPE

The altogether admirable thing about Stanley Kubrick's *Dr. Strangelove* is that it is the first American film to be thoroughly irreverent about everything the establishment takes seriously: atomic war, government, the army, international relations, religion, heroism, sex, and what not. Nor is this a fim in which the rebel against the establishment can be explained away as a Marlon Brando-James Dean type: sympathetic but underprivileged, an unhappily inevitable by-product of our essentially good society. Nor is the rebel a comedian, say, a W. C. Fields or a Chaplin, who can be laughed off as a marginal eccentric.

The rebel in *Dr. Strangelove* is nobody at all, unless you count the scenarists: Kubrick, Peter George, and, above all, Terry Southern. In the film, there are no rebels, only heroes; heroes of politics, warfare, science, all of them so repellent or, at best, nondescript, that the only rebels must be in the audience—amused, revolted, and ready to revolt. An audience of rebels, except for those few viewers and reviewers who wonder whether so much unmitigated irreverence can accomplish anything positive. Well, one positive, indeed necessary, thing it can certainly achieve: It can prove that there is an audience for satire, for devastatingly witty criticism of an ultimately serious sort, for attacks on institutions Hollywood considers almost as sacred as the box office.

Like any valid work of art, *Dr. Strangelove* is, of course, for something. It is for humanity, both literally and figuratively. Much more than an attack on its various targets, it is a *catalogue raisonné* of the ways in which mankind mechanizes or dehumanizes itself. There is the general whose dehumanizing lust for power is based on puritanism and stifled sexuality; and the other general whose lust for power is just hypertrophic animal lust, in whom all manners of grossness are neatly imbricated. There is the colonel in whom sheer stupidity caused dehumanization, and there are all those bigwigs in the Pentagon War Room where the buck is passed around the table as swiftly and mechanically as the ball around the roulette wheel. Above all, there is the B-57, whose complicated mechanisms, complex self-starting and self-locking devices, depersonalized code messages on which millions of lives—all lives, perhaps—depend, have become exactly as much or as little human as the bomber crew that mechanically tends them in an ancillary capacity.

And as a final grotesquely horrible symbol, there is Strangelove himself, exemplifying both hideous tendencies: the human body so full of artificial or artificially reinforced parts that little of it remains not a machine; and the rallying of these mechanical parts till it is they who come to a dominant—and catastrophic—life. The only hope in *Dr. Strangelove* lies in the efforts of such mediocre but well-meaning antiheroes as President Muffley and, especially Captain Mandrake, a kind of Ionescoan Bérenger, the lefthanded, out-of-left-field, but at least unsinister, human being.

High, though not necessarily unqualified, praise must go to the writing, directing, and acting, and not the least of it to Columbia Pictures for releasing the film. Two remarkable performances should be singled out: Sterling Hayden's well-adjusted maniac, and George C. Scott's maniacal adjusted man. The former is a triumph of realistic acting, the latter of making minutest idiocies and hugest beastlinesses larger than actual size. And Kubrick's generally fine direction is superb in the treatment of battle: the hand-camera captures it in the hazy, shabby, incoherent way of the documentaries. Here is ghastliness recorded with an exemplary sense of responsibility.

Ingmar Bergman's *The Silence* is, I am sorry to say, a disappointing film. We are in what might be called Bergman's Antonioni period. Like Antonioni, Bergman chose to make a trilogy about the emptiness, boredom, and lack of transcendental values in life; like Antonioni's, Bergman's third installment stringently divests itself of narrative content and shifts the burden of communication from incident to implication, from statement to symbol.

Like *Eclipse*, *The Silence* will have no truck with beginnings, but starts with a middle. And there is no end either, though it is an end in itself. Like *Eclipse*, again, *The Silence* deals with noncommunication, and, likewise, makes its points not by preachments but by concrete images. Whereas the basic metaphor in Antonioni's film was visual—the eclipse of man in a world dominated by things—the master-image in *The Silence* is auditory. Not only is the soundtrack full of the most disturbing sounds and stillnesses, but also the three main charcters find themselves in a country whose language is as strange to them as theirs is to the natives. Speech, the common denominator, has dropped out of the world and we are left darkling.

There is, however, a threefold inadequacy in *The Silence*. As in *Eclipse*, there is not enough forward thrust, not enough momentum to unite the specific points, the complementary but discrete images. The pearls are there, but the string is too weak to hold them. Again, there is not enough human content; there are hints of the past—rivalry between the two sisters, the father-fixation of the one, the excessive absences of the other's husband; there are suggestions about the present: incestuous and lesbian tendencies in one sister, promiscuity based on inferior intellectual endowment in the other. But the characters do not have enough space in which to develop, precisely because what space there is must remain empty to convey the message. The pearls are there, but we can scarcely see the neck on which they hang.

Lastly, for a film that proceeds by metaphors and implications, certain sensual details are too strong: masturbation, nudity, physical passion, however controlledly handled, loom too large to allow proper importance to such unstated questions as what may happen to a little boy who is dressed up as a girl by corrupt dwarfs and allowed to observe his mother's frantic infidelities. The pearls are there, but the baubles on the same string deflect our attention.

Which is not to say that there is no pleasure in such pearls as the exquisite performances, or in beautifully observed and meaningful details, as when Ingrid Thulin looks down on her sister's and nephew's seminude bodies and can barely suppress reaching out for her sister by switching the gesture into a comtemptuous flick toward the masculine nudity of the other body. There are symbols that are cogently conceived: the one sound that unites people who cannot speak to each other is a bit of Bach on a small radio; the dying aunt leaves the little boy a list of words she has been able to glean from the strange language. Art is universal, and so, potentially, is language; but we are, at best, beginning to learn its uses. The sisters who speak each other's tongue use it only to pummel each other with it; it flows easily only into foreign, uncomprehending ears. And best of all is Sven Nykvist's photography: it fuses the muted tones of the earlier Bergman films with the almost uncanny luster of the later ones, and plays across a whole expressive scale from matte to glossy.

Ermanno Olmi's second film, *The Fiancés,* is not so palpably ingratiating as his wonderful *The Sound of Trumpets,* but it is visually poignant, sensitively conceived, and marks a further technical advance. Young Olmi is one of the finest hopes of the movies, blending as he does the dedicated naturalism of the neorealists with the poetic humanism of Fellini. What *The Fiancés* does with great finesse is to combine the scope and severity of the documentary with the intimacy of a short story; the gap is bridged by a deeply perceptive, imaginative handling of memory and an unerring sense for montage.

It is one thing merely to mingle memory and reality. It is another to know the psychologically and artistically exact moment for the intrusion of remembrance and to recognize the tempos, stratagems, and very shape of memory. Here is a perfect binary rhythm by which the film moves fugally on the planes of reality and recollection—sometimes swerving even into the realm of wish fulfillment—asymmetric yet satisfying, a self-sufficient whole. With sovereign assurance the background music reminds us of the present while we are projected into memory; with supreme emotional logic images of actuality call forth corresponding mnemonic ones.

Olmi can make the most trivial piece of dialogue sound touching and true because of some minor but absolutely particularized incident that surrounds it—perhaps nothing more than a bitten, dirty fingernail during an embrace on the beach. The least gestures assume enormous significance: returning from a frenetically swirling fiesta, the lonely hero carefully screws back the cap on a tube of toothpaste. After the big, impersonal whirl, this decent, humble rotation becomes an act of devotion and piety. The final rainfall I can compare only to the snow at the end of Joyce's "The Dead," no small compliment.

Music, photography, words; everything is wistful, forthright to the point of vulnerability, good-natured, and slightly helpless, but uncomplainingly or complainingly hopeful in the teeth of feral odds. *The Fiancés* is full of landscapes, factories, faces either patiently waiting, or doggedly, dizzyingly juggling, jigging, racing to cope with

an unending barrage of demands. It is a small film, but
honest, beautiful and, above all, brave.

SURFACE SPARKLE AND INNER FIRE

Seven Days in May is a useful movie, serving an entirely
salutary purpose. It sets a standard for films that will not,
or cannot, be works of art or appeal predominantly to intellectuals, but that staunchly refused to compromise their
high standards of—not excellence—competence. This is
not exactly what James Agee used to call "intelligent
trash" but something rather better; perhaps "trashy intelligence" would be the name for it. It is not a case of intelligence going to work on making tripe look piquant, but
of canny observation deciding to play it not entirely
safe—yet safe enough.

Seven Days in May is like *Rigoletto* with Tucker, Mer-
rill, and Peters; like a good, *early* Bernard Buffet; like an
adequate red wine. It is to be enjoyed without feelings of
guilt, there should be more movies like it, and it has
nothing first-class about it.

Consider the scene at the beginning where a minor riot
breaks out in front of the White House. Had it been
directed by Otto Preminger *(vide The Cardinal)*, it would
have emerged pre-rehearsed, grandly violent but tidy:
tourist-folder photography—if there were tourist folders
inviting us to come to exotic Vietnam and see the glorious
fighting. Had it been directed by Stanley Kubrick *(vide
Strangelove)*, it would have had a spontaneous, unnerving,
newsreel quality, unspectacular but cruelly effective. It is,
however, directed by John Frankenheimer and partakes of
both modes.

True, it uses a hand camera; has movement that,
though carefully calculated, seems random and disorganized; and, best of all, has a nice rhythm to it with

just the right amount of gradual acceleration. Nonetheless, there are also slick camera angles, tricky panning shots, and rather sly cutting. Not that such devices are fundamentally wrong; they are merely out of place in such a nastily vulgar context.

Other virtues of the film are similarly ambiguous. This is the story of a military junta which is about to take over our government. An upstanding, sharp young colonel stumbles on the truth in the nick of time, tips off the aging and tired but able and right-thinking President and a band of his trusty aides, and together they foil the devilishly clever, Right-wing conspiracy. Its head is none other than the hero's venerated chief: a brilliant general, but, as it turns out, a fanatic.

Of the novel on which this is based, I know only that it was a tenacious best-seller and a favorite of Dore Schary—which, I'm afraid, is enough. But as a film, it has the obvious virtue of questioning the infallibility of our Army, which is a worthy endeavor, although since the Army-McCarthy hearings a breach has become manifest in the complacency with which Hollywood had viewed the Service. Accordingly the cliché Blustering General has lost ground to the cliché Nasty General: captious, bureaucratic, and meanly trig. But from the latter (say, as portrayed by Kevin McCarthy in *A Gathering of Eagles*) to the general who, though intelligent, intrepid, a master-strategist and sexy to boot, is also a brutal, neofascist traitor—and one who can carry most of our armed forces with him—we would seem to have come a long way.

And so we would have—if his psyche were adequately examined, if his language could rise above a judicious mixture of wisecracks and platitudes, if his actions were able to give him full three-dimensionality. Instead, Burt Lancaster makes him into just what he was meant to be: a figure in its two-dimensionality genuinely menacing, but not terrifyingly real.

So with the whole plot. Its bark, though very good indeed, is still worse than its bite. We are held by the story all the way, and on a lever above that of merely yielding to make-believe. But then, in the end, it is all a mite too quick, easy, bloodless: a bit smug, with everyone saying the right, only slightly hackneyed words, and we feel that we have perhaps been had, after all. I am told by a friend who went to see *Seven Days in May* a second time that the dialogue proves absolutely moldy on reuse; so it would seem advisable to see the picture only once.

Once, however, is good fun. Besides Frankenheimer's smartly profane direction—with occasional flashes of something better—there are also very good performances: Fredric March's President, ashen but still capable of smouldering; Kirk Douglas' Colonel, nicely suggesting the skin under the uniform; Edmond O'Brien's, George Macready's and Martin Balsam's sturdy supports to a President in need. Only Ava Gardner has a problem. Granted that she is meant to enact a woman left too long on the bough, the fine line between overripeness and marcescence proves too fine for her.

Pierre Drieu La Rochelle was one of those short-changed souls who came of age exactly as World War I broke out. He became, along with Montherlant, one of the writers who most clearly spoke for those who returned to post-war Paris morally uprooted and ideologically adrift. Americans will know this figure best from Colette's *Chéri* novels, but one must imagine a Chéri with exceptional literary talent and not only financial and amatory hungers, but also vast and fickle political appetites. Drieu veered from Communism to Fascism, wrote poetry, stories, and autobiographical novels with such emblematic titles as *The Man Covered with Women* and *Peculiar Journey*, became a collaborationist, and, totally disillusioned as well as aware of what awaited him, killed himself in 1945 at the age of 52.

Le Feu follet ("Will-o'-the-wisp") was a novel Drieu wrote as he pushed forty, and hell hath no fury such as a brilliant, charming drifter will unleash against himself when middle age surprises him *in flagrante* with the sense of his own gratuity. Seldom has an author so sardonically turned his fictional alter ego into a dartboard to riddle with the most fiendishly well-aimed epigrams. Now Louis Malle has turned *Le Feu follet* into a devastatingly accurate, wryly beautiful film, released here as *The Fire Within*. The film is as uncomfortably apt in the 1960's as the novel was in the 1930's.

It is the story of the last two days in the life of Alain, a delightful youngish man about to be released from a genteel private institution at Versailles as cured of alcoholism. But there is a graver ill of which he is not cured: himself. He has a rich and beautiful American wife in New York who keeps him, but keeps him at ocean's length. As the picture begins, he is in bed with one of his wife's best friends. As it ends, he is in bed with a bullet in his heart. In between, he revisits some of his old Paris friends (he has been in New York for years, then in the institution for months), like a good scientist seeking proof of his hypotheses—that life is not worth living.

The screenplay, also by Malle, is excellent in several ways. First, in its unprecedentedly incisive portrayal of neurosis and psychosis. Those sequestered at Versailles are pictured with uncanny exactitude: neurosis is just a little too much or a trifle too little of something; it is not weird and exotic, as amateurish films like *David and Lisa* would have it, only painfully ordinary and vaguely sordid. And we see it equally precisely, disturbingly, and unglamorously in those who are running around Paris —homosexuals, dope fiends, promiscuous women. But we see it most piercingly in Alain, who is so bright and appealing and yet such a cynical and irascible drain on himself and anyone who would help him. As clearly as perhaps never before in a movie we are shown what it is like to be confronted with someone who feels that life only humiliates us, and that he could never really hold anyone, anything.

The man is quite obviously going to kill himself. His adjusted friends want to help him: they want to convince him that life is good, but he only undermines their own faith in it. He is a beggar whom no amount of alms they can give will succor and who even insults them into the bargain. They end up loathing him, and themselves for loathing a sick man; finally they just stand there, stupefied, emptied out, mouthing some gilt-edged platitude. With the help of Maurice Ronet, a magnificently various Alain, and a spirited supporting cast, the film comes to aching, furious life.

But there is more. *The Fire Within*, even while honestly asserting the sickness of the sick (asking no pity for them—showing them both bad and good), insinuates with acidulous finesse its doubts: How healthy are the healthy? And just how much is health worth? The ambivalence of sickness and health, though, is never expressed sneeringly or snarlingly, but with flawless tact and a dignified sense of *lacrimae rerum*. And all this is couched in splendidly literate dialogue of utmost simplicity, untarnished even by lax subtitles.

Mostly, however, it is what is purely filmic that is so enchanting here. I am not even thinking primarily of the extraordinary photography, which is an object lesson in exactly how far one can push the artful without becoming arty. Or of the superb soundtrack, on which a wistful but proud bit of Satie piano music alternates with the clumsy, pointless noises of life. Or of the ingenuous way in which the camera comments on the bizarre objects and perverse little rituals with which Alain tries to bejewel the drabness of his existence. I am thinking, above all, of the way Malle has paced his film with a kind of double tempo: a lot of tiny, repetitious, senseless fastnesses which add up to a great, viscous, oppressive sense of barely moving. The panther in his cage, eddies in a stagnant pool, boxed pendulums—that is what Alain and his friends are. Marking time and marked by it, scurrying inside a huge immobility, they are slowly rushing to embrace a palpable nothingness.

What keeps *The Fire Within* from being a great film is the constricting effect of emotional grisaille relieved only by some flashes of black comedy. Nothing can keep it from remaining one of the year's best films.

IN THE CRUELEST MONTH

You should see *The Fall of the Roman Empire* if: (1) You can take a musician friend who owes you money. After ten minutes of Dimitri Tiomkin's score, he'll be limp; after three hours, you can safely remove his wallet. (2) Your grandparents are still ambulatory, and you want to give them the treat of reliving the Victorian romances: "Where could we go, Livius?—Anywhere we'd be, we'd be alone, Lucilla.—I'm Caesar's daughter!—You're a woman. That's a much higher rank." (3) You have been wondering about the stature of Will Durant as a historian. He was technical adviser for this mess.

Let us get a few more overrated duds out of the way. *Yesterday, Today and Tomorrow* brings together Loren and Mastroianni, who, according to producer Joe Levine, are the greatest screen lovers since Garbo and Gilbert. Is that any reason for putting them into a vehicle of roughly the same vintage? Vittorio de Sica gives us another glossy triumph of the neounrealistic cinema, and the scenarists bring us the same lovable Neapolitans, (Alberto) Moravian rich bitches, and whores whose hearts continue to maintain the strictest gold standard. So yesterday and yesterday and yesterday creeps in this petty pace, signifying nothing.

The World of Henry Orient is a clean, happy, dishonest little picture that is wonderful anti-intellectual fun for the entire family. What do you want to feel superior to? The arts? There is a poetess here who is an idiot, a concert pianist who performs incessantly at Carnegie Hall though he is a consummate no-talent, advanced modern music that is pure Mantovani with an occasional steam whistle added. Intelligence? Nothing more forsaken than a little girl with a genius I.Q. Psychiatry? There are so many patronizing jokes about it, you'd think psychiatrists are a minority group. The rich? They are unhappy as can be and their parties swarm with phoneys. (The poor, on the other hand, live in houses only a shade less sumptuous, and are happy as all getout.)

The values of the film are perfectly revealed when the *raisonneuse,* a scrumptious middle-aged aunt, remarks during the aforementioned Steam-whistle Concerto, "If this is music, what is that stuff Cole Porter writes?" Note that this critique is delivered in Carnegie Hall, where any less militantly anti-intellectual screenwriters than Nora and Nunnally Johnson would have substituted Tchaikovsky for Porter.

As for the acting, Peter Sellers is such an expert impersonator that one regrets his inability to add to his list of impersonations the Peter Sellers that was. Paula Prentiss is a lovely young woman, and there must be some other profession open to her. Of the two highly touted young girls, Merrie Spaeth seems to me extraordinary in name only, but Tippy Walker, with better direction, could yet make a real actress. For George Roy Hill's direction goes from terribly arty, terribly old tricks to passages of toal literal-mindedness, and the girls are allowed such bad diction as, "A blood pact means that we will hump each other as long as we live." (The word should have been "help.") In short, *Junior Miss* has grown up into a full-size miss.

The second Ian Fleming book to reach the screen, *From Russia with Love,* confirms the notion that James Bond is merely a fancy-pants Mike Hammer. But, I suppose, there must be status symbols even in protopornography, and those who prefer their sex and sadism in cutaways rather than dungarees must be so indulged. Speaking of the Fleming novels, Alex Comfort observed (in that highly challenging book *Darwin and the Naked Lady*) that Bond, "the eponymous hero . . . who tortures suspects, ravishes women and for preference shoots them afterwards, is the emissary of society—or at least he stands for authority and its uses, for the unlimited rights of aggressive behavior which it confers, and he is expected to carry the admiring acquiescence of his readers." Dr. Comfort (also eponymous) is all for sexual release even if accompanied by some violence, but, both as biologist and poet-novelist, he deplores what he calls affectless violence.

So, too, in the Bond films. Or in our censorship laws. Violence is granted every privilege of preening itself, and is made to seem thoroughly enjoyable—needless to say, you will not be so gauche as to identify yourself with the fellow who gets killed. Sex, however, must emerge ancillary, hasty, casual, *interruptus*; it is hard, if not impossible, to convey its joyful plenitude, but it is assumed that endless quantity can make it look as interesting as quality could. Yet the mind boggles at quantity; what it needs is quiddity. The fully rendered violence, the toughly cynical epigram-epitaphs with which each righteously murdered spy or thug is suavely dismissed, these are what is remembered. And they create a kind of snobbery of violence: the lush interiors and exotic scenery, and the lushly exotic dames, are only marginal enhancements of this aristocracy of brutality.

Now Mike Hammer is, at least, a bit of a slob; moreover, he represents an ultra-reactionary, unofficial point of view, and is a loner often in conflict with the police. But Bond is murderous, witty, condescending, frightfully in and frightfully chic; he gets, as a fringe benefit, all the female flesh he can eat; best of all, he is on the Side of Right! And when he lays his hands on the film his enemies secretly shot of him having intercourse with one of his girls, he cavalierly dumps it into a Venetian lagoon. This seems improvident, for it would have been the perfect follow-up in the series.

The acme of vulgarity, however, you have to seek in *What a Way to Go!* The mildest thing to be said about this film is that it is an abomination. It goes *Henry Orient* one better in its anti-intellectualism, it turns death into a running gag, it contains film-within-a-film travesties undistinguishable from the main body of the film, it has jokes to make the angels weep and costumes in which they wouldn't blow their noses if they were the only cloths of heaven; and it has Shirley MacLaine. Worst of all, this staggering concoction of Comden and Green's tries, cravenly, to have it both ways. Thus we are supposed to laugh at wealth even while being swept off our feet by it; we are supposed to admire the superior taste and wisdom that informs the movie while it makes tasteless fun of art and intellect, yet we must not take any of its inanities seriously; and we must accept every form of the *outré*— from dialogue to décor—as being at the same time glamorous and yummy. It is like a fat man entering a party with the exclamation, "Look at me, aren't I fat!" and bursting out laughing. We can respond neither with seriousness nor with amusement, only with embarrassed silence. At *What a Way to Go!*, the embarrassed silence is louder than the loudest laughter.

The Festival of French film classics at the 57th Street Normandie now yields two notable films not previously released hereabouts. *Les Dames du Bois de Boulogne* (1945), by Robert Bresson, has a screenplay by Cocteau based on the Mme de La Pommeraye episode from Diderot's *Jacques le Fataliste,* which had already fascinated Schiller. A proud lady, spurned by her noble lover, enables a charming slut and her mother to pose as retiring gentlewomen, makes her ex-lover meet them and fall in love with the girl, sees to it that he be driven by ungratified desire to marriage, and then informs him that he has married a whore. But forgiveness and love avert catastrophe.

Cocteau's dialogue is relatively restrained; even so, it is piquant to note the blending of the styles of *La Voix humaine* and the *Encyclopédie*. But whereas Diderot's was a moral tale, managing to forgive everyone with the possible exception of the girl's mother, Bresson and Cocteau give us a political allegory: there can be forgiveness for whorish collaboration and, by extension, Vichy France itself, if weakness is expiated and understanding prevails. In the film, it is the unforgiving mistress, smouldering with however righteous hatred, who is—if only by implication—left alone and lost.

The film could have been much more satisfactory if the overrated Bresson had not, as usual, directed with that glaringly naked literalism that some persist in admiring as economy of means. I, alas, cannot admire an economy based on sheer poverty. But I am full of praise for Maria Casarès' fire-and-ice-breathing wronged woman, and for Lucienne Bogaert's aging beauty torn between greed and love for her daughter, a touching mixture of solicitude and stupidity, a performance of unmitigated humanity.

Le Crime de Monsieur Lange (1935)—the translation cannot convey the pun, *The Crime of Mr. Angel*—is a film that is absolutely fine. It is a poetic parable written by that most marvelous of minor poets, Jacques Prévert, so marvelous that he almost makes the word "minor" meaningless. It is a completely touching, lyrically simple plea against simplicity, decency, and socialism. And true love. No one but Prévert could have brought off this ingenuous mélange of gently deadly irony, innocent hilarity, and sonnet-like rapture. No one but he could have made goodness look so dear, ardent, purblind and irresistible, victorious over everything from one of the most brilliantly suasive villains to the most exiguous English subtitles.

Jean Renoir has directed with quiet ingeniousness never encroaching on reverence; the murder scene alone can stand as an example of *sotto voce* artistry at its best. The actors are not only perfect, they are also quintessentially human, and beautiful down to their very ugliness. Jules Berry's villain, Nadia Sibirskaia's ingénue, and Jacques Brunius' enchanting comic bit with his dog, Daisy, are unforgettable. And there is a scene in which a young man forgives his girl for having been impregnated by the villain. Every word and gesture in it is a balm for all the crimes against mankind, from war to *What a Way to Go!* It makes you weep and laugh and proud to be alive.

OF 'PARADISE' AND PARASITES

What are the movies coming to? Any day now they will become so bad that we shall all have to go to the theatre. And then where shall we be? Film, which has captured the spirit of our age on screen and the attention of our audience in front of that screen, may well be losing both.

One of the most intelligent women I know told me recently that the only time she is really happy is at the movies, watching people doing things. "On the screen," I asked, "or in the seats around you?" What is there to be happy about at *The Pink Panther*, or *What a Way to Go!*, or *Weekend*, or *The Empty Canvas*, or *The World of Henry Orient*, or any number of other films now being shown? *Orient*, for instance, was our official entry at the Cannes Festival, and after you get over the shock of that, try to think of something much better they could have sent in its place, and after an hour of racking your brain you will really be shocked.

There are several recent films of some slight merit, to be sure, that I have not even reported on. It is precisely the slightness of the merit that makes them dull to write about: damning with faint praise or praising with faint damns is not a very inspiriting business. So I did not write about *Becket*—handsome, respectable, and boring; or about *The Servant*—moodily suggestive, well-acted, but petering out into a trickle of repetitious, unmeaningful nastiness; or about *To Bed or Not to Bed*—with its wonderful Alberto Sordi, stunning Swedish women, a few funny moments, and an idea that, though interesting, is handled much too sloppily.

Then one sees again *The Children of Paradise*, this time complete, with the superb Frédérick Lemaître episodes at last included and displaying Pierre Brasseur at his best, which is nothing less than genius; and one must say, no matter how unbearably the platitude hurts one, "They don't make movies like that any more!" Granted, Marcel Carnés's direction is nothing more than sound commercial work. But Jacques Prévert's story and dialogue are marvels: neo-Romanticism pushed to the limit beyond which there is only sentimentality, yet exhilaratingly cognizant of just where to stop and become hardheaded, funny, even matter-of-fact. In his novel, *Le Grand Ecart,* Cocteau says of Germaine, "Her beauty hovered over ugliness, but like an acrobat over death. It was a way of stirring you." Substitute "sentimentality" for "ugliness" and you have the beauty of Prévert's writing.

And the acting! Barrault in his heyday was unmatched at portraying a naïve, laughable, unworldly, and sublime adoration; and the sweetness, transparence, limitlessness of his love for Garance are equaled in masterly depiction by the unconscious, innocent cruelty with which he treats the wife he does not love. Arletty's Garance, a little past *à point* but not *faisandé,* inundates the screen with mischievous, headlong, seering femininity: exquisitely languid when not aroused, icy when not even tickled, but when fully awakened, torrential, transcending all dimensions, pure alkahest. And that voice, midway between a mountain stream and a gin-soaked parrot! Brasseur: a one-man compendium and epitome of the theatre—tinsel as good as gold; mendacious charm more beautiful than truth, and truer too; love, hatred, generosity, raillery, death-defying courage, all for effect, until effect becomes flesh and larger than life-size to boot.

Again, Maria Casarès as the desperate wife: Who else could have made nagging, choking, marathon jealousy look so touching, lovable, even heroic? How that plain face of hers can become transfigured with the humblest happiness; how, in the agonies of rejection and anger, its ugliness remains human. And what of those two great untimely dead actors, Louis Salou, as the Count, and Marcel Herrand, as Lacenaire the murderer? How contemptible this snobbish, humorless, manically possessive, superhumanly fatuous aristocrat, and yet try, if you can, despising him. Try not to feel the paroxyms of this lover, having without possessing, trembling with frustrated humanity under the impeccable sneer. And Marcel Herrand's foiled dramatist turned to the fine art of murder (as well as that occasional potboiler, larceny), investing it with spine-freezing mellifluence and bloodcurdling finesse, glittering hate shot through with sensuously sardonic epigrammatism. There are not enough Oscars in Hollywood or in Heaven to reward such performances.

Even those bits contributed by Gaston Modot as an all-seeing blind man; Jacques Castelot as the Count's crassly effete henchman; Pierre Renoir as the embodiment of true evil which is miserliness, hypocrisy, and mortal envy of other people's happiness: Etienne Decroux as Debureau, Sr.; and so many barely glimpsed others are wholly memorable. It is the sort of film that, no sooner ended, you want to see all over again. It is the sort of film after which your wife or husband looks as beautiful as on the day you fell in love. And it is the sort of film which, today, despite its first uncut showing, drew no crowds and was soon gone.

This is what worries me. Perhaps it is not the fault of the movies. Perhaps it is the fault of the moviegoers. Or nongoers. Consider some of the best films of recent times: Ermanno Olmi's artistically daring and humanly simple *A Sound of Trumpets* and *The Fiancés*, Malle's *The Fire Within*, Polanski's *Knife in the Water,* and, most recently, Vittorio de Seta's heartbreakingly persuasive *Bandits of Orgosolo*—how many of them were still there after one, two, or at best three weeks? Only Polanski's film had something of a run, but did it get a fraction of the acclaim given to that perfect piece of pseudoartistic mediocrity *Tom Jones*? This is, for once, not even the fault of the critics, who tended to do justice to those films—except to *The Fire Within,* which the higher-brow reviewers were blind and deaf to. This, then, ladies and gentlemen, is, I fear, your fault alone. And if you don't mend your ways, you'll get more and more *Yesterday, Today and Tomor-*

rows—Joseph Levine, the producer, has already announced such an annual Loren-Mastroianni delight around Christmas for at least five years to come, so put that into your stockings and smoke it. And more *Falls of the Roman Empire,* and the decline of practically everything.

One press agent blames it on there being no longer a hard-core art-house audience: a discriminating and dependable aristocracy among moviegoers, now superseded by a great, heterogeneous democracy hostile to excellence. But I wonder whether it was the artistic value of the first postwar Rossellini films, or *Bicycle Thief,* or *Devil in the Flesh,* or more recently, *The 400 Blows,* that guaranteed them an audience, aristocratic or otherwise. Or whether it was not something superficially new, superficially different, and —most superficial of all—something highly publicized that did the trick.

I can name you some excellent flops or near-flops from almost any period. Was *God Needs Man* a hit? Was *The Game of Love* (I mean Colette's *Le Blé en herbe,* not that ridiculous *The Love Game*)? Was *Il Bell' Antonio*? Could you have sold the early and best Fellini films except on the success of the later, less pure and less good ones? Or, nearer home, wasn't the one almost honest movie Billy Wilder ever made, *Ace in the Hole,* his one flop? (Not even changing its name to the more box-officy *The Big Carnival* made it smell sweeter where only success smells sweet.) And did *Paths of Glory* make any money? I could go on, but need I?

Let us concede that things were not necessarily good in the past. But at least there did not seem to be such wholesale discrimination against quality: *Bandits of Orgosolo* would not have disappeared after one measly week without even a follow-up run in one of the livelier neighborhoods.

What could be some realistic reasons for such large-scale audience delinquency? First-run movie theatres have become too expensive. There are too many so-called art houses and they have to offer something, consequently much trashy pseudoart is shown; this makes many people lose faith in all films and resist even the good ones. There is the assumption that it can all soon be seen, cheaper and nearer, as a rerun—or even on television—and unawareness that a poor first run may effectively prevent there ever being any second runs. There is the worsening of taste, possibly caused by TV fare; and the rise of an appalling cinematic pop art that subverts the younger and more enthusiastic movie audiences. There seems to be greater confusion in the minds of the reviewers, who find it progressively harder, in an era of proliferating pseudo-avant-gardes, to distinguish the fine from the fashionable, the far-out from the out-of-the-question.

The typical pseudoart film of today is something like *Disorder*, by a new Italian writer-director, Franco Brusati. There are a few good performances, notably Georges Wilson's, and a few routine ones; there is a genuine albeit second-hand cinematic sense; here and there a cogently directed scene; and outstanding editing by Ruggiero Mastroianni. But the thinking and writing in *Disorder* are almost unmitigated triviality and sensationalism, and faded sensationalism at that. The film is both frantic and derivative. It goes at it as if there were no tomorrow and, what is worse, as if there had been no yesterday.

RIDICULOUS AND SUBLIME

Satire may well be the most arduous artistic genre. Even before the satirist can get to the difficulties inherent in his art, he faces three liminal obstacles. There is the difficulty of finding a subject big enough to warrant a broadside; there is the problem of finding a large enough audience that will understand one's references; and there is the mat-

ter of exact timing: a premature attack alienates, an overdue one bores.

These preliminary hardships are exacerbated for the
film satirist. Film needs a much bigger immediate audience than literature, and large, far-flung audiences are
apt to break down into groups with parochial frames of
reference. Satire, moreover, appeals to a sophisticated intelligentsia whose suffrage the movies have not yet fully
obtained. Most of all, film industries and even individual
film-makers tend to be hidebound, or, more precisely,
celluloidbound. Film, to them, is more real than life.

In Hollywood, it is the formula that is supposed to pay
off. But in an insecure age satire is not going to be, or appear to be, a lucrative formula—assuming that it is reduci-
ble to one, in the first place. In Avantgardia, it is the
film-maker's individuality that is particularly prized. But
cinémathèque navel-gazers tend to have little individual
experience of the great universal problems out there in the
world. A general sort of impression is easily enough acquired: conformity, fear, sexual frustrations, spiritual im-
poverishment—such social ailments can readily be sensed.
But sensing them is not enough. The satirist must have an
accurate experience of the society's quirks, tics, pipe-
dreams, platitudes—its unspoken thoughts and unthought
inklings—before he can ridicule them distinctly and
devastatingly.

That Man from Rio is the latest film of Philippe de
Broca, the lavishly overrated confectioner of *The Love
Game, The Joker,* and *The Five-Day Lover.* This is meant
to be a crop of sex-and sadism spectacles, the killer-chiller-
thriller-dillers. It is plain enough why a film satirist would
pick such a subject: Movie audiences all over the world
can be assumed to have at least this one thing in common—going to the movies. Hence a take-off on movies
cannot fall on uncomprehending eyes and ears. Unlike a
musical extravaganza, however, satire is meant not only
for eyes and ears but also for what is behind them: the
brain.

And what does the brain do? It maintains that when a

genre becomes as palpably preposterous as the contemporary thriller, it is its own best satire; for example,
Mickey Spillane's most recent abortion, or the flimflam
Flemings, or such *mouvelle-vague* hyper-Bogartisms as
J.-P. Melville's *The Finger-Man,* (released here redundantly as *Doulos the Finger-Man, doulos* being the French
for finger-man). The brain further objects that a folly as
minor as this is hardly worthy of satire. What can be
disposed of with a few well-sharpened words does not require an elaborate and expensive two-hour color film to
puncture it; besides, on that costly and glossy a scale, you
cannot tell the punctures from the panegyrics. Lastly, for
such junior-size satire—pastiche—to be efficacious, it
must score bull's-eyes on identifiable targets; but the only
film of which *That Man from Rio* reminded me strongly
enough at times is *Black Orpheus,* fatuous claptrap but
hardly a thriller.

There are a few truly effervescent moments in *That
Man from Rio,* granted, and Jean-Paul Belmondo has a
real paprika-and-cucumber charm; Edmond Sechan's
color photography almost improves on the already perfectly sensuous or striking Brazilian backgrounds; Georges
Delerue's score is cajolingly atmospheric. There is also a
heroine, Françoise Dorléac, who can look ravishing in one
shot and like a death's-head in the next; and there are the
very considerable talents of Jean Servais and Simone Re-
nant, totally wasted. One can watch long stretches of the
film without feeling that it is reducing anything to absurdity, and there is nothing that it will have laughed out
of existence.

The Premise, a New York cabaret which has always
seemed to me likable but undistinguished, has now contrived a film featuring all of its original members and written by two of them. *The Troublemaker* has the opposite
troubles from those of *That Man from Rio*: this American
satirette is overstuffed with ambition and undernourished
in technique. By technique, I do not mean cinematography: Gayne Rescher's photography, though not
very remarkable or original, is better than what we

usually get in such minor independent ventures. What is lacking is a satirical technique, an understanding of how satire functions. No matter how seemingly free-floating a work like *Candide* or *Gulliver's Travels* may be, there is a discipline underlying it. There are no obtrusions of other, nonsatirical forms of humor; a consistency of character, however quizzical, is maintained; the overall structure is not lost sight of.

The Troublemaker concerns itself ostensibly with the efforts of a well-meaning, brave but naïve, hayseed to start a coffee shop in Greenwich Village without greasing the palms of everybody from the corner policeman to the four graftsmen of this apocalypse, the Inspectors of Fire, Electricity, Buildings, and Sanitation. So far, so good. But there is a subplot involving a would-be helpful but crooked lawyer and his fantastical mistress whom our hero wins over by his quixotic guilelessness, and though some attempt is made to treat this, too, satirically, a flavor of *Golden Boy—Born Yesterday* sentimentality syrups up the issue. The main drawback, though, is the intrusion of various kinds of slapdash irrelevance, like hands getting stuck in abstract statuary, seminude girls lounging about for the sheer nylon hell of it (shades not of the immortal *Candide* but of *The Immoral Mr. Teas*), lengthy and not particularly funny chases—a variety of not so comic ir-relevances or irrelevant kinds of comedy.

Why, for instance, that batch of old, forced, extraneous psychiatric jokes? Unfortunately, the most memorable thing about *The Troublemaker* is the brief appearance of China Lee in briefer costume even than the leporine one she was wont to wear at the New York Playboy Club, which still concealed certain key parts, at least from or-dinary key-holders.

Situated at the antipodes from satire is *The Organizer,* a socialist tragicomedy full of bittersweet sentiment and humor. It is slightly simplistic, somewhat old-hat, and ut-terly expert, moving, and lovable. This is a forthright tale of factory workers in Turin at the turn of the century; of how they manage to work up the courage to strike for a thirteen-hour workday, accident insurance, and a few fringe benefits; how the bosses oppose them bitterly and cunningly; and how, with the help of an eccentric, proscribed ex-high school teacher, they manage to win what seems like a partial victory.

Mario Monicelli has directed the film from a screenplay on which he collaborated with Age and Scarpelli, and this extremely able director, together with the brilliant cinematographer Giuseppe Rotunno and the superb editor Ruggiero Mastroianni, has created a work in which technical perfection triumphantly curbs the onslaughts of brute emotional appeal. The Italians are past masters of the difficult art of blending pathos and humor, and this is precisely what *The Organizer* manages with acrobatic skill.

If Marcello Mastroianni, as the former teacher, persecuted and starving, is being treated to a square meal by the obligatory aureate-hearted prostitute, Annie Girardot, the scene is on the verge of a sentimental commonplace. But Mastroianni tells Girardot he has a picture of his wife and children somewhere and fishes up several scraps of a snapshot, which she pieces together like a jigsaw puzzle and mutters a polite phrase about, whereupon he stuffs the pieces back into his pocket. The mixture of pride and clumsiness, of politeness and puzzlement in the characters, the unlingering offhandedness with which the camera observes this, the wistfully bantering dialogue—all these leave the viewer suspended between amusement and heartache in a state of intensified sensibility.

Again, there is a scene in which the scabs whom the bosses have imported are arriving on a train as the strikers await them at the station, to remonstrate with them or, if necessary, fight them off. It is a somewhat foggy day, and the moment is pregnant with melodrama. Suddenly we see shots of the misty landscape from the speeding train. Rotunno gives us images that have overtones of Turner, Monet, even Nicolas de Staël: landscapes reduced to hazy semiabstractions, dissolving forms, harmonies in grey.

Then comes the encounter of the workers: violent, comic, absurd, and finally tragic. But in the midst of all that jagged chaos, this interlude of crazy, lyrical scenery—a fleeting efflorescence of saxicolous beauty.

I wish I could describe in detail the last scene of the film with its split-second editing, not one frame too many or too few. Here the sudden apparition of a child determinedly trudging to a sweatshop, the disappearance of the child's head diagonally through the lower right corner of the image, a few seconds of gloomily empty background, then, abruptly, "The End," produce such an impeccable parabola and rhythm of surprise, pathos, beauty of movement, sense of loss and void that what might be tearjerking fills the eye not with dimming tears but widening vision.

Almost every point of the film is equidistant from tears, laughter, and awakening awareness. It is lovingly acted, and has the best musical score, by Carlo Rustichelli, since the great scores of Nino Rota. It observes people with affectionate tough-mindedness. It may oversimplify now and then, but it does not lie. It seems to be a living organism covered with pores exuding the sweat of humanity—one part stench and two parts glory.

THE NEW BYZANTINISM

Chabrol, one could see almost immediately, had no talent at all. In *Le Beau Serge* he was able, at least, to create an atmosphere of pervasive grubbiness, to unmask the French rural milieu as no one but René Clément in *Forbidden Games* had done it before. But each successive film only underscored Chabrol's mindless pretense at having a mind, his perverse obtuseness in the realm of psychology, and his mistaking of trickery for art. Godard started out promisingly, but soon revealed himself possessed of spirit rather than imagination, vitality rather than sensitivity, discrimination, or depth.

Malle scored splendidly with *The Fire Within,* but it will take more than one bull's-eye to cancel out all those previous misses. Resnais bore witness to a strange but undeniable sensibility and considerable directorial flair. But *Marienbad* already was a mere dance of death for an expensive puppet theater, and *Muriel* was only thirteen ways of looking at a vacuum.

That left François Truffaut, who had always been, at worst, inventive, and, at best, a shattering artist. Left him, that is, until *The Soft Skin* came along, severely jolting one's faith in him. Artists are, of course, fully entitled to occasional blunders in the pursuit of the experimental, but there is less excuse for fiascos of retrogression into the commonplace. What follows, though harsh, is written more in sorrow than in anger, and still more in sheer astonishment.

In *The Soft Skin,* which Truffaut also co-authored, a middleaged married writer-editor-lecturer has a clandestine affair with a young airline stewardess, falls in love with her, decides somewhat hesitantly to leave his wife and child, is rejected by the girl who senses his lack of conviction, and is melodramatically shot to death by his wife who discovers the affair. It is a banal old story, though French authors—perhaps not the very best ones—have successfully disseminated it on stage, screen, and printed page, dramatically, melodramatically, or farcically. But the success was due to a new solution or sharper insight: to the wringing of a keener cry of pain or brighter laughter from the situation.

Not so here. About the central problem the film has nothing to say that has not been said before and better. The one point it belabors is that everything important happens by coincidence. It is by merest chance that husband and girl meet, purely accidental that anything comes of it, utterly fortuitous that the wife finds out, and sheer rotten luck that the husband's contrite phone call doesn't reach the loving but vengeful wife in time. Coincidence is a tired old nag, but even tired nags have been known to win races—not, however, when saddled with the entire weight of the tale.

Yet that is the burden of Truffaut's story: the ghastliest disasters stem from the most trivial circumstances. And perhaps some life could still be wrested from this notion if the movie were peopled with real and interesting characters upon whom coincidence descended with sinister, brutal stupidity. But these characters are as hazy as their motivations, and the bitchiness of coincidence, not being pitted against any warm and moving realities, becomes the *only* reality and thus arbitrary. A game of dice may represent life, but if the dice are loaded by the film-maker, we can no longer call it chance. We must call it cheating.

And what of the incidental virtues, the peripheral successes that some have found in *The Soft Skin?* They are there, but even they tend to become contaminated or undercut. Truffaut tries, for example, to show contrasts—as between the phoney world of the man of letters and the simple sensuous existence of the stewardess. But the literary world emerges only as caricature of a catalogue of references from Balzac and Stendhal to Ionesco and Daninos. And the plain wholesomeness of the girl gets no more adequate objective correlatives than her alacrity to jump out of bluejeans into a skirt at the whim of her lover, or her ability to perform in the middle of a crowded dance floor a fairly ludicrous solo love dance which the intellectual lover savors from the uncommitted safety of their night-club table.

Again, there is absorption in detail for detail's sake without relevance to the whole. Truffaut is obviously interested in mechanisms, and so the replenishing of a gas tank and the revolving numbers on the dials of a filling station are photographed with loving accuracy, as are the slow but methodical ascent of an elevator and the darting progress of cars and airplanes. But this is nowise connected with plot, character, or ideas, for the power that sleekly propels a machine across the screen does not necessarily further our understanding by an inch.

There are, moreover, a number of hermetic incidents and statements that seem to be meaningful to Truffaut but are inscrutable to us. Much is made of a pair of sable-colored stockings the hero must procure for the girl, and though the device of the off-screen voice is quite uncharacteristically conjured up for the purpose of impressing on us the importance of the incident (which does, indeed, result in a derisory contretemps), no illumination results from it. A whole episode is built up only to enable the girl to inform her lover portentiously at its climax that women who wear imitation-leopard blouses are passionate in bed—a bit of *éducation sentimentale* as irrelevant as it is impugnable.

Knowing Truffaut's autobiographical bent, I suspect that these things have a private significance, but they strike me as the filmic equivalents of the tiresome personal references that neatly obfuscate Pound's *Cantos*. The invocation of the later Pound is not gratuitous. The New Wave is succumbing to a kind of Byzantinism that is no longer making it new, only esoteric, in-group-oriented and self-indulgent. Perhaps this is the ineluctable trajectory of innovation, but if so, the New Wave is traversing it with alarming speed.

Even the performances are merely adumbrations. Jean Desailly has the perfect physical equipment for the charming middle-aged weakling—that flabbiness and its concomitants that the French can tidily sum up with *veulerie*—but he is much less able to convey the desire or need or dazzlement sucking him into the affair. As the stewardess, Françoise Dorléac of the hauntingly skull-like head cannot communicate much more than the bare bones of innocent seductivity, though this may be the fault of the script. And as the wife, Nelly Benedetti is not given a chance to display anything but her pronounced dark fleshliness. The principals of *The Soft Skin* have the density of mere extras.

That leaves us Raoul Coutard's customary expert photography and Georges Delerue's economical and functional score. And there are a few moments when Truffaut

does capture the hectic corrosiveness of adultery poig-
nantly. Above all, there is the scene in which the hero
toys with and undresses his mistress who simulates sleep.
The camera movements up and down the recumbent
figure, the crosscutting from avid yet slightly frightened
face to rapt fingers gently exploring the texture of a thigh,
the chiaroscuro, the rhythms, the ability to suggest the ex-
tensiveness, manifoldness, delicacy of a girl's body and the
awe rather than mere concupiscence it elicits—these reveal the master. But such flashes are few and very far between.

Jules Dassin's new film, *Topkapi,* unlike other recent
works of his, is at least unpretentious. But one can go only
so far on a solitary negative virtue. In this tale of an
elaborate jewel robbery, Dassin returns to his happiest
poaching-grounds, the realm of *Rififi;* but whereas in that
movie he was cribbing from vintage John Huston, here he
is only borrowing from James Bond. In *Rififi* there was
genuine suspense, based on greater probability and
reliance on documentary technique, and more importantly, on characters who were both believable and
likable. In *Topkapi* we all too soon recognize the precarious structure of the fiendishly clever theft exposed by
unforeseeable accident, and the people are tawdry ciphers
who do not begin to engage us. It might be contended that
Rififi was predominantly serious business, whereas this is
intended as hokum. True, but hokum can be fun, as in
Beat the Devil which, in its own way, is scarcely inferior
to *The Asphalt Jungle; Topkapi,* however, is merely silly
and boring.

There are almost no funny lines and no funny characters—though Peter Ustinov's Herculean labors make a
standard petty swindler charming almost succeed. But a
comic talent at least the equal of his, Robert Morley's,
disappears into the maw of prevailing mediocrity. Since
the material is not such as to make us hold either our sides
or our breath, there remain the characters. Well, the
minor ones are just running gags, old enough to be rub-

bery, but not rubbery enough to stretch to the required length. And the principals are made yet more unbelievable by being Melina Mercouri and Maximilian Schell.

Schell sulks boyishly, smiles boyishly, and waxes boyishly tense. If a fetchingly cleft chin can be called a performance, Schell can be said to act. As for Miss Mercouri, her blackly mascaraed eye sockets gape like twin craters, unfortunately extinct. Her standard expression is a bemused, constipated smile which is supposed to convey everything from mysterious female canniness to irrepressible hormones, but manages to suggest only someone trying to look knowing while being talked to in a language he doesn't know a word of. And speaking of language, what Miss Mercouri does to English shouldn't happen to pig-Latin. Couldn't her dialogue have been dubbed by Katina Paxinou?

ESCAPISM INTO ART

Is Jean-Luc Godard's *A Woman Is a Woman*—as bad a film as anyone is ever likely to see—merely a product of crass stupidity, or is there something more to it? In it, Anna Karina, Godard's then wife, portrays a stripper who, apparently, works when she feels like it, and the rest of the time moseys around Paris and lives with Jean-Claude Brialy, who works in a bookshop but, apparently, takes off whenever he feels like it. When Brialy does not feel like taking off, Karina is being chased by her lover's friend, Jean-Paul Belmondo, who, apparently, does not work at all, except at making Karina.

The ostensible plot concerns Karina's repeated requests to Brialy to give her a baby (what this subnormal psychotic would do with a baby is too dreadful to contemplate), refusals by him, fights, his tossing her at Belmondo, her spiteful dalliance with the latter, Brialy's aroused jealousy and procreative possessiveness, and her final confidence that one man or the other—it hardly matters which—has impregnated her.

The ostensible human beings in the film are profoundly imbecile. When they are not juvenilely playing tricks on one another, they act out loving take-offs on moronic American movie musicals, spew allusions to or quotations from various "in" films (not excluding those of Mr. G.), make bad puns, partake in joint bouts of grotesquely unfunny tomfoolery. And so the time passes for them, though not for the audience.

And what does Godard deck this out with? He invents gimmicks for the characters: Brialy, for instance, bicycles around his living room; Belmondo skips out on hotels without paying and, when tracked down by his creditor, is allowed to insult his way out unscathed. Karina does mostly nothing, and when asked what she's doing, answers: "I'm thinking." Though she cannot cook, she can toss fried eggs up at the ceiling, go to the hall telephone and wrangle with her lover for a while, then come back and catch the eggs on the rebound. And there are the usual New Wave devices: stop shots, jump cuts, characters winking and talking out at the audience, portentously meaningless texts running across the screen (sometimes backwards!), and endless games. Thus the lovers are shown spending not one but two nights provoking each other via book titles: they keep bounding out of bed to pick up a book of whose title they cover some part, or to which they add in pencil a few words, so that insults emerge.

The dialogue is, of course, commensurate: "If I run my head against the wall, will that prove I love you?" asks Belmondo. To which Karina, distantly: "I ask myself if one must say 'evidently' or 'perhaps'?" (So he goes to the wall and thence to bed with her.) Or Karina may let drop this bit of ontological ambivalence: "It's unfair—it's always when one is together that one is not together and vice versa." Or Belmondo might crack, *"J'ai dit O. K. Vous ne comprenez pas le français?"* Then again Brialy and Karina might engage in a heated polemic about whether a certain song begins "ti-ti-ta-ta" or "ta-ta-ti-ti." But most often the principals just hurl *"pauvre con"* and *"pauvre conne"* back and forth at each other, which is, presumably, their daily exercise.

The tricks of the photography and musical scoring add their fleabite's worth of annoyance. More offensive is the way in which Godard wants the entire audience to masturbate over his beloved Karina, on top of whom his camera wallows almost incessantly. Even here he is not honest: whereas various other women are shown more or less nude. Karina is, after every kind of suggestive teasing, not allowed to reveal any flesh at all. She does, however, reveal consummate lack of talent, butchery of the French language, sticky narcissism, and a rather trivially pretty face.

It is worth inquiring why such a film is made, how it comes to win international prizes, how the *Times* gets to call it a masterpiece, and why a highbrow critic like Susan Sontag will declare (in this case, of its sister film, *Vivre sa Vie,* which Godard made the following year, again with Karina, and which is equally trashy but even more pretentious) that it is "one of the most extraordinary, beautiful, and original works of art" she knows. Clearly we have a problem here.

The answer seems to lie in a tendency rampant in today's cinematic world: the turning of escapism into art. Formerly the reverse tended to be true: The film, which was eminently capable of yielding art, was being systematically reduced to providing brainless escape. This process, needless to say, still goes on, and though its excess may be disheartening, it is at least harmless: what does not in any way approach art, cannot harm it. But today, a large body of film-makers, film reviewers, and film consumers have lapsed into a tacit agreement: the brainless, trashy, antihuman—provided only that it be tricky or pretentious—shall be accepted and hailed as art. Why?

The movies, alas, have become more and more the great communal womb to crawl back into. Television cannot be it, because your own living room is the place to run from, not to. Neither can it be the theatre, which is too expensive, far away, dressy, and (during intermissions) apt to expose you to scrutiny. It is, moreover, sold out far in advance and, more often than not, even less interesting than the movies.

So to the movies went flocking a curious coalition of disaffected intellectual drifters, neurotic young women, homosexuals in search of "camp," young people too lazy to read or go to art galleries and concerts, gadgeteers to whom a 16-mm. camera presented itself as a passport to Parnassus—an intellectual demimonde that recognized film as potentially the most energetic art form of our time, but that by its cynicism, pathology, immaturity, or lack of cultivation was hardly in the position to recognize real art when confronted with it. Youths who had never sat down with their Shakespeare—and certainly could not distinguish between a painting and a bit of dribbling —mingled with fingernail-biting wives escaping from home life by sitting through the same double feature twice; and both could, with greater or lesser proficiency, discuss the differences between the styles of Douglas Sirk and Nicholas Ray, the advances of Samuel Fuller over Otto Preminger, and, if they were particularly astute, describe a detail of a fight scene in a Raoul Walsh picture that no one else had noticed.

It is not that these people did not see good films as well, or necessarily discriminated against them. But here was a medium which offered as yet so little that was good, let alone great, and yet invited cultist worship from an immense but heterodox body of believers. An artificial hierarchy had to be invented, some kind of aristocracy had to be contrived to enable at least some of the damned to feel superior. Given the nature of the shrine and of most of its ministrants, affectations, curlicues, gimmicks—whatever falsifications of psychology, philosophy or history could elbow reality a little farther back—were greeted with especial rapture. And whoever had, escaping reality most stringently, achieved the most encyclopedic knowledge of the minutiae of the movies, naturally became a member of their aristocracy—and, in due time, a film-maker, film critic, cine-club director, film librarian or film festival organizer.

This is the background against which we must visualize the coming of the Godards, the Special Jury Prize of the 1961 Berlin Festival to *A Woman Is a Woman*, and its Best Actress Award to a Karina who perpetuates the insipid nonacting or pseudoacting of the divas of yesteryear. Out of this we may comprehend Archer's verdict in the *Times,* "very brilliant . . . rich rewards to a limited audience," that is, the aforementioned "aristocracy."

And it is out of this syndrome that we can fathom Miss Sontag's analysis of *Vivre sa Vie.* After demonstrating that there is no analysis, no psychology in it, only various kinds of dissociation and depersonalized assertion, and after explicating the philosophic meaning of dialogue like "A plate is a plate. A man is a man. Life is—life," Miss Sontag concludes that the film "both edifies and gives pleasure because it is about what is most important, the subject of all great art: the nature of our humanity." The nature of your humanity, Miss Sontag. Not ours.

After this, it is a relief to turn to good old vintage pre-*8½* Fellini. *Il Bidone* is the middle part of the trilogy that begins with *La Strada* and ends with *Cabiria.* As the former examined the struggles of itinerant mountebanks and the latter those of prostitutes (how different from those of Godard!) so this film probes the life of the confidence man (*bidone*) and grasps even the repugnant petty swindler's smiling but desperate humanity.

Who are these *bidoni*? Failed financiers, failed artists, failed Don Juans; and Broderick Crawford, Richard Basehart, and Franco Farizi make the three types both prototypical and highly individual. That these reverse Robin Hoods defraud the poorest of the poor makes them particularly unsavory; yet Fellini and his scenarists show them as witty, charming, resourceful, and having legitimate problems as husbands and fathers; whereas the poor are apt to be stupid, gullible, superstitious, and greedy. Hence no easy sympathy or cut and dried morality is exploited here: the predators are themselves humiliated by life, and the victims wear almost visible signs on their faces reading: "Kick me!"

Except for the end, which turns soupy, this is choice Fellini. Some of his best later effects are prefigured here, sometimes even surpassed. And while Fellini the psychologist creates irreducibly human figures, Fellini the poet, abetted by Otello Martelli's camera and Nino Rota's music, evokes moods that become fixtures of one's memory. The landscape, weather, and faces that surround the protagonist's last caper are quietly, heartbreakingly horrifying.

A DEMY PARADISE

At the meeting of the film-maker Jacques Demy and the musician Michel Legrand, the best we might have hoped for is Claudelian silence: *"Comme un pauvre qui trouve un plus pauvre et tous deux se regardent en silence."* For I doubt that two poorer specimens ever found each other, to produce, not dignified silence, but a ludicrous movie musical. *The Umbrellas of Cherbourg,* which won the 1964 grand prize at Cannes, is distinguished by the fact that its every utterance—from *bonjour* to "fill up the tank with super"—is subjected to a sonorous deviation alleged to be music and singing.

The plot concerns two passionately Platonic young lovers of Cherbourg: sixteen-year-old Geneviève who helps out in her mother's umbrella shop, and twenty-year-old Guy who is a garage mechanic. They want to marry and have a child named François. But Guy is called up for two years' service in the Algerian war; Geneviève threatens to die if he leaves, but on the eve of his departure she merely drops into bed with him and presto—I add this only for the benefit of those who have never seen an enchanting movie about young love—gets pregnant.

While away, Guy does not write much, for no very good reason, unless it be illiteracy. As her waist expands, Geneviève's faith shrinks, and *maman*, who has been struck by a sudden attack of poverty, urges her to marry a nice, rich jewelry merchant who pops up out of nowhere. Our Juliet consents to wed the County Paris, provided he will have her bellyful. Having no doubt learned from old Marcel Pagnel movies what the right thing to do is in such harbor-town situations, he marries Geneviève and they leave Cherbourg.

Now Guy returns from Algeria with nothing worse than a limp to find his dear godmother dying; neither she nor Madeleine, the lovely girl who has been giving her her camomile and penicillin, has apprised him of Geneviève's betrayal. He disintegrates: loses jobs, gets into scrapes, goes to the fleshpots, and refuses to shave. The godmother dies, leaving him money and Madeleine. Guy marries this angel of charity and they buy a lovely new filling station. His limp miraculously disappears. He starts shaving once again.

It is years later, Christmas Eve. Madeleine, with little François, has gone out shopping. A snazzy car stops outside for refueling. It's Geneviève, with little François. The former lovers exchange polite biographical data; then Guy sends Geneviève on her way and goes out to meet his returning wife and son. As the camera slowly draws away, they gambol jocundly in the snow. It is the longest snowy-gambol fadeout on record, but why boggle at what is the least of the film's interminabilities?

The music consists of three or four sickly little melodies, which would be saccharine but for a bit of fake chromatics to give them a modish plangency. With slight variations—and often without—we get the same monotonous intervals over and over again, now subsiding into recitative, now swelling into a veritable arioso. As you leave the theatre with the score oozing out of the back of your head, you are convinced that Legrand has risen from being the Mantovani of France to being the Menotti of Musical Comedy, but, then, so is Menotti.

As for the voices, they were dubbed in later, so that the actors (if it be they who sing) would not have to open their mouths unnaturally wide—a touching, though somewhat extravagant, concern for realism. Actually, considering the size and quality of the voices, the cast could have sung the whole thing on location without opening their mouths at all—through their noses.

Visually, *The Umbrellas of Cherbourg,* maintains its tenor of dishonesty. Jean Rabier is a good color cinematographer, but here everything is factitious, from fake rain to genuine Cherbourg houses which, however, Demy had painted chartreuse and shocking pink. There are one or two shots of the railway station on a wet day, when the colors are natural and the soundtrack actually shuts up for a few seconds—and the eye and ear experience an indescribable sense of relief. Needless to say, in the midst of their poverty, the heroine and her mother inhabit an apartment worthy of the Ritz, and sport clothes and hair-dos as gorgeous as they are anachronistic.

But the most painful thing about the film is the dialogue—or should I say libretto?—which is of a banality unsurpassed by the pure dross distilled in the alembics of Hollywood. There are platitudes in all colors, from chartreuse to shocking pink: "We're so alone since my husband died"; "I don't want you to ruin your life as I ruined mine" (spoken, naturally, by mother to daughter); or "One dies of love only in the movies" (which makes me wonder whether Jacques Demy has really kept up with the movies since 1930). Occasionally there is a bit of unintentional comic relief, such as "She hasn't married yet—you know how good she is."

The only reason I have gone into *The Umbrellas of Cherbourg* at such length is that it won, among its half dozen importent prizes, the International Catholic Cinema Award, which I can understand—it is, after all, a songful sermon on the Pauline text about the preferableness of marrying, however lovelessly, to burning, however passionately—and the Louis Delluc Award of the French critics, which I cannot understand, except as the complete collapse of French film criticism. We are told that in Paris the opening-night audience wept and the critics were ecstatic. It would have made a little more sense the other way round.

If anyone wishes further proof of Demy and Legrand's ineptitude, there is another horror of theirs currently on view, *Bay of the Angels.* This is a yarn about a young boy who gets sucked into big-time roulette, becomes enamored of a middle-aged divorcee who is a psychotic roulette addict, and is about to go down the drain with her. But he pulls himself up and out by his psychic bootstraps, and gets the patently loveless woman to follow him docilely out of the gambling hell into a middle-class paradise of making in a year what one won or lost in an evening. The fact that she is old enough to be his mother merely adds a touch of Oedipal *gemütlichkeit.*

The film has a good—but already somewhat routine—performance by Jeanne Moreau, dull photography by Henri Alekan, and a score by Michel Legrand in the best pseudo-Rachmaninov manner, vintage 1945, which was, as you may recall, a very good year for soup. Demy's technique here is a kind of imitation Bresson: the most literal-minded, dogged, barren concentration on two stock characters in a cliché plot and the most obvious settings, with no roundedness—no feeling for composition, detail, dialogue, minor characters. The images seem to come straight from the crude wirephotos that appear in the daily newspapers and scenario reads very much like the outline of a shelved Bette Davis vehicle.

Here again, what impresses me most is the sheer stupidity of the script, unrelieved by any trace of unpretentiousness. Whenever the hero and heroine go gambling together, there is a bit of dialogue going roughly like this: "What number are you playing?" "12." "No, you should play 23." "Why do you think 23 will come up?" "I don't know why; I just know." After the *n*-th variation on this inquiry, you'd think it would be time to stop asking. It is certainly time to stop watching.

The most poetic and profound film of recent times is Hiroshi Teshigahara's *Woman in the Dunes,* adapted by Kobo Abé from his own novel. This is the story of a Tokyo's schoolteacher lured by some seaside villagers into spending a night at a cottage in a sandpit where a woman works shoveling sand to keep if from engulfing the village. He finds himself trapped and condemned to a life of sand-shoveling, and the film tells of his efforts to escape until, finally, the primeval normality of an existence close to nature, with a simple but sensuous woman, and the chance to carry on scientific experimentation among the dunes, gradually obliterate his need to return to so-called civilization.

Everything in the film is a little stylized and phantasmagoric: the dialogue takes on a dreamlike antilogic which is nonetheless ineluctable, the editing is slightly elliptical to convey a disquieting sense of unexpected intensities in the midst of the quotidian, the unobstrusively brilliant photography is infinitely suggestive in its extreme close-ups in which every grain of sand and every pore of human skin is obsessively scrutinized until the ripples of flesh and flutters of sand merge in an orgiastic marriage of man and nature.

Toru Takemitsu's music—sparing, acerbic, elemental —acts as a bittersweet hymeneal, stressing the strains and rewards of this union. The performances, especially that of Kyoko Kishida, as the woman who changes from a homely, self-effacingly cheerful drudge to an irresistible earth (or sand) goddess, are memorable. And Teshigahara has directed with a contol and imaginativeness that prove judiciousness compatible with experimentation.

The total effect is of a world of harsh primary phenomena and impulses perceived through a gauze of

lyricism and compassion befitting that not quite realistic
realism that lifts *Woman in the Dunes* to the level of
timeless parable without the slightest loss in delicacy or
texture.

FIVE

1965

SEE NAPLES AND LIVE

Marriage Italian Style—let us forget the title immediately. It must have sprung full-grown from the Herculean brain of Joe Levine, the producer who provided the theatre and movies with the collective appellation "entertainment arts," in contradistinction to, say, music and poetry, doubtless to be known henceforth as "boredom arts." The idea is to cash in on *Divorce Italian Style,* a highly successful, entirely different, and considerably less worthy film.

Marriage is an adaptation of Eduardo de Filippo's play *Filumena Marturano* executed by the playwright and four other writers; it is one of those rare cases where the quality of the broth is unimpaired by the quantity of cooks. The work of Eduardo de Filippo, as Eric Bentley noted long ago in a perceptive essay, represents "what it means to live in a tradition—as against merely believing in tradition"; the tradition being the dual one of Neapolitan theatre and the city of Naples, "an infinitely suggestive and dramatic milieu."

162

Filumena Marturano, a young Neapolitan prostitute, falls in love with Domenico Soriano, a rich profiteer and playboy slumming in a brothel. She finds favor with him and he eventually promotes her to kept woman, household drudge, and business manager. When middle age has over-taken both of them, Domenico, the always unfaithful, decides to marry a young girl; instead, by a stunning stratagem, Filumena tricks him into marrying her. She has stopped loving him, but has, unbeknown to him, three sons who need a respectable name. The enraged Domenico proceeds to get the marriage annulled; Filumena, disgusted, raises no obstacles. But she tells him that one of the boys is his—without revealing which.

After a slew of comically abortive strategems by means of which Domenico tries in vain to identify his heir, he finally realizes Filumena's full worth. Not only his business but also his heart needs her—just as all three young men need a father. He marries Filumena properly but she will never tell him which of the boys is his.

In outline the story may sound like yet another dip into that greatest gold bank of all time, the pectoral regions of fictional prostitutes. But Filumena is not nearly so golden-hearted as she is sensible and tough: her protracted toiling for Domenico and endurance of his contumely are not mere emotion; they are a struggle for advancement for her sons and herself along the only path open to the likes of her—not labors of love so much as plain labor. And when devotion and decency win out in the end, the victory comes precariously and comes late. Its consummation is tears: tears of joy, certainly; but tears also, we realize, for the human condition.

The director, Vittorio de Sica, and scenarists have turned this into a film that ably combines the old and the new. The pace is leisurely and the characters, however minor, are resoundingly real. If some of them verge on comic types, no matter; the life of the *commedia dell'arte,* on native ground, remains inexhaustibly buoyant. But there are also newer devices such as making free and easy with the time sequence (though never losing the narrative thread), or using zoom and stop shots with youthful verve (though never without integrating them into a structural logic). If this happy wedding of the old and the new carries about it also something borrowed and something blue—the bordello scene must contain at least one unbuttoned fly—there is nothing into which an abundance of life and humor has not been breathed.

De Sica's best effects are often truly visual, such as the progress across a Neapolitan square seen in a long shot: the middle-aged Filumena, late for her long-awaited wedding, rushing and fussing with her dress; behind her, tiny and hobbling, her old servant also fussing with the gown. Or an effect may be potently auditory—as when a little boy has swallowed cherry pits and a great on-screen ruckus of hysterical adults is happily interrupted by an off-screen barrage from baby's tin chamber pot. De Sica's perfect *désinvolture* is always handsomely complemented by Roberto Gerardi's camera work, which gives colors a muted, velvety richness; even as your finger tips itch with desire to touch, your retinas are never overpowered.

Then there is the acting. Marcello Mastroianni balances Domenico precisely midway between irresponsibility and bonhomie, between egoism and charm—if there is such a thing as the pathos of brazenness, Mastroianni embodies it to a fault. Sophia Loren has often been excellent, here she is better yet. Whether as a brothel novice of 17 or as a tired but dogged fighter for her human rights of 48—or at any of the intermediate ages and stages—she is always cojolingly or fiercely female as well as humbly or burstingly human. Either because Filumena's story resembles Sophia's own, or simply because Miss Loren has finally become an absolute, nononsense actress, this may be considered one of the definitive performances in the contempoary cinema. The scene in which the scarcely literate Filumena is obliged to affix her name to a document—beautifully directed and written as it is—becomes a masterpiece thanks to Miss Loren's performance. Every outsize, titubating letter becomes a towering achievement: the invention of the wheel and the building of the Pyramids rolled into one. And the parturifacient concentration with which Filumena's face helps along her vile Italian hand is a tragicomic delight.

But probably the most tenaciously haunting sequences in the film are those in which Domenico's respect for Filumena is aroused, grows into admiration, and finally brims over into love. The hesitancies and recidivisms are traced with fidelity and tenderness, and as suspicion gradually gives way to headlong yearning and fulfillment, psychological truth and artistic pacing become exquisitely blended. No less satisying is the over-all rhythm of the film, masterly in its alternation and dosage of slapstick and sentiment, sensuality and common sense. True, Aramando Trovaioli's music lacks subtlety, and the subtitles lose a good bit of the flavor. But never mind. There is enough humanity and artistry here for the pride of the viewers to be second only to that of the makers.

Nothing But a Man is a well-made and moving film about Southern Negroes; if it is short on several requisites of a first-rate work of art, it nonetheless goes well beyond mere documentary convincingness, technical adequacy, and high-mindedness. As others have already observed, it treats Negroes as entirely unspecial people, however special and enormous their predicament may be. The psychology and dialogue of Michael Roemer and Robert Young's scenario never slip into condescension, idealization, glossing over, farcical or melodramatic exaggeration. Clichés are almost too scrupulously avoided, and there is heroic tact about how far one can go before sentimentality of Social Consciousness (with capital letters) gets in the way of sense or sensibility.

It is true that some of the picture's prestige comes from the mere fact that it deals with Negroes in Alabama and is, in that sense, unearned. The simple truth that a circumspect preacher and a shiftless drunkard may be equally incompetent in dealing with their children as long as they are all victims of social injustice would have less impact in any other context. And there is no denying that the words are not up to the extraordinariness of the situations; that the perception of character, though honest and lively, is less than profound. Even the direction of Michael Roemer and the photography of Robert Young are only substantial, where we might wish for the superlative.

But how much have we the right to expect from a pioneer effort? There is spectacular integrity in the understatement of what might scream at us and in the truthfulness of the details: When a young husband knocks down his pretty wife, she does not fall gracefully, pathetically, or terrifyingly; she drops ludicrously on her behind, her feet flapping in the air.

Yet even if the camera seems at times infatuated with mere kinetic energy, even if mood and ambiance tend to pass for insight, the picture is still good enough to stand not on "the Negro problem" but on its own feet. It is a fine example of what assured craftsmanship and independence from the major studios can achieve in terms of signficant and (I cannot stress this hard enough) *entertaining* film-making.

One thing, however, lifts this film immeasurably above mere solid cinema. And that, strange to say, is the facial expressions of its gifted actors. Every look is a look of courage. In Ivan Dixon, it is tinged with defiance, however guarded; in Gloria Foster, it skirts stolid resignation, without forsaking humane concern; in Abbey Lincoln, it is most beautiful: the slightly sad smile of a wise child, clothing with melancholy mockery its awareness of absurdity rampant in the world. It is a double-bottomed smile whose meaning reaches far beyond any specific time and place. I do not know whether these facial expressions constitute a histrionic or directorial achievement; I am inclined to think that, rooted in something deeper, they transcend both. They are the silences at the core of art in which roars the inexpressible.

As for Jean-Luc Godard's *Contempt,* it is portentous without having anything to say, improvisatory without imagination, full of esoteric references without relevance and in-group allusions without interest. Its puppets behave with meaningless meanness if not with sheer meaninglessness. To be sure, Brigitte Bardot's behind and quotations from Hölderlin have probably never been brought together before; but Godard might have pondered another passage from the Hölderlin poem quoted and pontificated about: *"Doch es zwinget/Nimmer die weite Gewalt den Himmel"*—far-ranging willfulness never conquers the heavens. Until we get an article from Miss Sontag proclaiming *Contempt* a near-masterpiece, we shall have to consider it trash.

FAKE DEATH, FAKE LOVE

Normal love is the title of a film by Jack Smith, who made *Flaming Creatures,* and judging from a sizable excerpt I saw, it has nothing to do with either normality or love. Granted that it is hard to posit canons for normal love, we nevertheless have as good a working definition of it as we have of, say, poetry—a term we can use to good effect without being able to define it definitively. What has happened to "normal love," then, in contemporary movies? Or even to "normal sex," a celebration of which in the cinema is apt to be a crashing bore like Jörn Donner's *To Love.*

It is instructive to examine the image of love and sex some current films convey. In the dreary and overblown *Zorba the Greek* (a film which, to my mind, proves conclusively the mediocrity of its once promising scenarist-director, Michael Cacoyannis, and the superficiality of its star, Anthony Quinn), sex is always awkward, stealthy, ludicrous or degrading, and the brutal murder of one's lovely sexual partner is to be accepted as a colorful bit of local folkways. In Jean-Luc Godard's abominable *Band of*

Outsiders, sex is yet another subnormal subhuman caprice perversely dubbed "love," and neatly blending with the Brownian movement of the brainless, feelingless particles passed off as people in this picture. Let us look in greater detail at two films in which love and sex are mauled and ridiculed, and at another in which, whatever the limitations of the film may be, sex emerges as the great and joyous thing it is.

How to Murder Your Wife, a film that has received assorted accolades, is the latest concoction of George Axelrod, who, after one charming comedy, *The Seven-Year Itch,* has supplied the stage and screen with ever more offensively unsavory and unfunny fabrications, the penultimate of which was *Good-bye, Charlie.* The noxiousness of that one was close enough to the surface—if one can speak of surface in something so two-dimensional—for even the reviewers to recognize its distastefulness. In *How to Murder Your Wife,* the corruption lies under several layers of varnish, and there is no dearth of eyes willing to be blinded by the gloss over the dross.

This is the story of a successful cartoonist living in a resplendent New York townhouse with a suave and prodigiously British butler, and, at night, an unending stream of willing beauties. The cartoonist first enacts for his butler's camera every breathtaking adventure of his cartoon hero, so that the camera's unlying eye can be translated with unimpaired authenticity into the daily syndicated comic strip. At a drunken stag party, an Italian beauty contestant emerges from a cake (oh, not nude, never fear, just nudish), and our hero, using the social pull great artists enjoy, intoxicatedly marries her on the spot.

Though at first full of Continental sweetness, and thus lying naked in bed all the time yearning to be made love to, the delicious creature is promptly reeducated by a middle-aged American wife. She now unremittingly buys expensive clothes, and what is worse, wears many of these integuments to bed. She has long since caused the butler to leave in disgust, and cooks starchy dishes which, by a peculiarly female black magic, fatten only her husband. She also redecorates the apartment according to the latest feminine mystique, and gets her husband drummed out of his last woman-free stronghold, his club.

What remains for our hero but to enact an elaborate ritual murder on a dummy representing his wife, and have this photographed and ultimately converted into coast-to-coast tabloid comic-strip fare. The lady gets the message and vanishes, whereat her husband is tried for murder and is about to be found guilty. He takes over his defense in a trial that bears even less resemblance to reality than the rest of the film, and, by means of an impassioned oration-demonstration, wins over judge, jury, D.A., and spectators to a loud roar of approval for uxoricide. He regains his freedom and his butler. But who awaits him with outstretched arms in bed? His wife, yieldingly nude again. She has even brought her remarkably youthful mother along, so that both master and butler can end up over-mastered—*happily* overmastered, mind you.

Decked out with gross gags and humorless witticisms, the film is infinitely more vulgar than a mere summary can convey; but the question is what lurks underneath the seemingly anodyne vulgarity? There lies, first, the masturbational wish fulfillment reverie of that lovely species of American male, the Eternal Freshman with Delusions of Sophomoricness, whom Axelrod tirelessly celebrates in all his works. Let no one tell me "caricatures, not celebrates"—next thing we'll be told that Al Capp does not love and envy *Li'l Abner*.

Anyhow, the hero of this inhuman comedy perceives marriage as the end of a blissful harem existence; getting married as an instantaneous albeit crapulous rapture; being married as a drag poorly compensated for by the gorgeousness, sensuality, and inexhaustibleness of a wife who is demanding and possessive; wife-murder as something one plans and executes with fiendish delight—but, of course, harmlessly, by proxy—and is, even if it were for real, exculpated of amid universal acclaim. Now, is this all Mr. Axelrod beats out of his typewriter or jerks out of his pen?

No, the best piece of self-abuse is yet to come. For Axelrod has not even the courage of his convictions, the guts to accept the consequences of his Steigian dreams of glory. After marriageless marriage and murderless murder, comes the most genuine 100-proof cop-out: The wife returns and is perfect down to her genitrix, and we get a double happy ending. It is the great American *Liebestod:* fake death, fake love, but honesty lies dead and everybody loves it. And let no one say, "But this is farce!" Honest farce comments on life, however waggishly; in bad farce, as here, the joke is only on the audience.

In *The Yellow Rolls-Royce,* Terence Rattigan, the writer, and Anthony Asquith, the director, have strung together three episodes in the life of a luxury vehicle. In the first, the car is bought by an *ante bellum* British peer for his beloved wife as an anniversary present, but when he finds her in it betraying him with a younger man, he disconsolately sells it. In the second episode, a gunman of the Capone gang, "vacationing" in his native Italy with his moll-fiancée, is suddenly recalled to the States for a little gangland killing; meanwhile the moll gets a chance to have her last happy fling with a lovable Italian gigolo in the capacious Rolls; thereupon, lest the boy be slain, she returns to her unlovable fiancé.

In the last episode, the handsome widow of an arch-Republican American millionaire ends up smuggling a Yugoslav patriot (he is clearly a Communist, but the film prefers to identify him as "patriot," going so far as to equip him with royalist sympathies!) into Yugoslavia in the trunk of the Rolls, on the eve of the German *Blitzkrieg.* During the bombing of Ljubljana and after, as chauffeur to the partisans under *Luftwaffe* strafing, the isolationist widow proves a committed heroine. Hero and heroine snatch a night of love in the Rolls, whereupon he gallantly insists that she do the best thing she can do—"go back there and tell them what you have seen here."

The film emerges as a great commercial for Rolls-Royce: first in love as in war, and indestructible either by age or by Stukas. It is, moreover, commodious enough to provide ample *Lebensraum* (or, perhaps, in this case, *Liebesraum*) for such unlikely lovers as the Athenaesque Ingrid Bergman and the smaller but hefty Omar Sharif, and can probably accommodate even the stepladder on which Sharif must have stood during the perpendicular love scenes. In *The Yellow Rolls-Royce*, love and/or sex are treated with a discreet smirk as the blinds of the Rolls come down and out comes Shirley MacLaines's bathing suit. Sex is hasty, furtive and blacked out: the little spiceless spice in some contrived, improbable or threadbare anecdote.

After all this, Kaneto Shindo's *Onibaba* (*The Demon*) comes as a desperately needed corrective. The film is nowhere near so good as Shindo's *The Island,* though it improves on it in one respect: the background music is no longer ladled from the same soup that usually fills the Hollywood Bowl, but intelligently combines Western modernism with traditional Japanese elements. Otherwise the film is chiefly distinguished by an honest treatment of the dehumanizing effect of war even on those behind the lines, some good photography (except for one gibbous moon straight out of *Madam Butterfly*), and rather trivial plotting.

But there is one all-important thing more. The film is the most ardent and unflinching celebration of sex. It shows with equal faithfulness the ecstasies of its fulfillment and the agonies of its frustration. The people involved are far from admirable, and the conditions of their intercourse are downright grubby. Yet what radiates from this sex is, in its humble way, comparable to the last chapter of *Ulysses*: a glorious affirmation of release, joy, and appeasement. This is the poetry of innocent animality, far more moving and meaningful when dealing with human beings than when gushing about tame lionesses and pet raccoons.

Today when the arts are more and more infected with deviant sexuality, and the no less unfortunate deviation of asexuality—posing, worse yet, as sexuality!—*Onibaba* is nothing less than a boon. It should be, if any compulsion were tolerable, compulsory viewing for all ages and all sexes. Instead, our society's most contemptible charlatans and hypocrites, the censors, have already snipped out part of one of the loveliest scenes of the film: a very long shot of the lovers, naked, chasing each other against a nocturnal background of river shore and tall grasses. If I knew what arms to take up against the sick minds of the censors, I would gird my loins forthwith.

CHRIST IN CONCRETE

God is unlucky in *The Greatest Story Ever Told*. His only-begotten Son turns out to be a bore. This is not the fault of Max von Sydow, whose Christ is noble in bearing, beautifully spoken with a slight Swedish accent, and penetratingly handsome in a way that, despite the black wig, is 100 per cent Aryan. What else could you expect from someone whose mother is Dorothy McGuire, her age and expression beatifically identical at the manger and at the cross? No, Sydow cannot be faulted; but George Stevens, who made the film, can.

Already the credits give us pause: "Screenplay by James Lee Barrett and George Stevens"; "Based on The Books of the Old and New Testaments, Other Ancient Writings, The Book 'The Greatest Story Ever Told' by Fulton Oursler, and Other Writings by Henry Denker." The whole "Produced in Creative Association with Carl Sandburg." Let us, in the spirit of Christian charity, refrain from commenting on the ancient writings of Fulton Oursler and Henry Denker, and the ancient creativity of Carl Sandburg. But it would seem that with this many tellers you don't tell a tale—you open a bank.

We begin with a starry sky in Ultra Panavision 70, the Star of Bethlehem, and an offscreen voice, not content with oil, throwing in myrrh and frankincense as well. And lo! there is the music of Alfred Newman, which at climactic moments, such as the resurrection of Lazarus, falls back on the ancient writings of George Friedrich Händel. As the Hallelujah Chorus explodes around us stereophonically and sterotypically it becomes clear that Lazarus was not so much raised from the tomb as blasted out of it. When Newman's score is his own, it runs the gamut from saccharine to syrup, and is, quite simply, awful.

The photography is inspired mainly by Hallmark Cards, and, come Christmas, should supply us with the greatest cards ever sold. There are some nice very long shots of figures milling around the mesas, canyons, and deserts of our great Southwest, but whenever a set appears, even pseudoauthenticity ends. The décor is almost without exception ugly and unreal, and if it suggests anything, it is previous décor. The costumes try for coloristic effects—as when everyone is in white except the woman caught in adultery, who is dragged about in red, which, as everyone knows, is what adulteresses wear. Taking a hint from this or from Eliot Elisofon, the color consultant, the photography aims for monochrome effects that are to create moods, but succeed only in looking stilted and garish. Particularly striking is the lilies-of-the-field sequence, where, by superimposition, a field of multicolored flowers wiggles in the middle ground before a background of mighty mountains, and the whole thing looks like—may the Lord forgive me—a superimposition.

The film is studded with "cameo performances" by guest stars. Evidently even the greatest story ever told cannot be trusted to bring in an audience unless a famous visage can be spotted peering out from under every third burnoose. To be sure, this does provide a few moments of merriment, as when Shelley Winters packs into ten seconds and one line, "I am cured! I am cured!" an entire course in method acting. Or when John Wayne, as the centurion in charge of the Crucifixion, drawls out of his helmet, "I believe this truly was the Son of God," in a tone to put the fear of the Lord into a saloonful of varmints. The principal performances are not quite so amusing, though Roddy McDowall's Matthew and Michael Anderson Jr.'s James the Younger are good for a snicker or two. And the late Joseph Schildkraut injects a touch of Old Vienna into the deliberations of the Sanhedrin.

George Stevens' direction is plodding and repetitious: whenever he has what he thinks is a fine shot, he is sure to repeat it several times; his groupings are studiedly picturesque, and a sequence like Christ's temptation in the wilderness is ludicrous throughout. Or take the scene in which the evils of everyday life are depicted in newsreel style with grainy photography, absurd in cinerama and color. Here a robbery, there a rape, yonder a murder—all taking place side by side along the main street, for Christ to look at, suffer, and do nothing about. It is sheer nonsense. As for pacing, the picture does not let you forget a single one of its four hours for a moment.

The whole conception is oh, so discreet, so defensively inoffensive. If this Christ says, "O ye men of little faith!" the apostles chuckle—it is all so pleasantly jocular. The stuff about rich men's difficulties in entering heaven, or the business of the money-lenders in the Temple—how painlessly it is all presented as if we had been given local anaesthesia first. Unlike Pasolini, who can make his Christ in *The Gospel According to Matthew* at least partly compelling through complexity, sternness, and a quality of fiery aliveness, Stevens gives us a milky, homogenized Jesus: no mention of his having come to bring the sword or to break up family ties, of barren fig trees, or of anything else troubling. Even the Lord's Prayer appears in the popular Protestant version!

What a seemly Crucifixion, what a relatively unlacerating ascent to Calvary, done without any other sound except that of Verdi's Requiem, the choir already foreshadowing Christ's triumph. And, of course, the word

"Jew" is never mentioned in an embarrassing context—if it is mentioned at all; even Pilate and the Romans have much to recommend them—there are good guys and a few bad guys everywhere. Judas himself, though he looks shifty and behaves schizoidly, seems to love his Master. Miracles are kept down to a decent minimum —three—and to the kind that with one exception would not tax a Billy Graham overmuch. Pasolini gives us harrowing poverty, disease, pain, and grief; here everything is sightly—even blood makes beautiful patterns on a white robe. Satan is shown merely as "The Dark Hermit," an unsavory fellow, to be sure, but nothing metaphysical—just a poor devil, really, and Donald Pleasence plays him exactly as he did Pinter's Caretaker.

Here and there the scenarists and director surpass themselves. Simon of Cyrene, who helps Christ carry the cross, is played by Sidney Poitier. His attire is blindingly white, and his face—could it be make-up?—appears blacker than it ever was before. Besides setting race relations immeasurably ahead, this reminds us that the values of the film are, underneath all that orgiastic color, plain black and white. There is the moment, too, when Christ, asked by the tax collector whether he has anything to declare, answers, "Only myself and my Father," which uncomfortably recalls Oscar Wilde's quip to the U. S. customs. Later when Christ is dead and Caiaphas announces, "The whole thing will be forgotten in one week," someone mutters, "I wonder . . ."—a tidy bit of resurrection from *Saint Joan*. Could these and their likes be what is covered by "Other Ancient Writings"?

Bosley Crowther assures us that Stevens' "reverence should captivate the piously devout." But what does it do for those whose religiosity, or English, is not redundant?

Lord Jim is a large, expensive movie with nice backgrounds and fine photography by Fred Young, and a contrived script and routine direction by Richard Brooks. Where some fragment of the Conrad novel survives, it rattles around uneasily in the alien and tinny context. Peter

O'Toole does another, much less interesting, Lawrence, but his blue eyes can still brim over beautifully with shattered innocence. Several capable actors do their standard bits, while Eli Wallach and Daliah Lavi remain substandard.

The Train begins auspiciously, and the earlier parts in which action—trains, aerial attacks on them, sabotage, collisions—predominates are properly gripping. But verbiage takes over the screenplay, and the action becomes drawn-out, repetitious, and predictable; the dubbing of the foreign performers is, as always, grating. John Frankenheimer, a lively enough director where images and movement are concerned, has no respect for writing. Once again he has settled for a script written by hacks, and what might have been taut and mordant dialogue yields platitudes and ostentatious emptiness. Some excellent performers, like Paul Scofield, Jeanne Moreau, and Michel Simon, are seen to poor advantage; while not so good ones, like Burt Lancaster, are seen too much. Nevertheless, the last few minutes of the film, after all talking has ceased (and the final bit of talk is particularly absurd), seem to me pure cinema of notable, though a mite obvious, forcefulness and again raise hopes for Frankenheimer's future.

Young Cassidy is a well-meaning but fairly lackluster pseudo—or screen—biography out of Sean O'Casey's autobiography. From a screenplay by the late John Whiting (though who knows what was done over his dead body) based on the memoirs of O'Casey's youth, one expected rather more. But Jack Cardiff, the photographer turned director, has merely blended the Struggling Writer Story with the Brawling Irish Story and wrapped it in gentle color photography. Rod Taylor is sincere but dull as a kind of O'Casey *cum grano* Charles Atlas, and the scenes at the Abbey Theatre and the lovers' final parting reach heights of unimaginative direction and improbable writing. Maggie Smith is a superlative actress, and Julie Christie a pleasure to behold, but Edith Evans is a less than likely Lady Gregory, and Michael Redgrave a bad joke as Yeats. There is one very effective scene of a street riot and its bloody suppression (which figures also in *Red Roses for Me*), but the Easter Rising falls flat. The rest is mediocre. Some of the blame may have to fall on O'Casey himself, who was less than the great writer the middle-brows try to make of him.

A Stranger Knocks comes from Denmark via our Supreme Court, which upheld its two scenes of fully-clothed sexual intercourse. One of the positions may be new to our backwoods areas and may revolutionize their sex life; the life of the cinema is certainly set back by the film a good forty years.

DESERT OF ALL COLORS

In his new film, *Red Desert*, Antonioni is no longer Michelangelo; at best, he is Rosso—not as in *Deserto rosso*, but as in Rosso Fiorentino. He is here a daring colorist, fanatical mannerist, and inferior artist. The color and compositions in this film are magnificent. It is not so much that the colors are used in an emotionally suggestive way (Giuliana and Corrado begin to make love in a walnut-paneled room but the consummation finds them among pastel pink walls); after all, even *The Greatest Story* tried for such effects. It is that the hues are chosen, juxtaposed, and reproduced more beautifully than ever before on film, and that Antonioni's painter's eye turns almost every frame of the film into an arresting composition.

But there already lies the first difficulty. This beauty is stationary, painterly, and the arresting image precisely arrests and retards the already moribund thrust of the film. And the color is so eloquent and thought-provoking that it emphasizes the vacuousness of what it envelops: plot, character, dialogue.

The chief theme of the picture is man's uneasiness in a

world full of the splendors and miseries of technology: factories, houses, furniture, paintings, toys, everything has become mechanized, functional, geometrical, its colors coldly or dazzlingly challenging. Even the slag heaps around the factories imitate junk art; even a foreman's cabin, crudely carpentered and gaudily painted, imitates pop. How is man to adapt himself to all this?

If the problem were examined in terms of a passably sane human being, it might be of interest. But Giuliana, the heroine, is frenzied and paralyzed by turns, terrified of all, "streets, factories, people, colors—everything." She is continually huddling in corners, climbing up walls, trying to commit suicide, talking and acting in non sequiturs. "There's something terrible about reality," she complains, "and I don't know what—no one will tell me." Or, as she is about to bed with her lover, "Everything hurts: my hair, my eyes, throat, mouth."

Thus the film heightens the old Antonionian theme of alienation to the point of insanity; at the same time it lowers the interest to that of a case history, and a far from clinically thorough one at that. No attempt is made to analyze Giuliana's evidently unhappy marriage, or her unsatisfactory relations with everyone around her, in short, how she got the way she is. And the partial cure at the end rings even less convincing than Bergman's notorious conciliatory ending in *Through a Glass Darkly*.

Stanley Kauffmann managed to see in Antonioni's new film "the prospect of full human life in the midst of whirling changes." From where or whom is this full human life to come? The heroine, as we have seen, is so neurotic as to be, much of the time, close to feeble-mindedness. But the two men, husband and lover, are scarcely Promethean bringers of light, either.

The husband is portrayed as a well-meaning but somewhat unmasculine man, not particularly alive to either work or play, except for a fit of verbalized sensuality during a peculiarly sexless orgy, about which more later. Carlo Chionetti does succeed in making him an amiable nonentity, and that, I suppose, is the best that can be made of a character who never says or does anything particularly wise, foolish, or different.

The lover, stodgily played by Richard Harris, is something else again. This was obviously meant to be a virile, alive human being, but, alas, a technologist. His bedside book, one may notice, is Max Frisch's *Homo faber*. Now the hero of that novel says, "I am a technician and accustomed to seeing things as they are. I see the moon over the desert of Tamaulipas—clearer than ever, let's say, but a calculable mass, which revolves around our planet, a matter of gravitation, interesting, but why an adventure?" Nevertheless, Corrado, though an engineer, gravitates quite unscientifically around Giuliana, and, though he makes some sensible remarks about politics and the future of the world, is not much more of a stable or purposeful figure than she is.

"We all need help," Corrado says, and says it not only to calm Giuliana. When she exclaims derangedly that at times she would like to assault someone, he asks what is wrong with that? He, too, after all . . . He laments, "There are times when I feel I have no right to be where I am," and demonstrably suffers from dromomania. Or he tells Giuliana, "You say, what should you look at? I say how should I live? It's the same thing." Truly, it is the same thing, a whole damned movie's worth of it. There are long stretches that affect us, despite immeasurable esthetic and technical superiority, rather like something that crawled out from the underground cinema of the Mekases and Warhols.

The people in the film are, according to Nelly Kaplan in the *Mercure de France,* "bound only by the astonishing force of emptiness." But emptiness as protagonist becomes forceful and interesting only when it asserts itself in some dramatic way. Thus Rochester's *Nothing* is appetitive, all-devouring: "The great man's gratitude to his best friend,/King's promises, whores' vows, towards thee they bend,/ Flow swiftly into thee, and in thee ever end." But the Nothing in *Red Desert* subsists on a much meagerer diet than Rochester's "Primitive Nothing"—it has become sophisticated, sated, and jaded, and what flows into it is nowhere near so juicy as a king's promise or a whore's vow.

"If there is anything this film is not," writes Stanley Kauffmann, "it is not 'once more' of anything." But what, except for the marvelous and somewhat scene-stealing color, is new here or different from what Antonioni has already given us in his Trilogy? The neurotic, exasperated, yet hopelessly searching heroine; the ineffectual, shadowy men; the listless nonorgies; the overshadowing of people by architecture or objects—if not exactly as here, by factories; the wispy love affairs that leave one nauseated and still hungry; the glimpses of simpler and happier people—but can *we* be like them?—all these things Antonioni has done to a turn in his three previous films. Now he is doing them merely to a return. And to diminishing returns.

There are three scenes in *Red Desert* that, I dare say, will be remembered. One of them seems to me quite false. It is the tale told by Giuliana about a real or imagined incident from her childhood. It does introduce a pink beach (a fellow-traveler of the red desert of the title?) and a child accepting such eerie mysteries an unmanned ships and disembodied voices singing proto-electronic music. It is a pastoral with the incursion of enigma on the childhood idyll, but enigma that can be accepted without producing a blot on the eclogue. The trouble with it is that the mystery is conceived, staged and photographed merely as something contrary to the normal or understandable. It lacks the kind of aura that the island search in *L'Avventura* had in abundance.

Then there is the scene in the quayside fog, in which people emerge, vanish, reappear, and the heroine panics. This is beautifully directed and shot, but loses much through the presence of Monica Vitti. According to Kauffmann, she is "one of those happy occurrences in the performing arts when the advent of the right executant evokes the best work of a creator." To me, Miss Vitti is an actress with a strictly limited repertoire, further limited by the fact that what she can do, she cannot do particularly well. Already in *L'Avventura* her poker-facedness alternating with studied grimacing was trying enough. How much better an actress is Lea Massari and how much more she brought to the film! Again, in *La Notte,* critics who traced the weakness of that film to Antonioni's changing his heroine were wrong: At least when Jeanne Moreau acts bored, neglected, and wasting away, one feels that a real woman is going to pot, and the actress elicits sympathy even where the character does not.

Monica Vitti, on the other hand, has no personality: it is all done with mirrors or lenses, with direction and cutting. And it is no use saying that the empty best portray emptiness; for a film about murderers, one does not recruit one's cast from Death Row. Several reviewers found that, in *Red Desert,* Miss Vitti looked like Barbra Streisand—a dreadful fate for a woman; to me, she looked more like Tony Perkins in a wig in *Psycho*—no fate at all for a woman. The sooner Antonioni's liaison with her ends, the better, I should think, for his artistic future. He can always bequeath her to the Actors Studio.

The third bravura scene is the already mentioned verbal bacchanal in which three couples lounge around a huge bed in a red frame hut, talk esuriently about sex, and indulge in a little arse-pinching and Platonic wife-swapping. The scene has resourcefulness of dialogue and staging, and a most attractive woman in Rita Renoir. It also takes place among red walls (a red desert?) which are, Kauffmann says, "painted a shade of red, off which, so to speak, the talk can rebound"—as if it could not rebound off cobalt blue or pale heliotrope. But this scene was done just as well on the yacht in *L'Avventura,* and is yet another bit of "once more." As the child, Valerio, remarks at one point in the film, "I'm tired of this game." From the mouths of babes!

WITH A CAPITAL A

Any attempt in America to make a film a work of art must be hailed. Usually, in the same breath, it must also be farewelled. Sidney Lumet's *The Pawnbroker* is no exception: its intentions are good, it earns our sympathy, but it serves mainly to illustrate how awesome the distance is between intent and achievement.

The Pawnbroker begins with a sun-drenched idyll that is only a memory. We know that it is only a memory because it's shot in slow motion. Children with flying hair are running in slow motion, a happy young parental couple gazes after them in slow motion, and a butterfly hovers in slow motion. It is all terribly Tennysonian, a little too long and a little too sweet. The clash of light and shadow is dazzling but also a trifle exaggerated, the butterfly gets caught—we are in for Art with a captial A. Yet art is something that should never be capitalized or capitalized on.

Sol Nazerman is a survivor of a Nazi death-camp in which his wife and children perished. We see him first in suburbia, at the brassy bosom of the American branch of his family: a setting and group enough to depress even the staunchest survivor. Next, he is off to the brass balls of the Harlem pawnshop he operates, making his living off human misery. By this time we have been initiated into the flashback technique which tells—first in extremely short, quasi-subliminal, seemingly disconnected snatches, then in longer and clearer sequences—of Nazerman's dreadful past experiences.

In the shop, a young Puerto Rican ex-hoodlum, Jesus Ortiz, is Sol's assistant; he is trying to learn the business from the saturnine Sol, and half admires, half resents him.

But the boy makes no more effect on this armor-plated psyche than does the widow of Sol's best friend. She and her husband were in the same camp with Sol; the husband died horribly, and she is now Sol's mirthless mistress. So far, so good.

But Sol's relationship with the racketeer Rodriguez, for whose operations the pawnshop is a front, is rather less convincing, more tritely melodramatic. A middle-aged female social worker appears on the scene, and attempts to befriend Sol. He rebuffs her. This, alas, rings a whole concerto's worth of false notes: there is even a shot of her holding out a shyly compassionate hand to Sol; he does not take it, but the damage is done—we have been tumbled into the *David and Lisa* pseudoworld.

Jesus has a girl friend who is a prostitute, but they love each other with a sweet, Annabel-Leeish love. It may be that this could be so, but it is not made convincing. Customers come before Sol with their little heart-breaks, little absurdities, little greedinesses. Along with their portable radios and wristwatches, they bring cuteness and sentimentality. Each customer is a tidy vignette, clearly labeled: "Pathos," "Comic Relief," "Sordidness." It is all simplistic, hard-edge painting; none of that commingling and shading of colors with which life and its true painters—a Fellini, an Olmi—would work.

Meanwhile the flashbacks have proliferated, sometimes effectively, as when a subway car turns into a hideous, jammed cattlecar transporting victims to the camps. Jesus' girl offers herself to Nazerman for some free-lance money that she wouldn't have to turn over to her boss but could contribute toward Jesus' going into business. Her bare proffered bosom takes Nazerman back to when he was forced to watch the Nazis raping his wife. The frightened prostitute begs Nazerman to tell Rodriquez, who, Sol realizes, owns him, too. He now tries to throw off the yoke of Rodriguez, but fails and gets beaten up by the henchmen. Why, however, did he get involved with the gang in the first place? Why did it take him till now to comprehend their evil? It may be that in Edward Lewis Wallant's novel these things are sufficiently explained; in the film, they are not.

Now, all of a sudden and for no very good reason, Jesus is shocked by a callous remark of Sol's. So the boy rejoins his band of hoodlums and leads a raid on the pawnshop, but when, against his stipulations, one of the punks pulls a gun, our Christ figure ends up by taking a bullet destined for Sol and dying for him—a rather capricious, not to say jejune, Jesus. Sol at last experiences true pain, though he has to confirm this by perforating his hand melodramatically—or, worse yet, symbolically (Nazerman—Nazarene, a veritable inflation in Christ symbols)—with a paper spindle. He emits over Jesus' body a silent howl worthy of Laocoön, and is now able to suffer fully and, I suppose, life-givingly. On the other hand, Rodriguez has threatened to kill him as soon as he starts enjoying life again, and, now that he is suffering so satisfyingly, his number may be up.

The questionable aspects of the plot need no further examination, but specimens of artistic insufficiency are in order. The subliminal, surprise flashbacks, for example, are a problem. Alain Resnais invented them in *Hiroshima, Mon Amour,* and put them (whatever shortcomings the film may have) to thorough and impressive use. Now, if this device is a mode of telling a story, it is, of course, at everyone's disposal; but if it is only a device, a personal idiom or idiosyncrasy, anyone else using it becomes an imitator, an epigone or plagiarist. I myself feel that this type of flashback is a brilliant but one-time-only (or, at the utmost, one-man-only) invention of Resnais', and that whoever adopts it becomes *ipso facto* an echo. The directors of the Spanish film, *Dialogos de la paz,* also made use of this technique, and here, too, an eclectic and borrowed look manifested itself, even though Font Espina and Feliü made the device a little more their own by fusing it with other techniques.

Lumet's originality is again brought into question with the vignettes of the clients confronting Nazerman. Here he seems to be copying partly the scene in *The 400 Blows* where the boy is being interviewed by an invisible psychologist, and partly the bravura letter-monologue of Ingrid Thulin in *Winter Light*. Again, Boris Kaufman's photography, though striking and incisive, resorts to certain cliché effects—and these, too, depend in part on the director—as when lights of the city start as a blur and gradually come into focus.

However, Lumet's limitations can best be illustrated with what is perhaps the finest sequence of the film. Hands, scores of hands, are extended over a sinister wire fence, and are being, one after another, stripped of their rings. This traveling shot of marriages, of very identities, being unmade on a production line, conveys far more piercingly the despoliation and rape of the victims than the inevitably unconvincing rape sequences can. In this sort of emblematic detail one can say all and still leave much to the imagination—rather than saying a little and leaving the rest to erotic fantasizing. But Lumet spoils even this bit by making most of the hands beautiful: sensitive, lyrical, ravished hands. No. They should be ordinary, shopworn, and raped.

What is Lumet good at? Intentions, underlining, and casting. Many of the performances in this overlong and overstated film are just right. I find myself frequently accused of not appreciating film as an entertainment, only as art. To indicate that this is not so, I lustily recommend two films that cannot be accused either of being dull or of being art. *Male Hunt* is a frothy, febrile comedy in which some of France's most attractive actors and actresses—as well as some who can really act—are put through intricate and diverting, though not exactly unfamiliar routines. Edouard Molinaro has directed this race toward and away from the zero hour of marriage (and sometimes both toward and away) with self-renewing vitality and inventiveness, and Michel Audiard's dialogue is consistently witty, even if the subtitles can cope with it only intermittently.

Il Successo is a kind of secondary cousin to *The Easy*

Life; not quite so resourceful, not quite so ebullient, but still to be watched with purring contentment. Vittorio Gassman again displays the select and enviable talent of being both comedian and actor in one: a funny man who is also very much, and very seriously, a man. Anouk Aimée is outstandingly restrained as this ultra-gogetter's wife, and the script is solid and by no means mindless entertainment, except for a rather too moralizing conclusion. Still, it is excellent nonart, and superior to any amount of pseudoart.

THE NEW MEN AS NONMEN

For those who have not read the book, the film version of John Fowles's novel *The Collector* is a splendid thing. For those who have read it beforehand, I cannot say, not being of their number. For those who read it afterward, as I did, it raises some interesting but troubling questions.

The hero of *The Collector* is a painfully ordinary young English bank clerk, distinguished only by his dour abstemiousness with women and passionate pursuit of the butterflies he collects. Then he wins a fortune in the football pools, and an extraordinary idea begins to obsess and possess him. He buys a country house complete with hidden cellar and equips the latter as a comfortable prison for his prize butterfly, the beautiful Miranda Grey. She is twenty, a gifted upper-middle-class art student; he has always adored her from a distance without daring to speak to her. Frederick Clegg abducts his *princesse lointaine,* pampers her, does not assault her physically, and madly assumes that by keeping her long enough he can make her love him. Their duel, as she fights for her freedom and he for her love, ends after a couple of months in her death. He grieves for a while, then the class resentment for his "la-di-da" victim gains a posthumous upper hand, and he sets out to kidnap a more amenable working-class butterfly, one whom he'll be able to "teach."

In the novel, John Fowles has attempted something ambitious. He tells the story (as the movie does not) from two points of view, Clegg's and Miranda's, and achieves notable results with the psychological and linguistic evocation of contrasting behavior, psyches, and diction. He also introduces (unlike the movie), through entries in Miranda's diary, her growing awareness that she really loves G. P., a middle-aged, untidy sensualist and brilliant painter—a Gulley Jimsonish character whom Fowles does not quite bring off. Anyhow, Miranda matures in her prison, and her death becomes not only tragic but also ironic: a terrible joke.

The book, furthermore, operates on several levels. Besides the psychological suspense story, there is also the myth of radiant aliveness exposed to repressed subhumanity. Since Clegg prefers to call himself Ferdinand, but Miranda is compelled to think of him as Caliban, variations on *The Tempest* establish a poeticomythical frame of reference that, I must admit, does not quite succeed. What does work very well in the book is the social level. Clegg is the kind of bloodless nonentity the English Noncomformist lower-middle-classes are all too apt to produce—no matter what heroic archetypes John Osborne or Albert Finney may prefer; his sense of beauty extends only to dead butterflies and Miranda's outward appearance, and his sense of duty has killed nearly every healthy impulse in him, to the point of rendering him physically and spiritually impotent.

Of course, society is to blame, but as Fowles demonstrates, the Cleggs, or Calibans, of this world are only too eager to meet oppression with a combination of servility, conformity, and mistrust of any generous stirrings, which makes them at least half responsible themselves. Miranda, who stands more for the natural and unspoiled than for any social order, attempts to save Clegg, pity for whom overcomes her loathing. In vain, for Clegg is one of those New Men who are coming into money and power in England and elsewhere, and whose ignorance, impotence, and clammy mistrust of the free play of the mind is more hostile to Miranda's gracious enlightenment than any overt violence could be. No wonder Miranda comes to resent the self-righteous respect with which Clegg treats her, the humbly unpresuming demands he makes on her, his spidery concern. To this tepid lepidopterologist it is incomprehensible why his golden butterfly should not thrive in a nicely padded captivity in which everything is available except light, air, movement, and communion with the world.

"You despise the real bourgeois classes for all their . . . snobbish voices and ways," Miranda tells her jailer in a speech significantly missing from the film. "Yet all you put in their place is a horrid little refusal to have nasty thoughts or do nasty things . . . Do you know that every great thing in the history of art and every beautiful thing in life is actually what you call nasty or has been caused by feelings that you would call nasty? By passion, by love, by hatred, by truth." But Clegg, though he may obligingly agree, understands none of it. Arrived though they are, the New People represent "the new form of poverty. The others hadn't any money and these haven't any soul." This aristocratic point of view is compellingly conveyed by the book, and generally ignored in the movie version.

The film is a very skillful, even artful, tale of a deranged man's weird action, and it does contain also some of the social facts: resentment, defensiveness, inability of the classes to communicate. But it makes important changes. It turns the girl into someone at times much too defensive, and thus, by implication, rather too guilty; it eliminates tellingly dreary details that evoke the Clegg world in all its grubbiness and sterility; it makes Clegg not only pathetic, which he is in the book, but also sympathetic—even his impotence is fudged over, and, most important, it does not connect Clegg's psychic aberrancy with his social background: it shies away from the central accusation, the basic allegory, the coming to power of the petty bourgeoisie as the death of the finer aspects of man.

Consider some typical changes. In the book, much is made of Clegg's garish taste in furniture, clothes, art. Miranda has to smash some awful plaster ducks with which his fine 1623 house is decorated; she can't bear to put on the dresses he buys for her; she cannot begin to make him understand about painting and literature. In the film, the furniture and clothes are just slightly off (clever work by the art director, John Stoll)—no plaster ducks!—and Clegg's arguments against *The Catcher in the Rye* and a Picasso reproduction emerge rather too convincing. Could it be that the director, William Wyler, was eager not to offend an audience who liked his *Ben Hur* and *The Best Years of Our Lives,* and who, no doubt, also likes plaster ducks? Does Wyler himself have a taste for them?

Again, one of the most chilling elements in the book is Clegg's amateur photography. He is unable to enjoy Miranda physically, even when she offers herself to him out of genuine compassion as much as desire to escape, and justifies this by declaring her a slut. He then proceeds to take seminude pictures of her under chloroform, and later, when she is already deathly ill, he binds and gags her and takes pictures in the nude. It is these pictures that he really enjoys, and, on one level, the book is a contest between painting (art, life, Miranda) and photography (non-art, death, Clegg). All this is missing from the film, whose aim is to make Clegg, except for his initial and final aberration, as likable as possible. From the point of view of sound dramatic conflict, this is, of course, sensible. But Fowles was after more than sound, sensible dramaturgy: he was evoking the horror of Clegg in the coolest, most commonsensical way—making him not likable but understandable and typical, and thus genuinely frightening.

I could multiply such examples, but I do not want to minimize the achievements of the movie. For Wyler has made, even so, an adult and provocative film, which, if one did not know the compromises it makes with the novel, would seem uncompromising. Evil, in any case, is allowed to prosper in the end, a step toward maturity in American movie-making that cannot be loudly enough hailed. The screenplay by Stanley Mann and John Kohn, within the strictures already noted, deftly telescopes the novel and creates cinematic effects that are both economical and equivalent to the verbal ones of the book—thus the single flashback tells remarkably much with great terseness. Wyler has added little directorial touches that are often quite beautiful, such as the trembling of dead butterflies in their cases when Miranda, in living indignation, slams the door of the collection room.

The photography, too, is admirably workmanlike; the preponderance of blues and greens, though, I suspect, unintentional, may actually enhance the mood of the story. Maurice Jarre's score is the most musically and psychologically satisfying work this intelligent artist has turned out since *Sundays and Cybèle*: I particularly liked the chamber-music quality throughout, and the dramatic effects achieved by bold changes in instrumentation from harpsichord to electronics. Most impressive, however, is the acting. As Clegg, Terence Stamp conveys the most complex shadings of a socially and sexually disturbed psyche with perspicuity but not obviousness. Down to the last wrinkling and unwrinkling of the forehead, to the in-choate little sounds over Miranda's dead body, this is performing of the highest, most illuminating order. Samantha Eggar's Miranda is almost as persuasive, and Miss Eggar has a wonderfully shrewd kind of loveliness, too, which seems to know when to be mere healthy Vassar-girlishness, and when to ascend into absolute beauty.

That leaves us with the great ultimate question. How is one to rate a film thoroughly successful on a lower level, based on a novel that is flawed but more ambitious, more meaningful, more in the realm of serious art? I think Wyler is to be praised for good film-making, and reprehended for imperfect integrity. Something more than plaster ducks has been ducked.

SARDINES AND WHALES

When there are whales to be had for the asking, who will remark a sardine? The fact that it tastes better than a plateful of whale steak is irrelevant: a whole school of sardines will pass unnoticed beside one totally unschooled whale. Today, when movies are getting more and more Leviathanish (the elephantiasis metaphor no longer suffices: to be caught inside a three or four-hour spectacular can be equated only with the fate of Jonah), exquisite little films have it harder than ever. One after the other, *Bandits of Orgosolo, The Sound of Trumpets, The Fiancés, Il Bidone, Variety Lights, Bell' Antonio, Family Diary* (to name only some recently released Italian films) vanish into instant obscurity, while hugely and yet more hugely bloated monstrosities are kept afloat on waves of pimping publicity, critical injudiciousness, and public indiscrimination. All this by way of introducing a very small, very unheralded, and wholly indispensable film, *The Fascist*; to miss it would be worse than a mistake—more like willful self-starvation.

The Fascist (Il federale) is the story of a mule-headed, thoroughly indoctrinated clod of a Fascist NCO who has to apprehend and bring back to Rome a distinguished anti-Fascist professor. The time is the last gasp of the Duce's era, with the Germans being booted out of the boot of Italy, and tempers, spirits, and discipline cracking amid the bootlessness of it all. Anyone with a sliver of common sense would give up; but Primo Arcovazzi has been so brainwashed, has such a bovine sense of duty, and is so keen on being promoted to a *federale* and wearing that gorgeous uniform worthy of the best Viennese operetta, that no footling cataclysm, no mere total collapse can make him desist. There is one hitch: he is a perfect bumbler.

Professor Bonafè, on the other hand, is a bit of an unworldly savant, but not an old duffer. He is neither crusty, nor lovable, nor any of the other commonplaces: he can be absurd but also amazingly resourceful. He is, like his antagonist, above all human and believable. As Primo and his prisoner trek toward Rome in a variety of rickety vehicles or on their own often highly wobbly feet, they encounter every sort of preposterous mishap that utter chaos can shower on them. These disasters are often frantically, and still more often subduedly, funny; through all of them, the Fascist and the professor debate dictatorship versus democracy, sometimes in open discussion, more frequently in insults or innuendoes, and always in attempts at oneupmanship. This burlesque contest, in which the antagonists are at times ludicrously forced to make common cause—against Germans, gun-happy teen-age blackshirts, or just hunger—serves ultimately as something bigger than a comic battle of ideologies.

For what the movie is finally about, and what it documents with a magisterial understatement that manages to be both sardonic and humanistic, is the eternal hostility of brain and brawn, of the speculative and muscular modes of existence. The conflict is depicted with impartiality and understanding: Though the intellect is perceived as the guiding principle, it can clearly learn a thing or two from the pedestrian but canny body. And the weaknesses of both are jovially lampooned.

Now, what makes the film remarkable is that it does not end in an apotheosis of democracy, intellectuality, reasonableness, or what have you—though it is anything but an apology for the opportunism and brutishness of Fascism. It ends with Primo and Bonafè accepting each other—but, again, not in any grand, emotionally uplifting way. It is a shamefaced, unexuberant, melancholy acceptance of one's own inadequacy made manifest in the other, and of the other's right to live without one's loving or even approving of him. A man saves another's life without any special fondness for him, only with mournful sympathy; the other receives the supreme gift without soul-cleansing gratitude, only with gruff incredulity. The sempiternal adversaries have gained a little grudging tolerance for each other—one of them is capable of an act of generosity—but they will remain adversaries. That a *Times* receiver should find *The Fascist* unmoving and "hardly profound" is only further proof of the unbridgeable gap that the film evokes with beautifully modulated humor, feelingfulness, and sagacity.

Under its bumptious slapstick, *The Fascist* is also highly sophisticated. Its basic unit is irony. This irony is visual, verbal, philosophical, and spreads out in concentric circles from the smallest incident to the ultimate significance, from the beginning to the end, which is no end. Irony is there in almost every utterance, as when the professor casually remarks during a Spartan meal that though pork may be scarce in wartime, there is an extraordinary increase in pigs. It comes out even more pungently in tiny episodes, as when the crass Primo saves two children abandoned in the path of a strafing plane by their devotedly screaming, absolutely useless parents, and then proceeds with his relentless hounding of Bonafè.

Or take the incident when Primo asks Bonafè for his precious, India-paper Leopardi, and the professor thinks he has converted his captor to higher values, only to find Primo ripping out a page to roll himself a cigarette. Whereupon the professor, noting that it was merely " '*Ad Angelo Mai*'—a minor work," tears out another page for his own smoking. But the irony does not stop there: an Italian viewer would know that the full title of the poem is "To Angelo Mai, on His Discovery of Cicero's Books of the Republic"—how apt that the Republic should go up in a trivial Fascist's smoke. And the little volume of Leopardi serves as an ironic leitmotiv throughout: The only sign of illumination in Primo comes at the end, when he is awestruck by the professor's sacrificing the page with "*L'infinito*," Leopardi's finest lyric. (There is, by the way, also an adscititious irony in the subtitles' translating, with their customary incompetence, "*Ad Angelo Mai*" as "To Angel May"!)

The young director, Luciano Salce, who also collaborated on the script, has directed with demonic abandon or brave restraint, as needed; and the editing is as incontestable as that of Lachesis and Atropos. Ugo Tognazzi as Primo, and Georges Wilson (Jean Vilar's no less brilliant successor at the Théâtre National Populaire) as Bonafè, give performances that are—in a word I am particularly chary of—perfect. The supporting cast, too, pitches in superbly. The rest, dear reader, is up to you.

Cat Ballou is another small film with its heart in the right place and with a mind of its own. Regrettably the heart is only medium-stout, and the mind only medium-sized. What's wrong with this comic Western is that it rears up in fear before really savage farce, and does not quite have the skill to ride high in the saddle of comedy. As it is, it has a few touches of pert satire, some quite funny lines, and three or four excellent sight gags which it would be unchivalrous to reveal. There is even a rather bold sound gag that occurs as the various doors of a bordello are opened, and about which I must also keep mum. Jane Fonda is one of our most desirable—in both senses of the word—young actresses, and Lee Marvin is two enormously amusing actors in his dual role. But direction, supporting cast, and interminable inept Western-style ballads used as running commentary, subtract much more than they add. *Cat Ballou* is a likable film; too bad that it isn't also a good one.

But *Ballou,* at least, managed to stay small. Another cat, *What's New Pussycat?,* which starts out as a nicely purring, playful kitten, comes to grief trying to stretch itself into a tiger in midstream. Woody Allen, who wrote the script, complains that the film was taken out of his hands and overinflated; it certainly has the look of two concepts, two modes, two films joined in loveless matrimony. For the first twenty minutes or so there is a good deal of freewheeling, irreverent—albeit erratic—merriment; thereafter follows a rather more consistent dullness. In an attempt to salvage some of this stale and insipid fare, all too liberal amounts of spice have been poured on out of oversize shakers labeled S and P (sex and perversion); but, unfortunately for all concerned, to make something enjoyably dirty, a lot of taste is required. What makes this especially sticky going is that a number of the principals seem to be acting out something not unlike their real-life problems. Peter Sellers and Peter O'Toole supply some genuinely comic moments; out of surely inadvertent modesty, Allen has written much less fun into his own part. Among the women, Paula Prentiss, Capucine, and Ursula Andress never rise above the level of ungifted amateurs. But Miss Andress' body speaks eloquently; more eloquently, alas, than most of the script.

A film that very nearly succumbs to its avoirdupois is *Those Magnificent Men in Their Flying Machines*. This pleasantly scatterbrained story of the antics and lunacies of early aviation—the putative plot concerns the farcical intrigues, private and political, and the farcical loves, for women and machines, surrounding an Edwardian air race from London to Paris—could have been a good bit funnier by being shorter. The winning time is 25 hours and 11 minutes, and by observing some sort of Neoaristotelian unity, the film seems to last exactly as long. There is many a likely gag in the film, but none that survives the second or third reprise. Red Skelton and Irina Demick, as a matter of fact, are too much even the first time around.

Still, there is quite enough here that is good for a not too discriminating laugh, and the crazily hyperexcrescent old flying machines are infinitely lovable. And the photography of Christopher Challis, with special effects by Richard Parker, is nothing short of stunning. Not a bad whale—as whales go.

SEVERE GLAUCOMA

If you do not care how ill-gotten and obscene your laughs may be there are two films to be seen currently that are guaranteed to have you rolling on the theatre floor—whether in fits of laughter or of apoplexy depends entirely on your temperament. *The Sandpiper* and Joseph Levine's *Harlow* will not widen your horizon, but they are sure to extend your rictus.

The Sandpiper is based on a story by the producer Martin Ransohoff, who clearly set out to prove that anyone who has been around movies long enough can write one, and if the price the viewer must pay is no objection, the case may now be considered proved. The screenplay is partly by Dalton Trumbo, and what *it* proves is that just because you were one of the "Hollywood Ten," your work need not be distinguishable from that of the Hollywood thousands. The film, with Elizabeth Taylor and Richard Burton, and directed by Vincente Minnelli, had every chance of being another piece of that mildly sentimental, reasonably vulgar, and vastly foolish nonsense that would have done this beloved genre proud. Instead, it took it in its puny head to be adult!

Against a background of Big Sur, this is a story that is meant to combine the devil-may-care lyricism of Edna Millay with the philosophizing randiness of Henry Miller (itself a combination not unworthy of the wax museums), but turns out to be merely Jack Kerouac strained through Kathleen Norris. We have here a free-thinking and free-loving Liz Taylor who supports herself and a small illegitimate son in a lush studio-made cottage by selling an occasional painting.

When a misdemeanor condemns her son to a posh West Coast Groton of which the Reverend Richard Burton (happily married to Eva Marie Saint) is the headmaster, ideas began to clash and bodies to mash. Before you know it, it is muscular Christianity versus adipose femininity; and confronted with Taylor's poetically bohemian, highly sexy atheism (she spouts about nature and sex, and her table is littered with poets in Penguin editions), Burton's latitudinarian—or, perhaps platitudinarian—churchmanship becomes so broad as to be expressible only in a horizontal position. Shades of Paphnutius and the Reverend Davidson! Moments of adulterous bliss are followed closely by hours of tormented responsibility, and the whole thing ends with Burton chucking his cushy job and going off on mission work to Mexico—he is an Episcopalian, but the iguanas, presumably, won't know the difference. And so he bids an eloquently understated temporary farewell to his wife, and an eloquently mute permanent farewell to his mistress.

Morality (as described above) will out, but first, what frank references to carnality! Why, the word "abortion" alone is mentioned three times. And there is posing in the nude, and guarded hints of an interracial affair, and beach parties that are implied orgies, and a few proto-four-letter words, and such bold wrangling about the existence of God. It is all rather like a five-year-old boy being dragged out of bed at midnight by his avantgarde parents to entertain their guests with a repertoire of dirty words.

Everyone will find his own favorite gems in this enlightened film; I can merely submit my personal choices. For intellectual stimulus: the moment after Liz's kid has uttered the first lines of the Prologue to *The Canterbury Tales* in Middle English and Miss Saint rushes to Burton to announce breathlessly that the child has just recited said prologue in the original Old English! For emotional catharsis: the moment when Miss Saint, who has bravely and forgivingly listened during a nocturnal car ride to her husband's confession, hears that he and Liz made love also in motels; at the word "motels" something snaps, and she leaps, blubbering, out of the car, to cover the remaining umpteen miles on foot. Moral: Adulterers who respect their wives should always ply their avocation in hotels.

It is also possible to get one's kicks merely out of watching Miss Taylor, who has grown so ample that it has become necessary to dress her almost exclusively in a variety of ambulatory tents. On the few occasions when she dares reveal her bosom (or part thereof), one breast (or part thereof) proves sufficient to traverse an entire wide screen frame—diagonally.

Harlow, on the other hand, is the exact opposite of *The Sandpiper,* and not only because Carroll Baker is concave where Liz Taylor is convex. Here we get the tried-and-tested formula of taking a luridly sensational story that everyone has heard or read about down to the last appetizingly aberrant detail, and presenting it as straight Louisa May Alcott interlarded with a measured amount of discreetly pornographic allusions. Our Jean, it turns out, had "the body of a woman and the emotions of a child," though, as we are also informed, "in that slim, delicate body is a woman as strong as a marble statue"; but, unluckily for the marble statue, "Oh, mama, all they want is my body!" High-minded as Jean is—"I couldn't love a man I didn't like!"—she learns that "a bedroom with only one person in it is the loneliest place in the world," but the script tends to eschew an excess of such profundities, realizing that "life doesn't move on philosophy alone."

Jean, in sum, was 'a little girl who suffered a big tragedy." She who was so pure ("Arthur Landau, you once told me that you never er . . . er . . ." "Procured?" "Yes—I couldn't think of the word . . .") naïvely marries a man who, announcing on their wedding night, "I'll give you love in every way," must be told, "Except the one that counts," which leads to the aforementioned big tragedy as the impotent bridegroom beats up Jean (off-camera). She moans, "There is nobody deader than I am right now," and, understandably, drifts into a life of drunkenness and . . . er . . . I cannot think of the word. When asked, "What do you want to prove?" she explains, "That I'm alive, every inch of me, every part of me!" So much aliveness must, alas, inevitably end in a heart-rending death scene in an oxygen tent:

JEAN: I promise I'll be a good girl, mama.

MOTHER (*shrieks something hysterical at Doctor that I did not get*).

DOCTOR: She's beyond help—*our* help.

LANDAU (*who has always been to Jean—more than her true friend—her agent*): She didn't die of pneumonia; she died of life! She gave it all to everyone else—there wasn't any left for her.

A pop singer then intones the theme song, "Lonely Girl," while a montage of stills of Carroll Baker in her glory (an ironic apotheosis, I presume) leads into "The End"—in more ways than one.

Regrettably, not all frightful movies are funny. There is, for example, precious little to laugh at in *Ship of Fools,* with the possible exception of the performances of Elizabeth Ashley and George Segal as a pair of sparring artist-lovers. Inspired by Sebastian Brant's lengthy and boring fifteenth-century verse satire, Katherine Anne Porter wrote a lengthy and boring nineteenth-century novel; now Stanley Kramer, the producer-director, and Abby Mann, his script-writer, have turned this into a movie that is not only long and dull but also obvious and pretentious, thus closing the gap between Sebastian Brant and Harry Brandt, after whom a chain of second-run movie houses is named. Kramer and Mann, I dare say, were already in the original *Narrenschiff* among those who "would be that which they are not/And think that all the world is blind."

Mann's dialogue, aside from leaden moralizing heavy enough to sink a Cunard flagship, abounds in conceits like, "Are you happy?'—"Who is happy?" or "I haven't lived!"—"Who has?" which are not very different from such tidbits in *Harlow* as, "There's something wrong with all of us, sweetheart, it just takes a while to find out." As for Kramer's direction, it is, as ever, attempting to perform pirouettes in astronauts' boots by way of harrying the cloddish into becoming art. When you are not being hit over the head with the symbolism, you're being punched in the stomach by would-be inventive camera work, while, unremittingly, Ernest Gold's score fills your nostrils with acrid exhalations.

Oskar Werner gives his usual somewhat hallucinated performance, but, at that, his bittersweet somnambulism is more interesting than Simone Signoret's by now cliché tough good woman or beat-up dreamer. Vivien Leigh is effectively type-cast; a newcomer, Gila Golan, plays awakening womanhood like a bear coming out of hibernation; and various competent actors exude an ichor of overemphasis to the director's palpable delight. Even the special photographic effects have about them a clumsy officiousness one associates with Kramer.

But the most disheartening thing about *Ship of Fools* is the favorable press it garnered and the queue of fools outside the theatres in which it is playing. There are films that are simply bathed in the odor of middlebrow sanctity. Let them be portentous multiple stories offering a cross-section of humanity, let them be bloated with sardonic political hindsight, let them be allegories of the World—let them, above all, be based on overpraised and underread bestsellers, and they are sure to be universally acclaimed. Sebastian Brant was wrong: the world is, if not blind, at least the victim of severe glaucoma.

What else but purblindness could account for the failure of Valerio Zurlini's *Family Diary* when it was first released? The New Yorker Theater revived it for two days, but what are two days? It is a terribly somber film and Vasco Pratolini's adaptation from his own novel remains, despite Zurlini's collaboration, disjointedly episodic. But the direction of individual scenes, the color photography of Giuseppe Rotunno, the music of the distinguished Goffredo Petrassi, and some overwhelming ensemble acting by Sylvie, Jacques Perrin, and Marcello Mastroianni—as well as incisive writing—make this one of the most moving movies of all time.

GRAVITY DEFIED

An Evening with the Royal Ballet makes ballet on film look even worse than usual. For one of its four offerings, it picked Ashton's insipid *La Valse* (further worsened by contrast with Balanchine's), it often chops off dancers' heads or feet, its color photography is undistinguished and its sound recording of an already slack orchestra appalling, and Drigo's music for *Le Corsaire* is so offensive as to make this old warhorse fitter for the knacker's than for the choreographer's art. But Fonteyn is one of the ballet's great artists, and Nureyev one of its greatest technicians; these two alone, even if it were not for the fine work of other soloists and members of the *corps,* could excuse the inexcusable.

Why is ballet *always* so unsatisfactory on the screen? There exist six, apparently insuperable, difficulties.

First, motion: a static camera setup is lifeless, yet the moment the camera begins to move it creates a choreography of its own, competing and conflicting with that of the ballet.

Second, composition: a ballet, like a painting, largely depends on the way in which bodies and movements are composed within the frame of the stage—on the relationships of soloists to one another or to the ensemble, even of bodies to scenery—and these groupings and proportions are lost sight of in anything but long shots.

Third, space: in watching live ballet, the spectator has a clear sense of how high a leap is, how long a *jeté,* how prodigious the distance covered by the most graceful *cabriole*; on the screen, dimensions and spatial relations lose their dramatic perspicuity.

Fourth, selection: the balletgoer at a live performance picks out the details that interest him most, that seem to

him to epitomize the moment—the arch of a foot on
pointes, the interaction of a dozen dancers in an abstract
pattern, a psychological reaction suddenly manifested in
the ballerina's *port de bras*; on screen, the camera forces
its choices on us and they are not always what we
want—in any case, the human eye can, to some extent,
concentrate on a particular and still see the whole,
whereas with the camera its either or.

Fifth, emotion: there is emotional play and byplay
among dancers in certain ballets, missed by the camera
while focusing on one or the other individual; even in a
pas de deux, while the ballerina is doing her variation, the
mere expression on her cavalier's face, his delight and
pride in her, is an integral part of the total effect.

Sixth, psychology: a moviegoer may know consciously
that he is watching an actual dance whose wonders are
honestly arrived at; subconsciously aware, however, of the
trickery of cinema, he cannot silence the still, small voice
that whispers, "Fake!" Seeing at one remove is not believing; at least, not utter, uninhibited believing.

If there is little hope for ballet on film, there seems to
be even less for integrity in a minor key. Time and again
these columns have sounded like eulogies for the untimely
dead or dying: heroic little films desperately needing an
audience from among the intelligentsia, because the
average moviegoer could do nothing with them. The in-
telligensia, however, in the year 1965 is still—believe it or
not—unconvinced that movies are of consequence.

Back in 1921, Hugo von Hofmannsthal wrote: "The atmosphere of the movie house seems to me the only atmosphere in which people of our time—those who make
up the masses—enter into a direct, wholly untrammeled
relationship to an enormous, albeit curiously contrived,
spiritual inheritance. Life faces life, and the jampacked,
darkened hall with its images flitting by is to me—I cannot put it otherwise—almost worthy of reverence, for it is
the place to which souls throng in an obscure urge for
survival, escaping from the numeral into vision." *Von der
Ziffer zur Vision*—it sounds fine enough, but if, instead of

merely dealing with ciphers, you are a cipher, there is no escaping. Or if you think that film is for "those who make up the masses" (true enough in 1921), you naturally stay away unless every reviewer happens to be raving about a movie, and then you end up with something like *8½*, and feel perfectly justified in reimmersing yourself in abstention. But Hofmannsthal was vatically right: A film like *Life Upside Down* is for "people of our time," even if it does not suit the masses, who, at all times, are of no distinctive time at all.

La Vie à l'envers, which should be translated as "Life Inside Out," or "Life in Reverse," is an ingenious and highly conscientious examination of alienation from one's milieu that leads to withdrawal, and withdrawal that ends as insanity. Alain Jessua, the young Frenchman who wrote and directed it, is a man of genuine talent, and not like Bernardo Bertolucci (over whose inept and pretentious *Before the Revolution* Pauline Kael was recently swooning in the pages of *Life*), a mere alert dung-beetle, making a film out of the droppings of half a dozen masters and *petits-maîtres* of cinema. Jessua is an original, in that his film reminds one of nobody, though a faint thematic parallel may be traced to Louis Malle's excellent *The Fire Within* (*Le Feu follet*)—itself, needless to add, a failure in these parts.

In showing us how an apparently ordinary, middle-class young housing-agency clerk removes himself from reality, quirk by quirk, Jessua accomplishes on his first try what the much-touted Bresson never quite brought off: the stripping of the story to its barest essentials of people, words, sets, and situations. While we have the feeling of perusing a scientifically complete yet concise case history, the wistful humor of the dialogue, the poignancy of visual details, and the rhythm of the editing give this case history the pregnancy of art. Sight and sound are put to resourceful uses that are, however, never mere trumpery—always penetration and illumination. A busy subway is swept clean of its multitudes; a pinball-machine parlor, emptied of people, reverberates with the bounce of self-propelled balls; a mistress's cheerfully ejaculated banalties shrink to a distant, ridiculously raspy, chirruping; a bed that a slatternly wife has converted into a cross between a beauty parlor and a cafeteria becomes pristinely virginal and wifeless; a common catalpa thrusts itself into the world with such gnarled, hyperexcrescent bossiness that it turns into a sacred fig-tree claiming a new Buddha.

The film is remarkable, too, for its objectivity. Though the good, average people and their social institutions are not spared a goodly number of well-merited kicks, and though the arguments of madness are presented with the greatest possible sympathy, it is still made to look mad and, in some ways, cruel; in the final reckoning, the ordinary world of doctors, police officials, simple-minded friends and benighted wives emerges as fumblingly well-meaning and pitifully likable. In the debate between not quite untenable insanity and not exactly prepossessing normality, there are no comfortable syllogisms or fulgurating epigrams with which to clinch the argument.

Life Upside Down, witty as well as wise, offers the warning that cannot be voiced often enough in a world in which easy solutions, whether in art or morality, are becoming more and more fashionable—and I am using "fashionable" advisedly: as never before, good or bad art, good or bad mores have become questions not of taste or belief, but only of fashion. This film is dedicated to demonstrating that neither the old fashion of simply condemning the madman, nor the new fashion of elaborately emulating him is to be unquestioningly countenanced. The hero of the film becomes absorbed in things—a lamp, a table leg—which for a poet like Rilke leads to truth, for a psychologist like Fromm to sanity, and for this fellow to dementia. Things are relative: One man's truth is another man's therapy and still another's poison.

The performances attain a degree of veracity that would be terrifying, were it not for a bizarrely comic streak in the writing; Jacques Robin's photography is particularly good at revealing the shoddiness of an ambiance; Nicole Marco's editing is full of surprising rubatos that, after the shock is over, leave us with the sense of their rightness. And to Alain Jessua goes the honor of having created a film that is amusing or disturbing depending on whether it is viewed from the outside or the inside, but perceptive and artistic whichever way one turns it. It is cause for rejoicing when honesty and imagination announce themselves so forcefully in the work of a young film-maker.

Jean-Luc Godard's *The Married Woman* contains a good deal of undeniable visual imaginativeness, a measure of somewhat more deniable honesty, and an incontestable surfeit of banality and intellectual confusion. These "fragments," as Godard himself calls them, concern a winsome but mildly imbecile young woman oscillating between a husband and a lover. What one sees is often very beautiful—human limbs and bodies entering into an infinite variety of erotic juxtapositions that partake of a stately dance as well as of a yearning colloquy; but what one hears is sheer tripe—either arrogantly dragged-in quotations and allusions or stupid maundering and pseudometaphysicizing to make the most hardened sophomore blush with the shame of recognition.

The heroine (engagingly played by Macha Meril) is a cute little narcissist who does not know the meaning of the word "equilateral" and thinks that Auschwitz was the scene of thalidomide trials, who indulges her most ludicrous whims while continually testing her husband and lover with portentous but pointless questionings. Nonetheless, we are supposed to care greatly about whom this frivolous goose will choose to be stuffed by: her lover, a fatuous, self-absorbed actor; or her husband, a well-intentioned but troubled commercial pilot. It could hardly matter less even to her, never mind us. And this short film is crammed to the gills with citations from or references to Molière, Bossuet, *Fantomas,* Dullin, Jouvet, *Yesterday, Today and Tomorroy,* Cocteau, Rossellini, Pierre Emmanuel, Apollinaire, Truffaut, *Bérénice,* Céline, Hitchcock, *Night and Fog,* Scarlett O'Hara, and a few others I missed. There are also some absurd puns, promulgated as serious insights, as when the girl gravely asks, *"Qu'est-ce que ça veut dire, 'regarder'?"* and is solemnly told, *"C'est garder deux fois"*; or when a sign reading "DANGER" is closed in on by the camera till it reads "ANGE," and another, announcing "PASSAGE," is split, ominously, into its components, "PAS"—"SAGE."

Worse yet are the endless monologues in close-up, during which an actor expatiates in unending platitudes and trivialities about some large abstract topic like "Memory" or "The Present," and registers little beyond the embarrassment at having to deliver such drivel at close quarters—or, if it is improvised, as in some cases it seems to be, at having to be caught with his metaphysical pants down; For what actor, after all, is a philosopher? Sample profundities: "If there is no present, it's not alive, it doesn't exist." "The present—it prevents me from going mad." "One must love young sages and old madmen."

There are, however, some compensatory visual devices, and Godard is able to handle these dazzlingly. Posters, headlines, record jackets are cut into the action to comment with wry cogency; the camera (in Raoul Coutard's capable hands) is made to perform every sort of gyration and *salto mortale,* including turning over on its side, sometimes with psychologically meaningful effect; there are tenderly intimate close-ups of lovers washing their hands together or struggling with the hooks of a brassiere, actions that take on the dignity of ritual; above all, there are those pertinaciously cropped shots in which parts of two bodies become synecdoches for the greater or lesser transports of love.

Even here, though, Godard's injudiciousness tends to get the better of him, and he ruins his best effects by excessive dawdling or repetition. What Appollinaire has called the *poésie des affiches* is finally reduced here to obstreperous pop art, and the sweetness of erotic dalliance is dragged out into compulsive doodling. Devices often misfire, as does a sequence of hectic shuttling between positive and negative exposure. All the same, there are four impressive scenes. One is an uneasy meeting between husband and guilt-ridden wife at an airport; another is the wife's partial overhearing of intimate confidences exchanged between two young girls; still another is the wife's measuring of her bosom to find out whether it is the ideal one as prescribed by a magazine article (the subtitles, by translating 20 cms. as 20 inches, also translate the Venus de Milo into the Hottentot Venus); the fourth is a sequence in which an emotionally stymied couple listen in their bedroom to an aphrodisiac recording of sexual laughter, while from the outside, into the middle of recorded giggles and pained, living silence, falls the chirp of a quizzical cricket.

Godard has told us what to do with young sages and old madmen; the problem of young madmen remains unresolved.

A note on Richard Lester, a young American ex-television director now making movies in England. His first film, *A Hard Day's Night,* blessed with four future Commanders of the British Empire and a clever scenario by Alun Owen, introduced a lively and endearing transposition of burlesque and absurdist jokes onto film; in the handling of the camera and in the montage, above all, Ionesco and Minsky were joined in unholy matrimony in the eye of Godard. All technology was enlisted in the service of the gag, and a kind of nuclear gagmanship exploded. But by the time Lester turned to gagging up Ann Jellicoe's charming play *The Knack,* the effects were more obtrusive, less spontaneous; the imagination more driven and less controlled. The New Beatles picture, *Help!,* proves after a few flashes of life, a deadly bore. Gags require a semblance of a plot or a point of view to hang them on; anarchy is piquant only with relation to an order. And so Lester becomes the John Bunyan of film, producing in sequence *Grace Abounding, Pilgrims' Regress,* and *The Life and Death of Mr. Gagman.*

FESTIVAL OF FAMINE

The first and second New York Film Festivals yielded two
or three indubitably fine films each and a lot of oppressive
ballast. The third Festival, just over, while increasing the
ballast to unendurable proportions, was unable to produce
a single first-rate film. Whatever the reasons, and they
may be complex, this is a depressing fact. Not one
outstanding film. Not one.

Incompetent, dreary films; inept and offensive shorts;
13 fatuous and flatulent symposiums; more programs than
critics could keep up with or judicious moviegoers begin
to contemplate. Of 26 features, three new ones and one or
two revivals proved valid or, at any rate, defensible; out of
24 shorts, four or five deserved to be seen. And all this
crowded into ten exhausting days. Weeping in heaven;
laughter in hell.

The first and best excuse that the Festival's directors,
Richard Roud and Amos Vogel, might adduce is that
there was nothing better to be found, or, at any rate, obtained for showing at the Festival. We might then be
inclined to doubt these allegations, but would, in all probability, be unable to disprove them. But there would remain at our disposal one insuperable answer: If that is the
best there is, forget it. Let's have a miniature festival: a
fistful of films, a few intelligent lectures and discussions,
one more or less Dionysian wake, and fifty-one weeks of
private prayers for better luck next year.

Jean-Luc Godard, the presiding genius of the Festival,
was represented by two features, one episode in a six-part
film, and several imitations by other film-makers. He also
appeared in the flesh. His new (though no longer newest)
work, *Alphaville,* with which the Festival opened, is a pretentious bore afflicted with pseudointellectual diarrhea. A

clumsy steal from *Brave New World* and *1984,* it is
decked out with references to Pascal, Baudelaire, and
Eluard on the one hand, and allusions to pop art, science
fiction, and comic strips on the other. There is a patent
failure of sensibility in attempting to make mass culture
and travesties of mass culture coalesce with high-sounding
humanistic platitudes and literary fragments shored
against the ruins of a disintegrating brain; the entire film is
a kind of Sargasso Sea in which bits of galleons and pieces
of drowned mariners churn in meaningless motion. The
cheapness and primitiveness of the execution, in which,
for example, present-day nocturnal street traffic blurrily
photographed is supposed to represent future interstellar
travel is emblematic of the arrogance of Godard's pretensions and the exiguity and paltriness of his powers.

The Little Soldier (1960), Godard's second film, is a
reduction of the Algerian crisis to a witless game of cops
and robbers, interspersed with the customary Godardian
philosophomorizings. Arab agents and Poujadiste reac-
tionaries are chasing, torturing, and killing one another all
over Geneva, ostensibly to influence the war in Algeria,
but actually to give Godard a chance to masturbate on
screen. Typifying the level of the film, the hero pursues his
designated victim through the busiest sections of Geneva
with a huge gun sprouting from his paw, without the victim, the police or the numerous bystanders finding anything amiss. Typical, too, is Godard's slobbering here (as
also in *Alphaville* and most of his other films) over his utterly untalented ex-wife, Anna Karina, who never plays a
part, only languidly toys with it. A film-maker who
confuses casting and directing with proto-sexual self-
gratification, and screenwriting with bang-bang-you're-
deading, is hardly to be taken seriously, no matter what
minor, peripheral felicities he may occasionally stumble
on.

Knave of Hearts, René Clément's 1954, English-made
film, shown here only briefly in a bowdlerized version, is a
good example of a sensible revival. Though the film is a
slight and somewhat worn story of a small-time Don

Juan's rise to a marriage of luxury and constriction, there is much charm in the script on which the witty Raymond Queneau collaborated, great *savoir-faire* in the acting of Gèrard Philipe and a smooth supporting cast, and an array of sophisticated niceties in the direction—not always novel, but always dapper.

Another revival of some, though lesser, merit was Antonioni's *Camille Without Camellias* (1953). This tale of a semitalented movie actress and unsuccessful wife and mistress, caught between her intelligence and her mediocre gifts, between her hopes of love and the shabbiness of her lovers, between the unacceptable alternatives of comfortable idling and unearned success, has possibilities; but, in this his second film, Antonioni was not yet able to supply more than rather good direction, the grouping and moving about of people being particularly praiseworthy. Like its heroine, the film suffers from intelligent mediocrity; it sorely lacks the originality, sharpness, uncompromisingness of Antonioni's best work, and, like Enzo Serafin's photography, displays a certain five-o'clock shadow where bright, merciless brilliance is crucially needed.

The other revivals were unqualified disasters. *The Wedding March* is the first part of one of those mammoth Erich von Stroheim films, reveling in lavish but indiscriminate reaction of physical details, in Stroheim's impudent display of himself as a supposedly irresistible seducer, and in an intellectual content straight out of the novelistic *kitsch* of Central Europe. The slowness, heaviness, mindlessness of this temple of unnaturalness through which man passes as through a forest of clichés defies description. Stroheim was an underprivileged Jew, clearly consumed with love-hate for the decadent splendors of *kaiserliche und königliche* Vienna, but he was no Schnitzler, nor even a Stefan Zweig—only an embittered sentimentalist with delusions of satirical grandeur.

Of Human Bondage is a totally obtuse concoction, serving only to demonstrate how untalented an actress Bette Davis was before she perfected those camp mannerisms that, while not heightening her artistic stature, did endear her to legions of miscellaneous innocents and misogynous inverts. *Les Vampires,* six-and-a-half hours' worth of a 1915 crime serial, is a pile of unmitigated trash, showing once again how yesterday's offal is transubstantiated into today's idolized camp. These three films (*The Wedding March* is not a little campy, too) added a queerly noxious odor to the otherwise merely stale one of the Festival.

From Sweden came Bo Widerberg's *Raven's End,* a well-meaning but old-fashioned and leaden-footed effort about a young writer's struggle to transcend the poverty and benightedness of his environment, in which an occasional neatly directed scene and two good performances hardly compensate for the glutinous mass of the whole. Poland also disappointed us with two films by Jerzy Skolimowski, from whom one opus would have been rather more than enough. Although Skolimowski has contributed to noteworthy films by Wajda and Polanski, here, as writer, director, and star, his work proved modishly rebellious, disconnected, and pointless. In the earlier of his two films, *Rysopis,* one could at least detect a certain panache; the second, *Walkover,* seemed like a giant dolly-shot exhibiting Skolimowski's artistic range from running very fast to slinking very slowly indeed.

It is the Czechs who emerge as the Pyrrhic victors of the Festival. *The Shop on Main Street* is overlong, derivative, ploddingly directed (except for an eruptive drunken dinner party), and ends with a final vision that is embarrassingly bad. However, its subject matter is genuinely moving and treated with a measure of restraint, its performances are authentic, and it is so imbued with infectious good-will that one can forgive some—though not all—of its shortcomings. *Black Peter,* by Milos Forman, is a pleasing film about teen-agers and their problems with parents, jobs, and one another; the acting and direction are engagingly spontaneous, and if it were not for a few *longueurs* and a sequence or two in which the improvisation (or script-writing) becomes silly, this would be a thoroughly satisfying minor effort, affably combining traditional techniques with *cinéma-vérité*.

James Ivory, an American who lives in India, offered his second film, *Shakespeare Wallah,* in which a basically interesting situation is inadequately explored. The disintegration of a third-rate English Shakespearean company that finds it increasingly harder to tour an India no longer responsive to crumbs from the British table allows for some penetrating and poignant observations, here only sketchily and spasmodically delivered. Instead, we are surfeited with a pasteboard love story, superficially conceived and amateurishly acted. The photography is humdrum and the sound, both in its recording and its dubbing, substandard.

Canada's *Caressed,* about the sexual entanglements of high school kids, is about as ragged and oafish a little film as ever came out of a cultural lag. Lawrence Kent, responsible for stuffing banality into the mouths of the sticks involved, and for falteringly shuffling them around, should at best be represented at a Southern Saskatchewan Film Festival. Equally objectionable and infinitely more pretentious was the German film (by Jean-Marie Straub, a young Franco-German), *Unreconciled,* a harebrained attempt to apply the techniques of the *nouveau roman* and Brechtian alienation to film and Heinrich Böll (on whose perfectly sane *Billards at Half Past Nine* this farrago is based), where they do not belong. The attempt to tell several stories in disjointed snippets, flaunting even the most impressionistic time sequence, and keeping the actors' faces and voices unremittingly blank, is bound to be stillborn.

France, even without Godard, failed to please. Actually, *Six in Paris* contains among its half dozen episodes by six graduates of the *Cahiers du Cinéma* one by —yes—Godard, scarcely the worst. But all the segments are cheap in conception and erratic in execution, as deficient in texture as in purpose. The whole venture, down to the garish color photography, is singularly unprofessional. Georges Franju's *Thomas the Impostor,* based on one of Cocteau's least filmable works (a youthful novella in the manner of Radiguet, blending patches of prose poetry with a kind of perversely telegraphic concision in the narration, and doing it less well than Radiguet) was, like other films of Franju, precise, evocative, even powerful in some of its images and details, but lacked a solid spine and produced no appreciable impact as a whole.

I did not see a bill of two TV films, one by Chris Marker, for whom I have little use, and one about Malcolm Muggeridge, for whom I have hardly more, and his return to India, which I was not aware that he had left. The American disaster, *Mickey One,* I shall report on later, if at all. There was also a triple bill of Buster Keaton films. The first, a travelogue for the Canadian Railroads, which should be shown only in tourist offices; the second, *Seven Chances* (1925), about six chances too long, but with a rousing final sequence in which Keaton is chased simultaneously by a horde of termagants and a malevolent rockslide. The last, mistitled *Film,* might with equal right have been called *Upanishad, Lobotomy,* or *Ginger Snaps;* made by Alan Schneider from a scenario by Beckett, it was a rickety but ultrapretentious superstructure erected over a gaping hole. Beckett really should refrain from supplying his middlebrow detractors with so perfect a weapon against himself, and one that is so irresistibly tempting even to his defenders.

A young Italian director, Marco Bellocchio, made his debut with *Between Two Worlds,* a murky, often muddled and always jagged, attempt at combining Chekhovian family and social disintegration with the violence of the horror film and New Wave techniques. It is an unattractive work, often quite unconvincing, but not without a certain directorial flair peeping through in places. The photography, too, has some merit, and two or three of the youthful performers exhibit promising talent.

Three so-called masters of the cinema, Visconti, Dreyer, and Satyajit Ray, were represented by films that,

if there are any doubts left about their makers' basic
fallibility, should surely dispel them. Since all three of
these goodies are certain to be commercially released, I
will now say only that Ray's *Charulata* and Dreyer's *Ger-
trud* are unutterably boring: based on second-rate literary
works to which they add no cinematic dimensions, they
merely drag themselves from verbal to visual platitudes
and back again. As for Visconti's *Sandra,* it is yet another
of his elaborately dressed store windows, its denizens, ap-
propriately, dummies. Everything here is artificial, attitudinizing, mawkish, and horribly hollow; Visconti is
what Gerald Weales has called Edward Albee—a juggler
without balls.

That leaves Kurosawa's *Red Beard,* a three-hour excur-
sion into nineteenth-century hospital soap opera; a mediocre enough script, but beautifully directed and flawlessly
acted. When, toward the end, two children, with their
lancingly truthful beings, take over the screen, soap begins
to look like marble—perhaps becomes marble—and the
New York Film Carnival begins to look like a Festival.

Among the short subjects, two cartoons, the American
Enter Hamlet and the German *A,* along with the French
live-action comedy *La Cloche,* deserve hearty praise; one
or two others might also pass muster. An Irish documentary, *Yeats Country,* with the most magnificent color
photography since *Red Desert,* was a Lucullian feast for
the eye, and ptomaine poisoning for the ear. Two
American shorts, *The Longest Bridge* and *Fist Fight,*
were, respectively, about as inane and as aggressively obnoxious as a short—or a long—can get. Robert Breer, who
squiggled or jiggled the latter, should return to the Underground Cinema, whence he crawled.

If the Festival served no other purpose, it accomplished
one thing at least: those of us who have gone around
glibly assuming that film is the one unquestionably fertile
and vital art of our time, were given upward of a score of
sharp, stinging reprimands across the knuckles. Then,
again, it might be mostly a question of management. Just
as it was necessary for the first theatrical duumvirate at

Lincoln Center to topple before meaningful things could happen, the removal of the present cinematic duumvirs may be the prerequisite for decent film fare. Judging from Roud's and Vogel's program notes and the mentalities they betoken, one surmises there must be a pair of press agents' niches waiting somewhere in which the directors should feel at home.

QUINTET IN THREE FLATS

One of the greatest problems of art—perhaps the greatest—is that truth is not beauty, beauty not truth. Nor is that all we need to know. The artist must find a way of bringing these two, if not inimical at least alien, concepts into a temporary liaison, lasting, let us say, the length of a film. In the case of *To Die in Madrid,* the dilemma was whether to try to tell every last ugly political and human truth, and have a shattering documentary but not a work of art; or whether to edit and editorialize, select and simplify in such a way as to have an eloquent elegy, beautiful but not the whole bloody and bloodying truth. It is to the immense credit of Frédéric Rossif that he has come as close to the all but impossible union as it is given to anyone approaching it not on the wings of fiction but on the feet of factual evidence.

Into his eighty-five-minute documentary, Rossif has striven to compress not all that *needs* to be said about the Spanish Civil War—for that would take either very much more time, or very much less—but all that *can* be said within the span of a remote spectator's endurance. And at one sitting we can take only so much horror, only so much heroism. Yet the Spanish Civil War was a supreme example of both; it was the rare case of a war in which right and wrong were clearly defined, yet in which, no less clearly, one could see the frequent wrongness of right as well as the occasional rightness of wrong. And as if that were not enough for Rossif to cope with, there was the additional burden of having to depend on available film footage, a limitation no Hemingway or Malraux had to contend with.

What Rossif and his text-writer, Madeleine Chapsal, have done is to look for the emblematic, the typical, the suggestive; to adhere, as much as possible, to a rhythm and variety that mitigate the monotony of utter gloom; and to fill in with narration whatever is not recorded on film. This last often proves a virtue born of necessity: where specific images have to stand in for larger verities, or were generalized views of landscapes, faces, fighting have to comment on a particular place, person, or deed, the double focus, tactfully managed, produces not blurring but breadth. The shifts are stirring: from famous people to anonymous ones, from events ensconced in history books to others denied any memorial.

The commentary, I gather, has proved too laconic for some who have already forgotten or never learned about this war; but that is the fault of human nature, not of Rossif and Chapsal. There is, however, one, and only one, more serious shortcoming. By this I do not mean that, despite a valiant determination to be fair to both sides, the sympathies of the film-makers win out. That seems to me inevitable and, in this case, right. What is not right is that the hideous infighting among the various Leftist factions and the sinister role of Moscow are not given their ghastly due. I was also a little troubled by cuts in the film, or in the English translation: the moving passages in the French text about Antonio Machado and his mother, and about the death of that other remarkable poet, Miguel Hernandez, were omitted.

Still, these are minor matters. It is indicative of the high merit of this movie that the additional footage—views of the Spanish land, many of them exquisitely evocative silhouettes—and the restrainedly mourning guitar score by Maurice Jarre achieve the same tragic intensity and control as the rest of the work. We leave the theatre with the frightening awareness that we live in a world, in a history, without justice. *To Die in Madrid* is not merely a film to be seen; it is a film to be memorized.

The Hill, also about war, marks a considerable step ahead in the development of Sidney Lumet. I have never before been impressed by this director's attempts to impress me, the moviegoer, with his artistic effects or significant statements, but much about *The Hill* comes off. This is a story of the unvarying degree of brutality to which prisoners of different degrees of culpability are subjected in a British military prison in Africa during World War II. Some of the paroxystic starkness of this protest against the military mentality may be due to the influence of that corrosive play, *The Brig*; some of the scenes in the cell block reminded me of *Shoeshine*. But much here is Lumet's own, and relatively free from the artsiness and heavy-handedness of his previous endeavors. It is unfortunate that, toward the end of the film, the rebellion of the Negro soldier, though gargantuanly comic, must strain the credulity of even the most credulous. The performances, however, are strong and flavorsome, and Sean Connery somehow manages to hold his own among a band of genuine professionals. At times, there is no escaping the feeling of *déjà vu,* and still less that of *déjà entendu,* but, on the whole, *The Hill* commands our interest and respect, though not, I suppose, our love.

A film that raises one of those doggedly haunting questions—should an artist produce mere entertainments?—is Roman Polanski's *Repulsion*. This is an intelligently made horror film about a psychotic girl whose fear of sex and hatred of men (to whom, however, she is irresistible) drive her into committing two murders before becoming engulfed by raving madness. Now, as a serious study of the causes of aberration, the film does not rise above the level of barbershop Freudianizing; even as a portrait of a cracking mind, *Repulsion* is superficial—say, on the level of *Darling*'s investigation of the psyche of a cocotte. But as a horror story, a genre for which I have little use, it seems to me entirely successful, because Polanski, the

maker of *Knife in the Water* and some excellent shorts, is
not the usual hack who turns out such films, but an artist
gone slumming.

Polanski has stated publicly that to him a film is a film,
and that its subject or category cannot make it more or
less desirable to him. In short, that there is not one kind of
film that is art and another that isn't; only that there are
good films and bad films. This, alas, is the same blunted
argument that one hears being resharpened for Simenon or
Lenny Bruce, for Pop artists or jazz musicians, meant to
prove that they are first-rate artistic creators. We are also
told that *Repulsion* was the only kind of film for which
Polanski could raise the money. In that case, there is some
excuse for his making it. There is none for his taking it
seriously.

As an entertainment of a macabre sort, though, *Repulsion* succeeds handily, if one overlooks a sort of *mélange
des genres,* which turns the unreal into the surreal. Still,
under Polanski's leisurely but sure direction, even
Catherine Deneuve gives something not unlike a performance, and the very garden of a convent adjoining the
site of the crimes manages to take on a cunningly
pseudosymbolic significance.

Opera on film is, at best, a frugal blessing. The more epic,
eccentric, or exotic the opera, the more it is likely to find a
moderately comfortable temporary home on screen; the
operas I can best visualize on film are things like *The
Huguenots* on the one hand, or *Aniara* on the other. Not
that I have a particular wish to see either. But *La
Bohème,* now filmed in the Karajan-Zeffirelli-La Scala
production, is of all things, a realistic opera—that is, if a
certain amount of *verismo* in the setting and a surfeit of
pathos in the story can be said to constitute realism.
Nevertheless, the moment that the real-looking snow that
is supposed to aggravate a very real lung condition proceeds to be nonmelting and inducive only of coughs
carefully spaced for the dramatic punctuation of an aria,

we are reduced to an equally nonmelting state. Again, it is unnerving when the starving artists in a garret are revealed in the most perfectly porcine rotundity; it is disturbing when the reputedly enchanting Mirella Freni, as Mimi, looks merely like a somewhat younger Leontyne Price, and looks it not from the safe distance of the stage, but from the mercilessly telltale proximity of the screen.

The point is that opera is not so exclusively aural an art form as purists might wish and myopics imagine. But even musically speaking, I found my enjoyment continually encroached on by the electronics: the sound was unnaturally loud, excessively harsh, and often did not correspond in volume or provenance to the position of the singer in the image, the filming and sound recording having been done separately and in different places—an opera house and a studio.

All this is particularly sad since Mirella Freni is, deducibly, an excellent singer, and, visibly, a fine actress, and Gianni Raimondi's Rodolfo was only a tone's throw from her Mimi. The others were fair to slightly overcast, but Rolando Panerai's Marcello, though vocally acceptable, was all ham. Karajan's *tempi* seemed faster at times than necessary, cramping some of the vocal climaxes. As for Franco Zeffirelli's staging (it is unclear whether he also directed the filming), it was adequately operatic but insufficiently filmic. This screen version of *La Bohème* can compete neither with a superior stage production, nor with a felicitous recording. In fact, it reduces the opera to the level of its libretto, and that is pretty dreadful.

Seventeen years after the fact, we were served up Visconti's early neorealist triumph, *La terra trema,* about the exploitation and disintegration of a family of Sicilian fishermen. There are a few moving passages in this very long film, clumsily written and cumbersomely acted by a cast of full-fledged nonprofessionals. The photography has its unassuming merits, but it is not helped by the ugliness of Sicilian faces surpassed only by the garishness of

Sicilian speech. Though *La terra trema* is superior to Visconti's later, stiflingly chic, vacuities, I agree with the remark of an actor friend: "Visconti has managed to pass from artlessness to artifice without ever touching art."

WHEREFORE ART THOU, JULIET?

If it were just for a handful of silver, just for a riband to stick in his coat, we could forgive Fellini that he left us. Where money is the cause of defection, it may yet, in time, be the source of liberation. And when a once-struggling artist sells out, we view it with a measure of indulgence, as we would a hungry man's stealing a loaf of bread from Huntington Hartford. But *Juliet of the Spirits* is a dreadful film: a little less arrogant, but no less vacuous and even tawdrier than *8½*. Fellini, alas, has sold out not for lucre, which he acquired, but for intellect, which cannot be commandeered.

Federico Fellini is a natural, and why not? Hard-core intellect is not one of the artist's requisites: Yeats never had it, and would have been better off not presuming that he did; Dr. Johnson had it, and *Rasselas* and *Irene* show how little it availed him as an artist. *I Vitelloni* is a masterpiece, one of the ten or twelve great films ever made; *The White Sheik,* on a smaller scale, is scarcely less admirable. All of Fellini's films from *Variety Lights* to *La Dolce Vita* contain strokes of genius that, so far, only about seven or eight film-makers have equaled. But somewhere in the middle of *La Dolce Vita* Fellini had to go and discover intellect with a capital, nay, a monolithic I, and the harm, the possibly irreparable harm, was done. Thus fell Fellini.

The history of this downfall and its various symptoms I have already described in my review of *8½*. And whatever went for that film goes double for *Juliet of the Spirits,* Fellini's *17.* It has been correctly observed that *Juliet* is a woman's *8½.* More precisely, as *8½* was Fellini's aggrandized autobiography, so *Juliet* is his embellished telling of his wife's own story—as it were, his *Autobiography of Alice B. Toklas.* Now there is an immediate and aggressive bit of bad taste in filming your wife's story, having her play herself in it, and appending the moral that if her husband cheats on her, she must endure it stoically—indeed, find in her acceptance of it her own liberation!

But before we get to the superabundance of bad taste, let us recapitulate the exiguous plot. Giulietta, a plain little upper-middle-class wife, feels obscurely that her husband is slipping away from her. Since her Catholic childhood, she has been having visions, or, more exactly, daydreams, in many of which she identifies herself with both a martyred saint whom she portrayed in a school pageant, and a classmate who drowned herself at fifteen out of unhappy love. More recently, she has been dabbling in spiritism and consulting mediums and gurus in the hope of finding what one of the spirit voices proclaims, *"amore per tutti,"* including herself. Giulietta is also the battleground of three family influences: memories of her grandfather, a free-thinking Garibaldian activist, who indignantly stopped the school play midway through his granddaughter's flaming ascent to heaven, and who himself flew off in a rickety biplane with a racy circus bareback rider; her beautiful, domineering, icily contemptuous mother; and her two sisters—one sexy, one elegant—whom the dumpy Giulietta cannot begin to approximate.

There are other influences: girl friends who propel her toward occultism or sexuality, an ebullient courtesan next door who stages slow-motion orgies of senescent appetites, an American lady-psychiatrist who urges Giulietta to leave her husband, and a Spanish business associate of her husband's who spouts absurd pseudopoetry in praise of what he takes to be her marital bliss.

Guilietta loves her husband desperately, amorphous a figure though he be, and only when the garish people from a detective agency confront her with incontrovertible evidence of his infidelity does she attempt to act. But her actions fail: She succeeds neither in becoming unfaithful herself at a neighborly orgy, nor in talking her husband or his mistress out of going on a trip together. She does, however, have a final vision or dream in which she rejects her mother's authority, unties her little-girl self from the blazing gridiron, and thus, presumably, frees herself from both earthly and spiritual authority. She walks out into the woods surrounding her villa; the troublesome visions have left her; she has become a free woman—heaven knows why, how, or to what purpose.

This précis does not begin to do justice to the disjointedness, irrelevancies, pretensions, and gaudiness of the film. Thus the various séances, voices, visions, consultations with an androgynous Oriental clairvoyant fail to illuminate Giulietta's or anyone else's situation; once again, Fellini is simply carried away with the visual and satirical possibilities of an ambience, and digresses *con amore*. But the tone is uncertain: The hermetic hermaphrodite is clearly a fraud, yet predicts accurately words to be spoken that evening by the Spanish visitor. Again, the lengthy episodes with the neighboring cocotte add almost nothing to our understanding of anything at all; they merely create a milieu with overtones of everything from Sade and *Flaming Creatures* (part of which Felini has seen) to accounts of Hugh Hefner's Chicago Xanadu, and enable the costume and set designer to have the kind of orgiastic fun no one on screen or in the audience is having. Relationships that might be significant, such as little Giulietta's to her grandfather and her mother, are not developed, but used as convenient and woefully unconvincing counters.

The central problem of the marriage itself is never gone into. Neither what made the rather dapper husband (who looks like a smoother version of F. F.) marry this unalluring woodchuck of a wife, nor what he really wants from her now, is made clear. Guilietta's visions are supposed to comment on her marital and mental state, but they consist of comic-strip figures (in New York, Fellini called on the publisher of Captain Marvel comic books) and pop-art props (he also visited Claes Oldenburg in his studio) that remain luridly opaque. The scenes at the detective agency have a certain zest to them, but the husband's relationship with the other woman, as it emerges from films, slides, and tapes, chiefly provides an excuse for a little tangential satire and a few bravura effects, as when the rising wife's shadow falls on the screen within a screen displaying the husband's gambols with his mistress. The sanctimonious head of the detective agency is always shown disguised as a priest, but whether this is meant to be a comment on religion, Catholicism, or the clergy is anybody's guess. Sensuality and spiritualism are, apparently, ridiculed equally as possible solutions, yet Fellini cannot refrain from drenching them with what looks like a genuinely felt, albeit sophomoric, relish and glamor. Worst of all is the final cop-out, when, with just one dream, Giulietta manages to free herself, presto magico, from a lifetime's guilts and fears.

In defending *8½* against my attack, Dwight Macdonald argued in *Esquire* that it is not necessary for an artist to resolve problems as long as he states them properly; that, in fact, some of the greatest artists never supplied answers. All very true, but the question is how important is the problem to which the artist addresses himself, how acutely does he set forth (if he is dealing with a dramatic medium) the alternative solutions, and how much light does he shed along the way on the human condition. Besides, behind the unstated answers, there should be a set of values, all the more compelling for remaining implicit. And there is the matter of efficient control of the form. On most of these counts Fellini failed egregiously in *8½*, and again, in the present film. To begin with, Giulietta is just too sketchy and lame a figure to make us care about her; and Giulietta Masina who, when she was younger, was capable of touching, though limited, enactments of low-life characters (in *The White Sheik, La Strada, Cabiria*) has, with age, become too unprepossessingly ordinary; furthermore, her expressionistic miming is appropriate to wandering waifs, but not to wealthy, middle-aged wives.

There are those who have defended *Juliet of the Spirits* for its sheer beauty, or vitality, or eroticism. As for the beauty, Gianni di Venanzo is a magnificent cinematographer and Piero Gherardi is one of the master costume and set designers. But where the emphasis is all on glossiness and chic, the more you succeed, the more you fail; what the film aesthetically adds up to is the incestuous marriage of *Vogue* and *Harper's Bazaar*. The colors are brilliant, precise, and tasteless—it matters little whether intentionally or not; the coloristic revel can best be described as The House of Revlon Rides Again.

As concerns the vitality, yes, Ruggiero Mastroianni is a superb editor, and the cutting, most saliently in the bustling opening scene, does create a bogus animation, as do also the clever camera set-ups. But what good is vitality where there is no life? Can a dose of benzedrine turn a bony, narcissistic fashion model into a great lover? Which brings us to the eroticism: Except for a brief shot of two young bucks being drawn up in a basket into a tree house by a strutting, seminude strumpet—the camera angled upward and the two heads rising toward the proudly jutting woman's crotch—which has some grit to it, and sexuality is of the onanistic schoolboy, or *Playboy*, variety.

Among the performers, only Caterina Boratto, as the mother, and Valentina Cortese, as an addlepated friend, make an impression. Even Fellini's last stronghold, the performances he was able to elicit, the penetration of life that he could accomplish through them, has crumbled. Fellini's lens, "*cette prunelle autant que l'océan profonde,*" as Victor Hugo, in a particularly visionary moment, foresaw it, has dwindled to a pool: at best a fashionable swimming pool; at worst, a cesspool. It is heartbreaking to listen to Fellini discoursing on the new sensibility, the new dispensation, his latest films have heralded. If it is indeed a new dispensation, it seems eminently dispensable.

SIX

NOTES TOWARD A DEFINITION OF
POP CULTURE

In *Thunderball,* the latest of the James Bond films, Bond
rescues two atom bombs from the hands of murderous
bomb-nappers; makes out, explicitly or implicitly, with
five beauties, usually in aqueous settings—the beach, a
shower-room, an underwater coral reef; has one of his
lovelies, as it were, shot out from under him; dispatches
more villains than I could count on fingers and toes; and
makes use of an array of prodigious weapons and devices,
some already invented, and others that science has been
waiting for the Bond scriptwriters to supply. *Thunderball*
begins and ends with Bond zooming through the air by
means of two entirely different gadgets, the true heir of
Superman; the rest of the time, again helped by a variety
of props, he is torpedoing around underwater, a veritable
Superfish, perfectly in keeping with the superficiality of it
all.

The screenplay stands on tiptoe at the outermost edge

of the suggestive and gazes yearningly down into the obscene; the only thing that prevents it from leaping is the still, small voice of conscience whispering, "Mightn't we lose money?" It is hard to say which is more ruthless in *Thunderball,* the mayhem or the sex. A typical amatory exchange runs, Girl: "What sharp little eyes you've got!"—Bond: "Wait till you get to my teeth." But the archetypal situation occurs on the dance floor of a night club, when Bond uses the beautiful villainess he has just had sex with as a shield against her accomplices' bullets, then seats her body at some unsuspecting revelers' table and remarks, "D'you mind if my friend sits this one out? She's just dead." Sex, murder, and sadistic humor triangulate the surface of the Bond world, and surface is all it has. This is not meant, however, to designate *Thunderball* a dangerous influence; probably no more people incur damnation through James Bond than work out their salvation through Louisa May Alcott.

Terence Young's direction is quicker than the eye and, therefore, beyond criticism. The performers are only around long enough to be judged by their looks, and I can report that the women are opulent, the villains ghastly, and Sean Connery capable of sustaining the same expression indefinitely, even underwater, where the face is that of a double.

Of course, we learn that the three previous Bond films have sold more than 100 million tickets, and 100 million ticket-holders, presumably, can't be wrong. But the fact is that the Bond series, dubious as it was from the outset, is getting progressively worse. Anything that depends merely on exaggeration must, if it is to continue beyond one shot, pull off ever bigger exaggerations, and the Bond films are now exaggerating themselves into a corner. Gadgets, women, and quaintly arrived-at corpses succeed one another at such vertiginous speed and in such dumbfounding quantity that the viewer, unless he happens to be a graduate of Dr. Pavlov's famous school for dogs, has barely the time to produce a response. As Richard Maibaum, the chief scenarist, proudly proclaimed, Bond is the universal wish fulfillment, which is yet again as far beyond mere old-fashioned escapism as escape is beyond reality.

However, even wish fulfillment, which is a kind of dream, must submit to the laws governing dreams. When the dream becomes too much for him, the dreamer awakes. When the wish fulfillment is put on too thick, the wisher, likewise, wakens—unless his sensibilities are so dulled that they require continual bombardment. And from the reaction of the majority of the preview audience, I am inclined to think that the question is not can 100 million ticket-holders be wrong, but can 100 million insensibilities be right?

A further trouble with this kind of exaggeration is that while it stimulates parodies, it also, in order to keep surpassing itself, ends up being indistinguishable from those parodies. There has been a slew of Bond take-offs lately, the most recent being *Our Man Flint,* which contains two or three scenes that have almost identical counterparts in *Thunderball,* though the parodists could not possibly have seen that newest Bond caper. The result is fatal to both the parody and the thing parodied—the one becomes ridiculous, the other ceases to be funny.

Sometimes, though, a film does not seem to know itself whether it wants to be wish fulfillment, parody, persiflage, satire, or what? This is the case with *The Tenth Victim,* Joe Levine's current attempt to trim our Christmas tree with an Italian sparkler. His previous Christmas specials have been Loren-Mastroianni vehicles; this time, Sophia Loren is replaced by Ursula Andress (the name has always seemed a spoonerism to me), and oh, the difference to us!

Altogether, *The Tenth Victim* features a curious lineup. Among its four scenarists are Ennio Flaiano, the "intellectual" half of Fellini's principal scriptwriting duo (Tullio Pinelli being the "earthy" half), and Tonino Guerra, who is Antonioni's main scenarist. The editor, Ruggiero Mastroianni, is especially associated with Fellini and Monicelli; the set designer, Piero Poletti, is Antonioni's man; the cinematographer, Gianni di Venanzo, has worked for both Fellini and Antonioni. And, sure enough, the film is a mixed bag.

The Tenth Victim takes place in the future, when war has been superseded by something called The Great Hunt, an organization in which warlike individuals from all over the world alternate as hunters and victims—either of whom can legally kill the other—to the vicarious satisfaction of the rest of humanity. When a member of The Great Hunt has bagged ten scalps, he can retire to a life of honor and riches. Needless to say, owing to the cleverness of the members—and to titillate the moviegoer—the mode of these slayings has to be refined to a point of sinister subtlety that would have left the Borgias at the starting post. Probably the most celebrated of these demises will be that of an Oriental killer who pursues his appointed victim, Ursula Andress, into the Masoch Club (!), where she performs a mildly sadistic dance number almost naked, and thus ostensibly harmless, only to shoot her enraptured hunter with her metal brassiere, which is really a double-barreled, or double-breasted, gun, dispensing mammary justice.

Now the locus of *The Tenth Victim* is somewhere between *Brave New World* and *Alphaville,* between *1984* and *Thunderball,* and, to make matters shakier, it won't stand still, but shuttles back and forth among all four. Characteristic of the prevailing confusion is the use of pop art throughout: in the décor, the clothes, the music even; amusing as this sometimes is, it is never clear whether we are supposed to laugh at it or with it. Too bad, for here was a chance at another *Dr. Strangelove*; indeed, at a few, a very few, points some valid and funny satire on our own age is achieved—yet how much more of it there could have been under the immunity granted by couching the action in the next century.

Instead, most of the picture reduces itself to Godardian chases and gun duels that are supposed to be endearingly inept, or to slightly travestied Bondian gadgetry. Among the gadgets, the most engaging is a kind of computer turned pet, a mechanical animal that can be programmed to infinite fidelity as well as to carrying concealed guns, and that looks like a cross between a dog and a bug. One would be tempted to call it a "dug" or a "bog" if, in the vicinity of Miss Andress' bust and the script's *longueurs,* this might not give rise to misunderstandings.

Some of the technical aspects of the film, no less than its technological ones, show considerable expertise, and there is particular hope for the director, Elio Petri. But when one thinks of the number of gifted men who have labored to produce this wobbly jape, one is struck by the fact that, of all the arts, film can be the greatest waster of talents.

There is one thing, though, that all these films have in common, no matter on what level of pseudoseriousness and proto-funniness they operate. And that is, regrettably, their scornful dismissal of love. In the older escapist fare, love was the sunset-colored panacea, the supreme reward of the hero, the last stop on the road to romance. In their pitiful way, these films did at least make a plea for quality over quantity in man-woman relationships. Once that standard is unconditionally reversed, not only love becomes meaningless, but even sexuality escalates itself out of being a refined pleasure into becoming a production-line opiate. I repeat, I do not think that film trash can seriously affect our lives, but it may be that even the most unreal films reflect a nascent historic reality. In that case, *sauve qui peut.*

TWO FROM BELOW

In Kenneth Anger's *Scorpio Rising,* the color photography is perfectly acceptable, and the pop songs on the soundtrack are fully audible. For the technique of an underground film to scale such heights of adequacy is unusual indeed. The subject matter is less surprising: the motorcycle cult—bright chrome, black leather, blonde boys, sadistic homosexuality, and no plot.

The beginning is sober enough: motorcycles are being worked on or polished with rapt solicitude by stolidly dedicated youths, while the soundtrack bleats out "Fools Rush In"—this might be wry social comment. But presently the boys gird their loins: male nudities, lovingly dwelt on, are enveloped, in careful, fetishistic ritual, by tight jeans and bulging jackets; arrogantly studded belts are redundantly topped off with sinister chains; leather bands are coiled ominously around wrists. The soundtrack croons with campy transvestite yearning, "She wore blue velvet . . ." A leather boy gets up from a large cone-shaped highway marker; another youth handles a huge flashlight in front of his crotch. No more detachment: the atmosphere is sultrily pederastic.

One sequence shows the cyclist at home. As in a Dutch genre painting, we linger fondly over an interior complete with such *objets d'art* as Jimmy Dean photographs, "No Parking" signs (stolen), a pinned-up discharge from the Marine Corps (honorable), a skeleton in black hood and cape, a noose, rings with ruby-eyed skulls on them, an Al Capp comic strip that translates the Freudian vision into lower moronic, and a tabloid headline reading "CYCLE HITS HOLE AND KILLS TWO," the fittingly monosyllabic epitaph for heroes of our time. The television is on, with Marlon Brando and his fellow delinquents in *The Wild One* careening across the screen within the screen: cycles within cycles, wheels within wheels, world without end. Or is this it?

The cyclist sequences are frequently intercut with something like bits from the 1927 *King of Kings,* in which Jesus looks subnormal and his burnoosed followers like Bedouin cutthroats. Thus when the cyclists, wearing garish masks and costumes—or nothing at all—pile into an orgy combining sodomy and sadism, we cut to Christ and the Apostles entering a house; as the boys torture one of their gang and the soundtrack features distorted screams, we suddenly see Christ watching with expression-less but sedulously unaverted face. At other times, Nazi rallies and Hitler's harangues are intercut with motorcycle hoodlums zooming about in devil masks and swastika armbands, or vandalizing a church by celebrating a black leather mass in it. The message is clear: Christ, Hitler, the Motorcycle—one cult is as good as the other, and today it's bikes, buggery, and bestiality.

As for Jonas Mekas's *The Brig*, it is a totally inept on-stage filming of Kenneth H. Brown's bitingly effective documentary play about a Marine stockade, as performed by The Living Theatre Company. The soundtrack has severe laryngitis, and the hand that held the camera Parkinson's disease. Mekas has declared that critics who accuse "the new film-maker of shaky camera work and bad technique" are "hopeless." With underground films like *The Brig* and *Scorpio Rising* rising above ground, what is there to be hope*ful* about?

KEEPING THE DOCTOR AWAY

David Lean's *Doctor Zhivago* does for snow what his *Lawrence of Arabia* did for sand. From blue, through white, to silver—baleful in storms, pristine in the moonlight, boding in time of war—the snow is decorative on a Moscow street (in suburban Madrid) and majestic on the Urals (in northern Finland). Under Lean's fastidious direction and for Fred Young's inspired camera, the snow waltzes like an intoxicated *corps de ballet,* forms little parasitic stalactites on a wandering man's moustache, cowers submissively under sibilant sleighs. It makes the blood of the Cossacks' victims look redder; shored against window panes, it frames and isolates the faces behind them more broodingly than mere glass could. It is present even in absence: the summer scenes, because of it, harbor a pang in their rapture. Soon, we feel, they too will be snowbound.

I wish something else about *Doctor Zhivago* were as beautiful as the snow. Well, most of the photography is, except for an occasional false note, as when Lara's face emerges from the corolla of a jonquil. At such a moment, the imagery is less indebted to Boris Pasternak than to that even better-loved poet, Walt Disney. But, for the rest of the time, one reacts to this film rather as G. K. Chesterton did to nocturnal Times Square: "What a glorious sight for someone who couldn't read!" What a movie this would be for someone who couldn't hear—and, if possible, think. Still, such an image from the film as that of two slanting red flags atop a moving train that reach out, like arms, to take possession of endlessly white lands, is, for primordial beauty no less than for its color symbolism, the equal of many a masterwork that has settled on a museum wall.

But let us begin at the beginning, with Pasternak's novel. I do not think it is anywhere near the masterpiece that a world hot for uncertainties from the land of arrogant self-assurance took it to be. It is not so much the chary characterizations that bother me, or the symbolically charged but arbitrary and tiresome coincidences, which would have it that hardly a character can appear after a certain point in the book without being someone from before, transmuted or merely transplanted—until the unexpected can no longer travel incognito. More bothersome are the dialogues, which, even when they are not reluctantly disguised monologues, turn into set pieces or arias. Most enervating is the fragmentariness, the decentralization, the rebarbative deviousness of it all—partly because this clandestine autobiography must serve as vehicle for contraband disclosure; partly because, as a lyric poet, Pasternak lacked the fiction writer's patience and respect for development and linkage; and mostly because so much of the novel is metaphoric, symbolic, anagogical while yet striving to be "realistic," that its texture cracks from self-contradiction. Even the central, proto-Christian resurrection motif rings more willed than true.

Although the reader may disagree with my evaluation of these elements in the book, he will have to concede that they are hardly calculated to make transposition onto film easy, or even possible. And what must be counted as the twin strengths of the novel—its exultant leaps into poetry and its tireless imaginative proliferation (in a letter to Pasternak, the already dying Rilke thanked him for "*was Sie in sich so wunderbar vermehrt haben,*" the "marvelous multiplication" that describes also this novel's economy)—cannot be readily transferred to the screen. For such copiousness, even a film of some 200 minutes is not capacious enough; and for images such as Pasternak distilled, having, as he said, "brilliance and unimperative quality" and "interchangeability," film has no equivalent: for the brilliance, yes; for unimperative interchangeability, no.

Edmund Wilson correctly notes about the book's principal characters: "The personalities of Yury and Larisa stream back into wider reaches, a realm in which their contours and features are lost, in which they become indefinables, unclassifiable poetic elements that can only be conveyed by imagery; and it is not only the imagery of these metaphors but their rhythms of recurrence, their alienations, their confluences and interfusions that express the real sense of *Zhivago.*" As excellent as this may be in poetry, so dubious is it in prose fiction, and so inconceivable on film—at least commercial film, as it is now practiced. When David Lean proposed to reduce this to a "highly personal love story" for which "the Revolution simply provides the canvas" (he must have meant "background" or "setting"; not even the most toweringly personal love story can be painted across an entire, huge, impersonal revolution), he had already missed every possible point. The love story is not highly personal, except in some of its details; it is exemplary, symbolic, mythopoetic—its actors, besides being individuals, are signposts of history, religion, ontology, and teleology. And the Revolution is not the décor but the eternal antagonist: the danger of coarsening, collectivizing, dehumanizing what must remain inviolably individual and intimate.

I do not know to what extent Robert Bolt, the scenarist, is to blame. His plays have ranged from poor (*Flowering Cherry*) to very able (*A Man for All Seasons*); his screenplay for *Lawrence of Arabia* took considerable liberties with history but remained artistically sound. Here, however, he is taking liberties with art. Thus the killing of an idealistic Red commissar of upper-class background by a mutinous faction of the proletarian soldiery, becomes in the film the murder of a Tzarist captain by populist deserters at the front. The fault of the commissar is, according to Pasternak, his St. Petersburg accent and high-pitched voice; according to Lean and Bolt, the captain is guilty of ruling-class slogans, "My country! And proud of it!" In both cases, the speaker is shot grotesquely in a barrel, but how the implications have been altered!

One more example will have to suffice. When Zhivago and Lara return to Varykino for their last, doomed idyll, the house they inhabit is merely deserted and sparsely furnished; parts of it, in fact, are quite tidy. In the film, they return to a house into which snow has fallen and in which ice has gathered, so that the interior is like something out of an Andersen fairy tale, or, more precisely, an earlier David Lean movie—Miss Haversham's cobweb-encrusted parlor in *Great Expectations*. Aside from the fact that such a snow palace would have to be roofless and uninhabitable, this is turning oppressive reality into mere Gothic romance.

But, it might be asked, what does the film accomplish independently, as film? Mostly melodramatic oversimplifications and the standard romantic pablum. The episode of Lara's attempted assassination of Komarovsky turns into arrant theatrics, with Komarovsky condescending to Yurii and belittling Lara like a perfect cad, and Pasha appearing as the gallant rescuer: a chance for acrid humor and social raillery deteriorates into a conventional *scène à faire*. Yurii's return to Moscow from the war instead of revealing small, ominous changes creeping up from everywhere, plants him in something rather like the last part of *Ninotchka:* a ludicrous pair of petty officials, male and female, ordering about a teeming houseful of socialized scarecrows, and joining with them in bullying the Zhivagos. And the bitterly splendid last thirteen days of Lara and Yurii at Varykino yield lines like, "We'd have got married and had a house and children . . . If we had children, Yurii, would you have liked a boy or a girl?"

The performances are less than outstanding. Julie Christie and Rod Steiger make the most flattened-out versions of Lara and Komarovsky, but Omar Sharif and Tom Courtenay cannot coax conviction out of this Yurii and Pasha. They don't, at that, make fools of themselves as do Alec Guinness and Ralph Richardson, as Yevgraf and Gromeko. Most disappointing of all is the Tonia of Geraldine Chaplin, who seems to have inherited only some of her mother's looks and none of her father's talent. The editing is not up to what we expect from a Lean film, and shows drastic departures from the shooting script, especially some Draconian cuts. A few incidents do come off, such as Zhivago's mistaking, on his terrible wintry foot journey back to Yuriatin, a family of frightened refugees for his own.

Maurice Jarre's music is usually his third-best when geared to the American market; in *Lawrence,* it was pulpy Tchaikovsky; here it is piddling Rimski-Korsakov, atwitter with balalaikas. That leaves us with the images. If none of Zhivago's artistic and metaphysical concerns come across anywhere in the film, something of Pasternak's poetry is caught in a rufous gleam hovering just above Lara's sleeping face at Varykino. As this ruddy glow defies the surrounding gloom of emerald and amethyst, as the sleeper smiles in a dream no more frail than reality, some approximation of one of Zhivago's moving stanzas is achieved (my translation is even more approximative):

> *But who are we and wherefrom*
> *If of all that the years begot*

Gossip alone survives
In the world where we are not?

A much more successful—though much less arduous—screen adaptation is that of *The Spy Who Came
in from the Cold*. Like the John Le Carré novel, the film
presents the world of espionage and counterespionage as,
to be sure, fiendishly and wisecrackingly clever, but also
drab, squalid, and fraught with a mortal danger lacking all
glamor: it strikes you dead in the dark, from behind,
without a peroration.

The film, departing from the novel in minor ways only,
questions whether it is possible to tolerate the traffic in
lives that spying and counterspying involve—particularly
the dastardly business of sacrificing one's own good men
to protect some swinish double agent whom expediency
places above all. It questions also the still less tolerable
business of using innocent bystanders as decoy ducks that,
however, get killed as very real ones. And just when one
can feel sympathy for an honest enemy, one must cause
his death for the sake of a monster with whom one finds
oneself allied.

The protagonist, Leamas, is burdened with a conscience
and a girl he cares for; when his bosses in British counterespionage destroy the girl and all but crush the conscience, he opts out and prefers to die. As Richard Burton
plays him, he has only two basic moods: a stolid, almost
impassive, agony; and a quivering, humane cynicism. But
by expert gradation or sudden change, Burton wrests such
a repertoire of shadings and shocks from the role, that he
turns in a master performance. Those pained eyes and
lips, that cantankerous voice, becoming very meaningful
to us, and very dear. As the girl, Claire Bloom exudes
youthful good-will and perilous naïveté; at film's end, she
ages before our eyes, and the sadness of bruised innocence
radiates from her final moments.

A large and excellent supporting cast, in which Oskar
Werner, George Voskovec, Peter Van Eyck, and Robert
Hardy especially distinguish themselves, manages to con-

vey much more than the brief and often one-dimensional parts would seem to permit. Martin Ritt has directed the crisp screenplay with restrained efficiency; even the occasional bravura process shot or tricky camera angle does not disrupt the seedy starkness. *The Spy Who Came in from the Cold* comes out of the cold of mere suspense into the warmth of concern.

A movie such as this one does, however, present one very serious problem: the problem of not being art. If you have not read the book, the details of the plot are a bit hard to follow, and the characters seem, though credible, a trifle skimpy. And you wonder if the whole thing isn't just a shade far-fetched. But you enjoy it none the less. If you have read the book, you are impressed by the general fidelity to the text, but the suspense is gone, and without suspense, what is left of a spy thriller? I went back to see part of the film a second time, and was still impressed by the performances and over-all conception, but it struck me that this was not the sort of thing to see more than once, and that even having read it beforehand may constitute a *déjà vu*.

Art is that which gets better with reexperiencing; nonart is what can be fully relished only once. It would be foolish to argue that there is no room for the perishable pleasure, the impermanent work. It would be slipshod not to evaluate it, too, according to its greater or lesser interest. But it would be wrong to make too much of it; it would be wrong to call it art.

PEARL THROWING FREE STYLE

Not long ago, Sir Tyrone Guthrie deplored Sir Laurence Olivier's wasting his energies on the British National Theatre, work that "could be done equally well by several other people, none of whom could play Othello, Macbeth, Lear, Faustus . . . which, at present, he has no time to think about." Soon thereafter, Sir Laurence found time to think about *Othello,* at any rate—to co-direct and play it at the National Theatre, without relinquishing the managerial reins. Sir Laurence seems actually to have had too much time to think: his Moor, though exceedingly black, is sicklied o'er with the pale cast of thought.

Before getting into the specifics of the movie version, let me discuss certain problems of the underlying stage production, which I caught two years ago at Chichester. Olivier and John Dexter, the co-directors, fell into three traps. First, they were influenced, as Dexter has declared, by F. R. Leavis' essay "Diabolic intellect and the Noble Hero, or The Sentimentalist's Othello," one of the master's shriller pieces, which, considering his talent for shrillness, is no mean piece of stridency. It is also not a little foolish.

Overreacting to Bradley's established interpretation of a super-humanely noble Othello and an arch-fiendish Iago, Leavis tried to reduce the Moor to a forceful, valiant, but far from magnificent or even maturely loving fellow, and Iago to a verminous, but hardly especially inspired, villain. According to Leavis, it takes Iago a ludicrously short time to undermine a supposedly immortal love, and Othello, in his quick collapse, is revealed as more bloated than great. If Bradley's view was indeed swooningly sentimental, Leavis' corrective is nonetheless worse than the offense. Fortunately, John Holloway, in *The Story of the Night,* makes mincemeat of Leavis' arguments, even to the point of catching the master out in some quite unscholarly sleight-of-hand, and restores, without going all the way back to Bradley, the play's dignity and magnitude.

The second trap, related to the first, was, I think, an attempt to play a classic in the modern way, that is, in the manner of Brecht or Beckett—if not, indeed, of Jan Kott —and, rather as in Peter Brook's recent *Lear,* to play down all heroic and romantic values. The third trap was the opportunity to capitalize rather meretriciously on contemporary racial problems, to make this Moor *plus ca-*

tholique que le pape, which is to say blacker than black, almost blue, so as to milk (if I may be allowed to mix my colors) Othello's *négritude* for all it is worth—or, rather, for all that it isn't.

Let it be said that Olivier plays this misconceived Othello spectacularly, in a way that is always a perverse joy to behold. The make-up (it took Olivier two hours each day to get into it) gives us a handsome jet-black Jamaican with incarnadined lips, palms, soles, and with a melismatic Calypso accent: What he does with the vowels A and O alone introduces an exotic marimba into Shakespeare's orchestration. But already he is in trouble: at moments when the poetry must swell, soar, or subtilize itself, Olivier is forced to abandon the accent.

Whenever remotely conceivable, the actor is barefoot, indulging in that swaying, lilting, almost prehensile walk of jungle-dwellers—which, too, must be jettisoned in scenes of courtly or tragic splendor. Again, he is the black man inconclusively converted to Christianity, and still prey to fetishistic impulses; around his neck hangs an oversize cross that he fondles or kisses on the slightest provocation—though he kisses with equal alacrity any number of tokens of the Doge's authority. When the stress finally becomes unbearable, he tears off the cross, and reverts to prostrations and abasements suggestive of Mohammedan ritual or voodoo. All this is fascinating, but diverst our attention from what the play is about, when it does not downright clash with it: The Othello solicitous for Desdemona's salvation ("I would not kill thy soul.") conflicts with the image of a regressive barbarian.

But contradictions of all kinds are common to this Othello who combines in himself the psychic geographies of Barbados, Aleppo, and Senegal. Thus, for example, after sanguinely referring to "men whose heads/ Do grow beneath their shoulders," Olivier suddenly and unaccountably waxes skeptical and looks at the Venetians with amused complicity, as if to say, "We know that such creatures don't exist." Or, upon discovering the bottomlessness of his tragic error, Othello, having jumped into bed with the dead Desdemona, passionately rocks back and forth with her body, and erotic overtones coupled with frenetic emphasis on blackness embracing blonde whiteness run riot—or should I say race riot? It is an awesome sight, but unmoving.

Here let us stop and state what ought to be a truism but—such is the power of capricious reinterpretation—may sound inflammatorily reactionary: *Othello* is a play about jealousy, about loving passion turned to hatred, about the ineffable fragility of goodness, intelligence, love. Desdemona is goodness, but how weak that is; Iago is intelligence, but how corruptible and corrupting that is; Othello is love, but, once its molecular structure has been disturbed, how like its opposite that is! True, these people are no Bradleyan saints and devils; but not even a host of thundering Leavises or rampaging liberals can turn this tragedy of love gone bitter into a drama of gullibility or of a noble savage victimized by white Venetian cunning. Granted, Shakespeare makes Othello a Moor, to add some precariousness to his prominence and make his downfall more credible, but to forfeit the emphasis on the pitiful morality of love "were such perdition/ As nothing else could match."

Actually the best Othello I remember seeing was the late Aimé Clariond's at—of all places—the Comédie Française about fifteen years ago. Clariond modeled himself on some archetypal Bedouin chieftain, a figure in whom prideful grace and cruel animality calmly cohabit; moreover, Clariond's schizophrenic voice, like a superb bell with a sinister crack in it, carried the split in Othello into his farthest-flung syllables. Which is not to say that Olivier's Othello is not impressive—as impressive as he is wrong.

The supporting cast does well enough, with three reservations: Frank Finlay's Iago is very good, if you can accept the Ancient as a clever little Cockney snake in the grass; Maggie Smith's Desdemona is fine, if you like your *Othello* with two Emilias in it, and can see this Venetian pearl as one of the horsier daughters of Albion, say, a field hockey coach at St. Trinian's; and Derek Jacobi's Cassio is just plain bad—priggish, doltish, and effete.

Now there are, curiously, some ways in which this filmed version of a stage play—usually anathema to sophisticated and demotic moviegoers alike—turns out to be superior to the stage production. On stage, Oliver dominated the proceedings to an uncanny extent; Finlay, whose elocution is a bit moss-overgrown anyway, tended to disappear altogether. Film, what with close-ups and recorded sound, acts as a leveler in this respect. Again, by transferring Jocelyn Herbert's sets to a movie studio, the production acquired a profitably increased acting area in which to stretch its legs; the linking together of scenes was also facilitated. Incidentally, the dominant color of this *Othello* is a kind of purplish brown, to be found in Venetian painting from Gentile Bellini to Carpaccio, which creates an atmosphere of appositely somber foreboding; it also, regrettably, tends to make Olivier's face merge with the décor. Much use is made of backlighting, presumably to create the illusion of sea and open skies around Cyprus without having to resort to backdrops, but the effect is only that of very theatrical backlighting.

There is value in the film's experimental poking around at the frontier where the realms of ·film, theatre, and television meet: three Panavision cameras were used with television-style editing of shots, and the whole venture was filmed in three weeks, incorporating much of the original stage blocking. However, one does become aware of the somewhat limited range of shots for the film director, Stuart Burge, to choose from, and the entire *mise en scène* seems, some of the time, to vacillate in a no-man's land between stage and screen. Certain features, like the crowd movements, seem too stagily conventionalized for film; others, like an unexpected and incongruous overhead shot, too cinematic for what is still largely photographed theatre. Geoffrey Unsworth, the photographer, has brought a refined discretion to his color work, though I wish he could have found a way around the shadow-play effects the backlighting often elicited.

No doubt about it, this is the best filmed *Othello* so far, vastly preferable to such a previous version as Orson Welles's, despite the exquisite Desdemona of Suzanne Cloutier. Indeed, as filmed Shakespeare, this *Othello* is surpassed only by Oliver's own *Henry V* and *Richard III*. Even so, with talent such as Olivier's and the British National Theatre's, what a chance was here for a definitive version of this tautest, swiftest, most concentrated of Shakespeare's major tragedies. The production, however, is "one whose hand,/ Like the base Indian, threw a pearl away/ Richer than all his tribe." Still, it is throwing away in the grand style. The thing is worth watching—not so much for the pearl as for the technique of the throwing hand.

LOVING EXPLORATION

There is cause for genuine, albeit temperate, rejoicing over the new Swedish film, *Dear John*. Here is a film that does not remind us of Strindberg or Bergman or Sucksdorff or Sjöberg—no offense meant to any of them, except that it is nice to come upon something unexpected. Swedish films have tended to be readily classifiable as paeans to the brief Nordic summer tremulous with pantheistic nature worship, studies in suicidal neurosis exacerbated by a lowering ambience, ponderous preachments creeping through a forest of symbols, or creaky frameworks for the display of programmatically wholesome nudity.

In the hands of a master three of these categories can be redeemed, but masters are few and have a way of slipping into self-parody, and, in any case, the new always augurs well when it is not merely a gimmick. In *Dear*

John, which Lars Magnus Lindgren adapted and directed from Olle Länsberg's novel, there is something that might, at first, smack of a gimmick. This is Resnais' Marienbad (or, if you prefer, Hiroshima) Strategy of breaking up the time sequence by suddenly introducing previously un-shown episodes from the past, or repeating previously shown ones, identically or somewhat altered, to suggest the characters' thoughts, recollections, or the modernity of one's cinematic technique. In *Dear John,* the intense simplicity of the story, verging on triviality, does not seem to require—and perhaps cannot even sustain—the weight of such complexities.

But in Lindgren's tactful handling, these premonitions and remembrances take on the quality of refrains or in-cremental repetition in a ballad, and what could be simpler than the story of a ballad? So here the story of how Anna, an unwed mother full of passion hemmed in by the proud choosiness her position demands, and John, captain and owner of a small merchant vessel and a man whose marriage was anything but smooth sailing, find a way toward each other—tentatively, gropingly, ex-uberantly, falteringly, and at last radiantly—is com-monplace enough. But it is also universal and, when told with respect for human idiosyncrasies, affectionate atten-tion to detail, words and images that eschew banality, it emerges as something spirited, tasty, and engagingly alive.

The film abounds in filmic values. Take, for example, its sensitivity to the time of day: time made tangible through changes of light and dark, fluctuations of the rhythm of life, modulations of moods. Here morning ex-plodes on the scene, with the hero performing ecstatic cabrioles on the way to a matutinal swim, the heroine visibly filling herself up with the fuel of freshly distilled sunlight, and her brother pronouncing with an authority the most confirmed noon riser could not question that "breakfast is the best meal of the day." As a Sunday out-ing begins, space opens up in all directions—even inward, into the hearts of a young mother, her delicious little daughter, and her tenderly avid would-be lover—to be gradually stuffed to bursting with human and animal activity at the Copenhagen Zoo. The child becomes the happy mediator between man's wariness and the naturalness of the beasts: A fateful gap is bridged as an elephant's trunk swoops down on a proffered carrot, and the successful imitation of a penguin takes on the vast dimensions of joy.

But Lindgren's direction is not only alert to time and space, it is capable also of dominating them. Thus he is not afraid of lingering for long, slow seconds over a sitting man's head looking out to sea from a promontory at nightfall, and, next to it, a woman's betrousered hips and thighs, erect and immobile. Perhaps this is symbolic: the man may be discovering, to his surprise, that life can hold more than escape into seafaring, and he may look away from the woman in his amazement at her having come to mean so much to him so quickly; in turn, those gibbous haunches may represent the woman's long-dormant physical desire awakening to incontrovertible intensity. Or the whole thing may be no more than a lovely pictorial composition: the woman's white garments still resisting the dark to which the man's face has already succumbed while only his fierce golden hair rides like a comet through the night. Rune Ericson photographs it sensuously, and the director stays with it, sunk into a rich, drowsy wordlessness.

Many are the scenes informed by inventiveness and delicacy of perception. Take the walk of the couple to the promontory, with the music gently arpeggiated, while the moon and its reflection in the sea spell out that inverted exclamation mark we cherish in the paintings of Edvard Munch, and the camera dollies in the opposite direction from the ambling couple until, in an extreme long shot, the figures dissolve into the darkening seascape. Equally effective is a comic montage of extreme close-ups of John brushing his teeth and a sailor's brush swabbing the deck; or the crossing of the sky above the lovers, now by brashly ejaculatory jet planes, now by yearningly honking wild geese.

Psychological observation is minute and exact: John running through a repertoire of critical faces as he scans his waistline in a mirror; listening analytically to the sounds of Anna preparing herself in the bathroom; freezing his private parts as he rummages, naked, in Anna's refrigerator; fiddling, embarrassed and indignant, with a box of chocolates for the girl who seems to have rejected him; Anna silently debating with herself whether to reprehend or respond to the nocturnal mating call of pebbles at her window pane; the friendly skirmish, during an embrace, of offensive male and defensive female hands on the battleground of a woman's body—the number of such intimately reverberating insights is legion. And the dialogue is commensurately intelligent. When, for example, in the quiescence between bouts of lovemaking, John casually hints at marriage, Anna protests, "You mustn't say that—you're not in me now"; to which John replies with touching plainness, "*You* mustn't say that."

Sex is handled with integrity and artistry in this film. Though it is omnipresent either implicitly or overtly, it is always relevant to the furthering of the plot and the unfurling of character, as well as subtly and elegantly depicted. The composition, for instance, of three diagonals parallelly crossing the image from upper left to lower right—Anna's thigh, John's head and chest, Anna's face—is memorably beautiful; so, too, is a female hand traveling up a male arm, the slow progress emblematic of all loving exploration. One is reminded of Godard's *The Married Woman*, except for the much greater air of spontaneity here. The dialogue is equally lightsome. When John is busy with the kitchen sink, Anna inquires from bed, "Are you washing him in cold water?" "No," John laughs, "just cleaning some beer glasses." Sex and domesticity are propitiously blended. When Anna asks the aroused John to dance, his ithyphallic embarrassment is implied by a look and a mere "I can't"; "It doesn't matter," she smiles and clings to him, assenting. The excitement of the discovery of erotic reciprocity is friskily conveyed. And not a word or picture too many.

As John, the mercurial Jarl Kulle is all generous volatility: his expression leaps into swaggering boyishness or hurtles into depths of manly feeling; his movements and inflections reveal, facet by facet, a manysided simplicity. In Christina Schollin's Anna, the tartly mettlesome peasant, the anxious, unfulfilled girl-woman, and the smilingly serene young mother merge into absolute believability. And the director is always unobtrusively there, driving the characterizations home. The lovers have their last coffee together under the tree on which their bathing suits are hung up to dry: the man's trunks are immobile, while the woman's suit, exposed to the wind, is flapping frantically, prefiguring her imminent flight.

What is it that nevertheless prevents the film from attaining full artistic stature? For the splendid parts fail to build a whole greater than their sum. Is it that the context of these lovers remains a bit too sketchy? Or is the dialogue ultimately a little too thin? Might it be that the spaciousness of a novel becomes too cramped in the narrower compass of a film? Or perhaps the idyll is simply too weary a craft to dodge the shoals of our skepticism. Still, *Dear John* is a film to feel along with in a state of blissful consanguinity.

Not much need be said about *The Group*. Mary McCarthy's novel was unreadable; the movie version is readable enough. Sidney Lumet's direction is pleasantly bouncy, except for his panning around the Group once or twice too often. Sidney Buchman's script is workmanlike. Yet the characters refuse to come alive; social and sexual problems, though not wholly evaded, have no more urgency than five-finger exercises; and the male figures—thanks, no doubt, to the author herself—are mere caricatures of good, bad, or silly guys. As evidence of the film's wavering courage, "yid," "commie," and "lesbo" are blurted out with uneasy bravado, while the famous pessary is euphemized into a mere "whatnot."

When Larry Hagman, who plays Harald lumpishly, fumbles his elementary Latin and declaims, "*Morituri te*

salutemus," the lapse is prototypical: one cannot ever tell
who is blustering ineptly—the character, the novelist, or
the script-writer. There is a great meeting here of tangled
superficialities, which Boris Kaufman's well-defined color
photography only underlines. The performances range
from Joan Hackett's amiable but exaggerated Dottie,
through Jessica Walter's merely exaggerated Libby, to
Kathleen Widdoes' hermetically lifeless Helena. *The
Group* has nowhere to go, but if of a rainy evening you
should have the same problem, you might want to go there
together.

GORILLA TACTICS

Morgan! would appear to be the first underground movie
made above ground. It is based on a BBC television
play by David Mercer, stars two acclaimed young
Shakespeareans, David Warner and Vanessa Redgrave,
and was directed by Karel Reisz, whose *Saturday Night
and Sunday Morning,* though greatly overrated, exhibited
no cultist hallmarks of the underground. *Morgan* (I shall
henceforth spare you that punctuational phallic symbol
with which the American title has been decked out) is,
nevertheless, a paean to the pop mentality, although the
ending is a palliative cop-out. Cop art?

Morgan Delt is an eccentric young proletarian painter
now being divorced by his upper-class wife, Leonie, who
married him "to achieve a sense of insecurity." But when
he shaves a hammer and sickle into her poodle, she proceeds, despite occasional sexual relapses, to divorce him.
She is already living with Napier, Morgan's smooth art
dealer and friend, and plans to marry him. Morgan is introduced to us at the zoo, studying the gorilla with whom
he identifies himself: large, strong, clever, herbivorous,
friendly until aroused—all these things Morgan is, except

perhaps herbivorous; however, the gorilla is not a Marxist, which evens the score. The movie tells of Morgan's ever more grotesque stratagems to win back his wife, of his troubled but tender relations with his marvelous Cockney-Marxist mother, and of how his brushes with the bourgeoisie and the law, as he assaults Leonie's privacy, lead to his final crack-up and consignment to a mental institution.

To illustrate Morgan's view of himself as a gorilla and of people around him as other species of African fauna, the human action frequently switches to more or less corresponding scenes of jungle wild life. At other times, Morgan has fantasies based on old Hollywood movies: sometimes he is Tarzan-Weissmuller disporting himself with Jane in a lagoon and fighting a crocodile barehanded in her defense; sometimes he is King Kong, frenziedly but pathetically defying the world in lovingly lustful pursuit of Fay Wray—here film clips from these oldies are intercut with the roughly corresponding events in Morgan's life. At still other times, he has grandiose hallucinations, which, in technique, are derived from the daydreams in *Billy Liar* and *The Knack*. When all else fails, Reisz speeds up the film.

Morgan goes to the gorilla and considers his ways. His studio, in Leonie's and his house, had a beast in view, in the shape of a stuffed gorilla; in the living room hangs a huge painting of the beloved ancestor. In clothes and hair-do, Morgan does his best to emulate his shaggy god, and whenever the spirit moves him—which may be in the subway, to confound a ticket-seller; on a ritual Sunday outing to Karl Marx's grave, as a funerary offering; or in his wife's bedroom, by way of jungle wooing—Morgan starts thumping his chest, grimacing, bellowing, hulking, and shambling, in prime primate fashion. But he has other ways, too, of making a nuisance of himself, by playing practical jokes on Napier, Leonie, her family, as well as on a bemused policeman. These include blowing up his mother-in-law with the bed supposed to explode under Leonie and Napier, kidnapping Leonie and holding her prisoner by a chilly Welsh lake meant to be romantic, disguising himself as a gorilla to break up her wedding, sneaking loudspeakers into Leonie's bedroom and blasting her and Napier out of their embraces with recorded pandemonium, or merely shaving a hammer and sickle out of Leonie's favorite angora rug, which cannot appreciate it even as much as the poodle might.

A very little of this is funny. A sight gag involving a raw egg with which Morgan demonstrates the assassination of Trotsky to a bewildered bobby is modestly amusing; so, too, is Morgan's answer to the befuddled peeler's, "You want to watch it!"—"Yeah, but where is it?" But the jokes are seldom more than pranks, nastily dangerous ones at that; the liveliness is never more than frenzy, the devices repetitious and overexploited.

Worse, the point of view is subhuman, and, to top it all, lacks the courage of its convictions. The hero is clearly conceived of as being in the right: His *anomie* is really bonhomie; his anti-intellectualism, parasitism (he lives either off his wife or off his mother), destructiveness, selfishness are presented as spontaneity, naturalness, freedom from inhibitions, and self-realization. It is the unhealthy conformity of our society that is to blame for Morgan's end: The asylum symbolizes middle-class suppression of the free spirit—as it has before, in a number of films, novels, and plays. But in the past the victim was someone who stood for something genuinely or arguably superior to middle-class values—for Franciscan charity, like the heroine of Rossellini's *Europe '51;* or for a kind of nirvana, like the hero of *Life Upside Down*—not for mere primitive gorrillaism.

It is emblematic of the intellectual and moral anarchy of this film that the hero is for the reversal of mankind's march up from the ape; that atavism is made to look like liberation and advancement; that bestiality is put forward as virility. "I've been born into the wrong species," says Morgan, and the context implies that the species is wrong indeed. Which, let us remember, it well may be, without thereby making the gorilla right. Morgan's supreme tribute to his wife, his *Morgengabe* (or Morgangabe), is, "Nothing in this world seems to live up to my best fantasies, except you." But what are Morgan's best fantasies? Bits of *King Kong* and Tarzan movies—not even original fantasies, only crumbs from another man's trough.

Even so, the film does not dare to conclude openly in Morgan's favor; in his last hallucination, Morgan must be shown to be really mad. Thus his institutionalization is made to appear, at least superficially, justified, and we are not obliged to take any of the previous sympathy for him seriously. Yet the truth is that the Morgans of this world are not certifiably mad, and that they do not end up in asylums; they are merely chronically immature and irresponsible, and they inherit the world. Neither are their opposites particularly recognizable in what is shown here. And, above all, the relationship between these elements of our society is both more comic and more pathetic than *Morgan* begins to let on to. Where in *Morgan* is there anything as ludicrous and appalling as the real-life fact of the latest Andy Warhol "films" being shown to an invited audience in the conference room of the Rockefeller Foundation?

The final scene, the ex-wife's visit to the now sequestered hero—feebly reminiscent of the last act of Stravinsky's *The Rake's Progress* and of the close of Buñuel's *El*—is a lesson in how to equivocate. The fact that Morgan is unreconstructedly planting a flower bed in the shape of a large hammer and sickle is meant to represent a botanical Pyrrhic victory; that the child Leonie is about to give birth to is, as she tells Morgan, his (how she can be sure, having blissfully shuttled between her ex and her future, none neither knows nor cares), presumably constitutes a zoological Pyrrhic victory. Such devices, plus a distracting bit of montage, are supposed to make us overlook the final cowardice and confusion of the film.

Not even the acting, except for that of Irene Handl as Morgan's mother, amounts to much. David Warner (whom I saw at Stratford-on-Avon as a good Henry VI

and a poor Richard II) leaves Morgan as superficial a
character as he finds him; Vanessa Redgrave's Leonie is a
compilation of clever little mannerisms. The excellent
Robert Stephens doesn't have a chance as Napier. And
Karel Reisz's direction merely tries to win the British
Gimmick Derby, whose previous winners were Tony
Richardson on *Tom Jones* and Richard Lester on *Help!*

But where is the ultimate pop-camp-underground
consummation attained? In two separate scenes, when
Morgan feels put upon, he smiles with engaging sheepishness and ingenuously flicks out a switch-blade knife.
To the pipe-smoking college sophomore who, with his
date, sat next to me, this proved so uproariously funny
that he detonated a laugh of whose decibel content no
gorilla at mating time need have been ashamed. Something
like that laughter seems to be ringing in the raves that our
reviewers have showered on *Morgan*. But, someone will
say reading these lines, why take it all so seriously, when
it's all in fun? For fun, I'd rather lead apes in hell.

At that, *Morgan* is nothing short of a masterpiece compared to its current American near-equivalent, *Lord Love
a Duck,* George Axelrod's self-styled "black comedy" that
is merely a dirt-grey joke-book. Axelrod's scenario and
direction are the *ne plus ultra* of cinematic bad taste,
blending in equal and unsurpassable measure vulgarity,
pretentiousness, inept imitation (usually posing as parody), stupidity, and such a proliferation of stomach-
turning jokes as would take your average smut peddler a
lifetime to assemble. But then, Axelrod wasn't exactly
hatched yesterday, either. Thus there is, as described by
Rex Reed, the "bit where Miss Weld gets a secretarial job
to the principal of [her] high school by sitting on his desk
and playing with her breasts while he proceeds to scrawl
'69' on his memo pad—drool running down his chin—then
calmly eats his pencil."

I take this scene to be an allegory. Tuesday Weld is Axelrod's infantile, pseudosexual Muse, the obscene scrawl-
ings are Axelrod's works, and the eating of the pencil,
going far beyond mere suggestivity, symbolizes Axelrod's

ability to have his naughtiness and eat it, too. When the long overdue Pornographers Anonymous is founded, *Lord Love a Duck* will undoubtedly be part of the daily shock therapy. Meanwhile, whatever is smeared on children's thumbs to prevent them from sucking them, should be carefully applied to all of Axelrod's pencils.

YOUNG AND COOLISH

Modern movie screens no longer have the black border the screens of yesteryear were equipped with, but for the film fare of the past season, as I look back upon it, a black border seems mandatory. Most of the films we have been seeing—avant-garde, rear guard, off-guard—jointly spell disregard for minimal requirements of a civilized adult. And as one's filmic disaffection increases, one may, perhaps, be excessively susceptible to the shenanigans of disaffected youth, as seen in a brace of films just in from England and French Canada.

The Girl-Getters is a modest, skillful, charming, inconsequential, and fairly dishonest little picture, to be enjoyed and deprecated in roughly equal measure. It deals with a bunch of youths in a typical English summer resort—in other words, a perfect bit of hell on earth and water—who have organized a syndicate that preys on middle- and lower-class girls seeking to sandwich in a little romance between sea and sunshine. The boys, one feels, would have no difficulty making out with the girls each on his own; the syndicate would in reality be for money-making along with the lovemaking, all the more so since most of the boys seem to have no other visible source of income. Indeed, some of their wintertime girl friends turn to prostitution during the summer—though this, too, is glossed over.

Where the film is good is in depicting some of the

techniques of the syndicate; showing their contemptuous attitudes toward the tourists—complete with a special derogatory slang; illustrating some interesting interactions among members of the gang; and setting all this bustling activity against a background of general shabby exploitation and suggestions of the deadening doldrums at both ends of the short season. I say that the film is good in these things but must add that it could also be a lot better; more should have been made, in particular, of the contrast between the *morte saison* and the brief, flashy, desperate doings of summer.

The main plot concerns the adventure of Tinker, leader of the gang and street photographer who uses his job to obtain the victims' addresses, with Nicola, spoiled rich girl and professional model who, for not wholly plausible reasons, spends part of her summer at the resort. Tinker and Nicola are a prosified juvenile version of Benedick and Beatrice, though their hipsterish oneupmanship and counteroneupmanship is not without interest, especially in the interplay of social and sexual elements. But even here the film is facile in the way it allows the kids to revert speedily to romantic young lovers, and in a contrivedly ambiguous bittersweet ending, convincing neither in its actual bitterness nor in its potential sweetness.

Many of the incidental episodes—Tinker's casual affair with the neglected, unhappy wife of a vaudevillian; his humiliation at the hands of Nicola's posh Oxonian friends; his exploitation by a mean, sanctimonious employer—have an all too familiar ring to them, yet manage to introduce an occasional sharp, novel-sounding tone cluster into lovelessness's old sour song. Though Peter Draper's dialogue intermittently rouses itself to a good, crackling bit of impudence, and the acting is lively and authentic, it is the director, Michael Winner, who most deserves our attention.

Winner has a strong feeling for detail: not always imaginative or even accurate, but always intense and sometimes incisive. One has the impression that every patch of the cinematic image, every movement that con-

tributes to the action, has been thought about, molded,
worked over with the total form, mood, and impact in
mind. At times these details misfire, as when Tinker, having just seduced a sweet, silly, overweight blonde who
thinks she has found true love, shoves her out of his flat
and falls against the inside of his door in that mingled
weariness and relief with which countless comic or romantic heroes have applied their backsides to studio-built
doors. But Tinker is neither comic nor romantic; he is
cynical and mechanistic, and he would, once the door was
shut, simply resume his daily routine. Again, as Tinker's
and Nicola's affair progresses, the walls of Tinker's digs,
previously lined with a casual medley of photographs,
blossom out with ever more numerous, ever larger por-
traits of Nicola, until the parting scene is played against a
veritable seraglio of larger-than-life-size but two-dimensional Nicholas—fine, except that Tinker would have had
neither the time nor the money for such darkroom orgies.

At other times, however, details are powerful. As a
used-up piano that played all summer long is about to be
ceremonially drowned in the sea—a farewell offering to
the departed season—we watch the boys cavorting as farcical pallbearers to the deceased instrument. At one point
they file past the little part-time whore who sits, forlorn,
on a parapet, and during that very moment we catch
her—yawning. The yawn is just right: It is perfectly
unassuming, yet it deflates pathos and merriment both at
once. Again, at the wedding of one of the gang, considered
by most of them as a betrayal of their unprincipled principles, every gesture of false gaiety, every mumble of
pseudojovial hostility is captured in masterly fashion. And
the beach bacchanal that follows, at which the human-
sized effigies of bride and groom are burned in a frenzy
that goes far beyond Guy Fawkes Day toward the autos-
da-fé of Torquemada, the fun erupting into hate is har-
rowingly realized.

Michael Winner, whose debut this is, should turn into a
noteworthy director; he will, in due time, learn also that a
device must be integrated into the whole to earn its keep.

Thus he has conceived a clever mode of transition: A sequence ends in a stop-shot, the camera then moves laterally across to another, unrelated still, permitting us to see parts of both, side by side, until it reaches the second completely and continues with normal filmic forward motion. But this flamboyant trick is not properly motivated, and, after a while, it is dropped as conspicuously as it was introduced. On the other hand, Winner has elicited telling performances from a large and motley cast, and has got himself two highly personable principles in Oliver Reed—who might, to good effect, imitate Brando less—and Jane Merrow—whose figure and demeanor were not exactly those of a fashion model but all the more desirable for it.

From Montreal comes Claude Jutra's *A tout prendre* (meaning "after all" or "all things considered" and not *Take It All,* as officially Englished), a vastly self-indulgent and derivative film that, nevertheless, manages to have moments of sardonic *éclat* and enough quizzical effrontery in between to keep it from wholly dissolving in undisciplined copycattiness.

The main trouble is that the story is too much Jutra's own, and the technique too much everybody else's. In a manner that is 2 per cent Antonioni, 2 per cent Cocteau, 26 per cent Truffaut, 69 per cent Godard, and 1 per cent of uncertain provenance (though closer scrutiny would find a source for that, too), we are served up the tale of a squalid love affair between a young film-maker and a Negro actress-model in what seems to be every trivial and sordid detail (leaving out only the essential motivation, of which Jutra is either unaware or afraid) and which is, worse yet, enacted by its real-life protagonist, Jutra, and Johanne, his actual ex-girl friend. Not content with mere undigested autobiography, the movie revels in in-jokes about the Montreal film scene, which is carrying esotericism to new peaks. As for Jutra's borrowings, they are not only excessive in quantity but also insufficient in taste: even something like Godard's camera's awful,

endless shuttling between two faces with a lighted lamp
between (from *Contempt*) awaits us in this magpie's nest.
Moreover, whereas Johanne and a few others are able actors, Jutra himself is lumpish and boring. Lastly, the film
was shot in 16mm. and in being transferred to 35mm. lost
much of its photographic definition.

What, then, is good about *A tout prendre?* There are
two extremely funny scenes: one in which the hero recites
poetry as he plummets off a jetty, and another in which he
takes out a bank loan for an abortion. There are several
other nice episodes: one in which the hero tells his mother
(astutely played by Tania Fedor) that he is about to
marry a Negress; and one in which the hero's buddy and
neighbor climbs, as usual, across a ledge into his friend's
place—only this time he has just left a mistress in his bed
and finds an ex-mistress in that of his pal. There is also a
mock-heroic off-screen narration that can be quite amusing (except when it tries to be genuinely heroic and
poetic: "What I'd like to do is to challenge death, dirty it,
defile it!"), and the hectic dialogue and still more hectic
cutting of the film also have their moments. The English
version by Leonard Cohen is adroit, though it tends to
outbid the original in literary conceits: thus "*Une larme?
Tout un chagrin!*" becomes "A drop? No, a fall."

With his customary aplomb in plumbing the obvious,
Karl Jaspers remarked, "It is in our love that we are what
we actually are." But, unfortunately, it is precisely in his
love that Jutra becomes tenuous, vacuous, a nonentity;
and his film, accordingly, lacks center. Sheer disaffection
does not provide a sufficient thread to string anything on:
pearls, or even swinishness. And that is the paradox that
emerges from *A tout prendre* and films like it: that where
the disaffected young—charming creatures that they
are—are most real, they are least real. It becomes progressively clearer that should the world end, it will be
neither with a bang nor with a whimper, but with a colli-
sion in outer space of those mighty unmanned missiles,
Marshall McLuhan and Norman O. Brown. The resultant

explosion—more of a sexplosion or implosion—will produce such a fallout of fatuity that survival will be, not impossible, but undesirable.

GROWING YOUNG GRACELESSLY

That turn-of-the-century comic genius Alphonse Allais
wrote a short sketch called "*Sancta Simplicitas,*" in which
a husband, wife, and lover do the most extraordinary and
outrageous things to the accompaniment of polite,
unassuming little platitudes, and without batting one
eyelash among the three of them—because they are
"simple people." This grotesque may well have inspired
Agnes Varda's *Le Bonheur:* only what Allais treated suc-
cinctly and sardonically, with perhaps a grain of pathos, is
here lingered over, idyllicized, and rhapsodized about. It is
as if a *Playboy* joke were rewritten as an erotico-
sentimental novel. The result is again a joke, but an unintentional one, rancid and embarrassing.

Le Bonheur is the story of a young carpenter from the
Paris suburbs who works for his uncle and lives comfortably and happily with his lovable blonde seamstress
wife and two adorable children. One day he meets a postal
clerk who is as blonde and lovable as his wife, and even
prettier. Before you can say Jacques Robinson, they have
an affair. The mistress is radiant in the transports of sur-
reptitious passion snatched usually during lunch hour; the
husband is ecstatic, what with the illicit joy spilling over
into the licit; and the wife has the double bliss of matrimony and ignorance. But after a month, during one of
those family outings that act as a refrain in the film, the
husband is persuaded to share his secret happiness with
his wife. With a grand, heuristic image, he explains:
"*C'est simple, tu sais.* You, me, the children, we're like an
apple orchard inside a fence. Then I see an apple tree out-

side the fence, and it's in bloom too. There are more apple blossoms, more apples to add to ours . . . do you see? *Et puis ça me fait tellement de plaisir.*"

By way of winning over his mildly jolted wife to a *ménage à trois,* he bolsters up his horticultural trope with a tentacular one: "It's as if I had ten arms with which to enfold you, and you too had ten arms for me. Then I feel as if I sprouted some additional arms . . . You don't find that I love you less? . . . And it's so stupid to deprive oneself of life, of love." Whereupon our pomiferous octopus proceeds to make mad love to his stunned but obliging and loving wife. While he sleeps the sleep of the just, or of the just fagged out, she drowns herself in a near-by pond. After a couple of months of mourning and summer vacationing, he marries his little postmistress. There is no demur from within, no murmur from without—the new wife has better taste in books and clothes, anyway. We end with the new family going for an outing in the same woods in which the old family gamboled in the start of the film. Everyone is uncomplicated, guiltless, and happy. Ah, those simple people.

A clue to the artistic and intellectual integrity of this film, which Agnes Varda wrote as well as directed, is provided by that fruity image. If the wife, children, and mistress are all apple trees, one presumes that our hero is an apple tree also, and trees do not go about picking, or picking up, trees across the fence. If, however, he is the apple grower, the image implies the most brazen kind of double standard, whereby the women become subordinate—indeed objects—and our fellow can go gathering apple buds to his heart's content, while they are condemned to be sedentary, passive, and complaisant. Just as Mme Vardia's husband's movie *The Umbrellas of Cherbourg* was one of the silliest films ever made, so *Le Bonheur* strikes me as one of the most amoral *and* one of the silliest.

Everything in the film is smooth, casual, soft, pretty. No voice is ever raised, no one does anything ungainly, no setting is less than delectable, nothing jars. One might think of it as a fairy tale, except that the fairy-tale world has its own distinct morality, as well as poetic symbolism; here, there is neither enough reality nor enough fantasy, and the film is ultimately neither fish nor fowl, merely fishy and foul. For reality, we get a Paris suburb in which nobody gossips, parents don't blame their son-in-law for their daughter's suicide, children who don't miss their mother in the least, a husband and mistress completely free from guilt over the wife's death, etc. For fantasy, we have such snatches of dialogue as Emilie, the mistress, telling the hero, François, when he asks whether she understands him, "*Oui, je comprends le français et le François*"; or François' response when Thérèse, his wife, announces that they are going to a movie with no horses in it, "No horses? Then it must be a French film." Actually recent French films tend to omit only the front part of the horse.

But what of the much vaunted visual beauty, the style of the film? There is no denying it, *Le Bonheur* has style, most of it Godard's, every one of whose devices is present; the rest of it Resnais', Truffaut's, and Antonioni's. The reviewers have raved about the Renoir-like quality of the images, an erudite insight they gleaned from Mme Varda's own program notes. True enough, the outdoor photography is that blend of lushness and winsomeness characteristic of Renoir's paintings, but, let us face it, Renoir was a sentimental, second-rate painter, and to imitate him is no better than, in music, to imitate Tchaikovsky. (When the images in *Sundays and Cybèle* suggested Corot, and in black and white at that, the effect was much more satisfying largely because Corot is worthier of emulation.) But Renoir is not the only model: in certain blurry effects one recognizes a hint from Monet, some of the indoor compositions evoke the Postimpressionists, and there are two or three flower vases straight out of Redon. Many of these images redound to the glory of the cinematographers, Jean Rabier and Claude Beausoleil, but they look top-heavy and self-conscious in a film where nothing else competes with them for our attention.

No less irritating is the Mozart score; not only because

the same bit of music (don't ask me which, I'm not a
Mozart man) becomes boring after a while, but also
because its courtliness and control consort ill with the
unrestrained and demotic goings-on. Equally inept are the
typically new wave interpolated tributes to fellow artists:
Emilie reads Jacques Prévert's *La Pluie et le beau temps,*
someone referred to is named after a Truffaut character,
Thérèse takes François to see *Viva Maria,* a television set
is playing Renoir's *Picnic on the Grass.* This last, at least,
makes some sense: on the TV screen, a character utters
the line that has been taken as the theme of *Le Bonheur,*
"Happiness is perhaps submission to the laws of nature."
(I shall return to this.) But a typical dragged-in homage
runs thus: Emilie and a woman at the post office are looking at some recent stamp issues, one of them with King
John the Good on it. "*Jean le Bon,*" one of the women
wonders, "d'you think he was the husband of *Anna la
Bonne?*" *Anna la bonne* is a dreary verse monologue that
Cocteau wrote for the chanteuse Marianne Oswald, and
there is nothing in it with the slightest bearing on *Le
Bonheur.*

Some people have found the sex scenes exciting. About
the only interesting thing in them is that it usually takes a
while before one can tell whether François is in bed with
wife or mistress (get the point?); otherwise, they are
either so static, or so artfully contrived in composition and
choreography, as to deny us any illusion of spontaneity or
intensity. And though Marie France Boyer as Emilie has a
good face, and Claire Drouot as Thérèse a good-sized
bust, there is nothing much else about them to justify all
the poring over their anatomies.

Does Varda, as director, contribute anything? Well,
there is François' first visit to Emilie who has just moved
into a new apartment. They are both eager to embrace,
but careful not even to brush against each other. From
these conflicting impulses there results a veritable ballet of
near-collisions, evasions, sudden spurts, and suppressions
of movement—quite as if the *clinamen* of Lucretius were
being dramatized—which, against the background of the

unsettled-in quarters, achieves a wonderful, nervous expectancy. Again, when François, with the two children, is looking for Thérèse in the woods, and stopping periodically to ask people whether they have seen her, the pacing of the action through both subject and camera movement, dialogue, and editing is anguishingly and expertly accelerated toward the dreadful discovery. But then Varda has to spoil it all by crosscutting from François holding the dead Thérèse to one-frame flashbacks (*à la* Resnais) of her drowning—sheer gimmickry.

And now what of happiness being submission to the laws of nature? The proposition as such is dubious: We have come a long way since Rousseau and *Sturm und Drang* toward recognizing that, in human behavior, we don't know the first thing about natural laws, if, indeed, they exist at all. But *Le Bonheur* does nothing to illuminate this or any other proposition. If it is natural law for François to have an affair, why is it not so for Thérèse? And why stop at one extramarital relationship per person? And is it natural law to stay together as a family? Why not have bastards all over the place? But the people in *Le Bonheur* are a trifle too elaborate to be animals, and quite a bit too simple to be human beings.

If there is anything more dispiriting than the New Wave trying to be quintessentially and encyclopedically new wave, it is the sight of the Old Wave having a desperate and disastrous go at it. In *A Young World,* Vittorio de Sica and his scenarist, Cesare Zavattini, make an objectly humble genuflection before the younger generation while also trying to assimilate recent film techniques. Alas, coming from these old-timers, the *dernier cri* emerges as the last gasp.

A Young World tries to say that though the previous generation, that of today's parents, is indeed much to blame—even if they were heroic in the War, they became jejune in the peace—some pity and appreciation might yet be spared for them. The young on the other hand, are shown as spontaneous, pure, fun-loving yet aspiring to a better world, but are asked to remember that they don't hold all the answers, either. Moreover, they have not so wholly transcended the so-called conventional values as they might think. And this lovely combination of breast-beating and propaganda is packaged in what the old boys think is the freewheeling style of the New Wave, replete with its best tricks, and then some! (Hold on to your stomachs, here we go.)

A young Italian photographer, the rebellious son of a rich lawyer, is trying to make it on his own in Paris. At an orgiastic medical students' ball, he meets an appealing young student and, without a word spoken, makes love to her on a secluded balcony. He, next, falls afoul of the cynical and lecherous photographer he works for (a small, dull part on which Pierre Brasseur's prodigious talents are prodigally wasted). "He doesn't like women's behinds," says the boss from his bed shared with a concubine, "*c'est un intellectuel*." But our hero (a stock part to which Nino Castelnuovo does uninteresting justice) tells the middle-aged slob off: He is merely green with jealousy of youth's vitality and hope. He quits, in order to photograph, not girlies, but faces in the street, in which he perceives the history of mankind, including the next world war. We are allowed to wallow in these faces on the boy's wall, and I must confess that I saw about as much of World War III in them as of the Second Punic War, but I could understand why the magazines weren't buying them.

Meanwhile our hero is yearning for his lost Cinderella, and he seeks her all over the Medical School until he finds her in a large lecture hall. After some rather old-fashioned (and belated) hesitancies and pursuit, they become lovers. Unfortunately, the girl (passably played by Christine Delaroche) managed to get pregnant, in best old wave style, on that very first occasion—perhaps the fact that she is only a first-year medical student might be considered a mitigating circumstance. Now comes a tug-of-war between the girl and the boy who is afraid of marriage and bourgeois mediocrity like that of his parents: "They promised us big things, then they did nothing . . . They want us to be like them; they want our complicity."

For a while he veers toward marriage, then he avoids the pining girl. Finally he returns and recommends abortion. Having made the rounds of a dismal maternity ward in the retinue of an eminent but heartless gynecologist (the older generation again!—and what a waste of Georges Wilson's talent), the girl acquiesces. The boy turns gigolo for a night to a middle-aged woman (the gifted Madeleine Robinson in a puny role): How corrupt can the rich elders get? The boy, after all, does it for unselfish purposes, for his girl and for his principles; the woman only for sex! She gives him all the money he needs for an abortion, yet cautions him against such an act. But she also gives him a good address: "Two sisters—they are even very cultivated."

And so they are, the evil old things. They live in decadent old-world elegance, but their essential nastiness is epitomized by what hangs on their walls: ghastly paintings of Napoleon and his campaigns by Meissonier. On the way to the operating room, the girl passes a glass book case containing a complete set of the Pléiade—all the French classics in suspiciously mint condition. She can't go through with it. (After all, she is a baker's daughter from Clermont-Ferrand, where Pascal was born and the First Crusade was preached!) As one of the abortionist hags angrily slams down her *Remembrance of Things Past* (culture, you see, is not worth much), our heroine runs out past the Empire furniture, and we cut from Meissonier to the lively pop art on the pinball machine with which the hero is playing while waiting for his girl.

They go to a movie: a big, noisy western. As she confesses that she did not get the abortion the film-within-the-film ends. They look miserably at each other. The word "FIN" appears on the western's screen and extends to our eastern screen. Ambiguous ending, as in any number of new wave films. And, of course, there are the other new wave paraphernalia: a tribute to another film-maker, in this case Marcel Carné and his *Hôtel du Nord*; establishment of a character through a book he reads, in this case a volume of Aimé Césaire on a Negro medical student's shelf; lingering of the camera over a variety of still photographs on someone's wall to set a scene in what is taken to be a very filmic way; using a hand-held camera wherever remotely possible, etc.

Perhaps the only wholly successful scene in *A Young World* is an auto accident with the victim lying in the street and various bystanders reacting in diverse ways. Though this, too, becomes partly an indictment of middle-aged callowness, the neorealist, social-documentary approach to life in the streets makes itself tangibly manifest here. The lesson to be derived from all this is a melancholy one: In film, styles change very fast and a creator is likely to be out of date well before he is ready to retire. De Sica and Zavattini made some remarkable neorealist dramas like *Shoeshine, The Bicycle Thief,* and *Umberto D.;* they managed to make the jump to the next fashion, low-life comedy with sentimental or social overtones, such as *Gold of Naples* and *Marriage Italian Style*—the distance, after all, was not so great. But what came after is simply beyond them. They should not, however, try to copy, apologize, and plead. It is undignified, and it is bad art.

WOOLF DOG

According to an announcement from Warner Brothers, their forthcoming thriller, *Chamber of Horrors,* will feature "two important motion-picture health-safety devices—the Fear Flasher and the Horror Horn." Whenever the movie reaches its "Supreme Fright Points" these devices, by blinking and buzzing right off the screen, will alert the "weak-of-heart" to run, hide, or "face the consequences." It is to be regretted Warner did not develop this device in time for *Who's Afraid of Virginia Woolf?* which, aside from being generally mediocre, has enough Supreme Fright Points to have benefited from such warnings. But I suppose the Fear Flasher would have been mistaken for one of the director's arty light effects, and the Horror Horn for Elizabeth Taylor's voice.

Albee's play was, barring the inept metaphysics and the unconvincing business about the imaginary child, an effective piece of theatre, full of ugly but potent humor, cutting or at least sideswiping language, venomous but believable characterizations, and generally convincing bedlam. This is not the place to analyze why that fictitious son, or, at any rate, the way he is used, is psychologically unsound and dramatically dishonest; why the metaphysicizing—for the most part omitted from the movie, anyway—is bogus; and how the ending is a sop to the public's yen for a more or less edifying message. (Indeed, the NCOMP, which stands for National Catholic Office for Motion Pictures, and not, as you might have thought, for *non compos mentis,* allowed the picture to squeeze by because of that terminal uplift.) We have all talked and written ourselves out on the subject of the play, and there is enough to worry about in the movie.

The mere fact of the film adaptation smacks of the supererogatory: *Virginia Woolf* is not the sort of work that can bear much repetition. Because of its prominent place in an impoverished theatre, many people saw it twice, or saw it and read it, and that is about enough; unlike major works of art, this one palls. Where the essence is repartee—and not, as in Wilde, for example, repartee plus style—the jokes and surprises use themselves up. But in the play, at least, the jokes functioned so as to make the living-room in which the three long acts of nastiness pile up a more and more unlivable-in place, filled with the smoke of human bitterness and the stench of thwarted lives. For this the stage is indispensable: the single set slowly hardening into a cage. In the film, the scenarist Ernest Lehman chose to spring this confinement

by transposing parts of the action to other rooms, the garden, a speeding car, a roadhouse. This may be cinematic
necessity; it is surely a dramatic blunder.

But film is otherwise unkind to this play. One need not
go so far as Friedrich Dürrenmatt, who contends that a
close-up is in itself an indecency, to feel that a piece of
foolishness uttered in a close-up comes out more foolish
than the same line spoken on a stage where it is absorbed
to some extent by the plurality of available sights and
mitigated by not issuing from a larger-than-life-size head.
On screen, some of the shoddier bits of Albee's writing
emerge shoddier yet. And when the occasional bathetic
badinage is underlined by Alex North's banal and inap-
propriate score—the final scene, sentimentally directed
and played, features marshmallowy passages for the cello
that would bring tears to the eyes of a Rostropovich, and
nobody else's—the result is stultifying.

Where the film irrecoverably falls down, however, is in
the acting and directing. Mike Nichols has done some extremely inventive directing for the stage, but always in the
medium of cabaret or comedy; here he is doubly
transplanted: to film and to drama. We are treated to the
choicest directorial commonplaces, from a naked light
bulb swinging and casting ominous shadows to the ring at
the end of a window shade (or was it a lamp chain?) nervously jiggling away; from a neon arrow flashing on and
off behind an irate head to a revolving disc of colored
lights drenching dancers in black and white—what a waste
of a grand color platitude!

Whole scenes are hammily conceived; the one, for
instance, in which George goes to get a toy gun with which
he pretends to shoot his wife. In the play, too, this is
meant to produce a brief scare, but here the fetching and
carrying of the weapon are milked for a prolonged melodramatic effect unworthy of either the wit or the
seriousness of the context. Or consider the needlessly obvious silhouettes-on-window-shades shots for Nick's and
Martha's sex bout; or Honey dancing by herself, staged

like the village idiot trying to impersonate Isadora Duncan. The film as a whole is unmemorable and so is each of its scenes.

Among the participants only Richard Burton can be dignified with the term performer. Though he makes George yet another one of his underwater creations, a diver descending ever more deeply into a sea of nausea while little bubbles of contempt and self-hate rise to the surface, he is at least repeating a performance, if not creating one. Burton's mannerisms have become predictable, and he lacks the demonic quality with which Arthur Hill so brilliantly invested the part on Broadway —weakness, yes, but one that knows how to smash its image in the mirror of another's weakness. Burton broods over his sarcasm rather than brandishing it, and when Martha kicks her hatred at him, he plays goal keeper rather than opposing center forward.

But at least he does not fumble. Elizabeth Taylor, on the other hand, is a total flop. Made up to look middle-aged and frumpish, she remains a pretty, soulless child, the age and slovenliness painted on, and even the fat, though genuine, looking like baby-fat on her. The voice and accent are, as always, those of a spoiled and untutored brat (this is supposed to be a college president's daughter, aged 52!); the gestures are even more regressive. Martha, whom Uta Hagen made so richly, rottenly ripe is here still on the throes of a difficult puberty: except for the tinny nastiness, it might as well be *National Velvet Rides Again*. Clearly, Miss Taylor has been coached down to every intake of breath and flutter of eyelashes; but behind those robot-like mechanics there is no discernible human being.

As Honey, Sandy Dennis accomplishes the well-nigh impossible feat—oh, let's be generous, the quite impossible feat—of being worse yet. The part calls for a simple, dull girl who gradually uncovers a cache of hysteria, only to revert to superficial wholesomeness again. Miss Dennis acts, from beginning to end, demented, but demented in the most simperingly phoney way, so that the always

tenuous boundary between the worst kind of method acting and raving madness disappears altogether. Why Mike
Nichols' directional hand—or, at the very least, a strait-
jacket—never clamps down on her remains a mystery. As
for George Segal's Nick, he is one-sided and obvious.
Where George Grizzard, on stage, brought out an iridescent variety of emotional coloration under the outward
innocuousness, Segal takes us only from nonentity to
loutishness and back to nonentity again, which may well
be the last remaining nickel ride.

That leaves Haskell Wexler's photography, craftsman-
like despite a slight overindulgence in chiaroscuro,
and the astute art direction of Richard Sylbert and
set decoration by James Hopkins. Except that the place
looked much more like that of an English professor than
that of a historian (photographs of Marianne Moore
and Isak Dinesen, books like Edith Sitwell's autobiography, *Catch 22, The Tin Drum,* and a copy of *The Paris
Review*), the sets and properties joined with gusto
academic clutter and slatternly topsy-turviness. I particularly enjoyed the visual pun of a map of Martha's
Vineyard on the wall. But all that is small comfort.
Thomas Mann once mused about a film adaptation of his
Royal Highness: "It should succeed. There are rewarding
parts in it, even the infallible one of a beautiful dog."
Perhaps instead of making *Virginia Woolf,* Warner
Brothers should have filmed *Flush.* Better start with a dog
than end with one.

How much of a film's success depends on the vagaries of
release! If *Sweet Light in a Dark Room,* a Czech film
made six years ago, had been released here before *The
Shop on Main Street,* it would have garnered the plaudits
Shop received instead of getting clobbered with invidious
comparisons. Actually, *Shop* is rather less good than has
been claimed, whereas *Sweet Light* is considerably better.
Both pictures have the same naïve honesty which does
not preclude an almost innocent tendentiousness ("Look
how good we Czechs were to the Jews!"—who would

have the heart to confront such well-meaning pseu-
dodocuments with the "Hmm?" of historicity?), a somewhat homemade or thrift-shop look, and passionate
but not unbridled humanitarianism. The dialogue is uninspired but felt and persuasive, the cinematography un-
sophisticated but as compelling as a painting by a good
primitive; the direction fallible but with many penetrations
into the dark heart of things; the actors simply and un-
selfconsciously there—as a fence, livestock, or the sound
of footsteps is there.

Sweet Light tells of a young Aryan student's hiding a
Jewish girl in a storage room, of their nascent love as he
risks his life by harboring her, of their shy hopes surrounded by murderous madness, of the boy's mother's revealing to the girl the danger she represents, and of her
composed departure into death. Dana Smutna, the girl,
has a face in which lyrical and tragic poetry are equally at
home, and Ivan Mistrak, the boy, has the disarming spontaneity of genuine, youthful talent. In the scene in which
the Nazis come and get, not him, as it turns out, but a
friendly young neighbor couple, and his reaction is frantic
laughter with just a hint in it of sobs, the camera abuts on
ultimate revelation. And there are several more such
scenes in Jirí Weiss's film, scenes that are not to be tri-
fled with.

TECHNIQUE TRIUMPHANT

A Man and A Woman is mostly a woman: Anouk Aimée.
There is not anywhere on today's screens a more intense
yet mellow, a more striking but at the same time soothing
presence than hers. The angular, elongated face has an architecture full of surprises: a sudden softness where one's
eye pursued chiseled acuities; and so, too, the body:
velvety womanliness is stopped short unexpectedly by the

sexless grace of child or angel. Is this an adolescent, a girl, a woman? Her movements have learned the art of amorously caressing the air they cleave; yet her voice has the slightly strangulated modesty of a virgin bride's "I do." There is something of the scimitar about her sinuous sharpness, yet everything in her speaks of a gentleness that only long nights of loving could have instructed in groping its way to the core of human darkness. And on top of all that she can act.

It is as if Anouk Aimée had reduced the palette of emotional responses to two colors: a boundless, world-conquering smile, and a deep, delicate anxiety. Her face, voice, movements dip freely into these colors, allowing them to overlap almost imperceptibly, suffusing each with the other, or drawing undauntable lines of demarcation between them and immersing her entire being in the one pure color or the other. To put it another way, it is as if she were profoundly aware that every gesture, expression, sound is to be situated in its exact place on a carefully calibrated scale between the greatest joy and the ultimate anguish: between the act of love and the act of dying. And so her every response is precise—in duration as well as placement—and bears just the right amount of love or death in it. And what is even more amazing is that she makes us cognizant not only of the locus of an utterance or movement on that scale, but also, simultaneously, of the invisible presence of the two extreme points, the finiteness and infinitude of our existence.

But, of course, this gift goes far beyond technique; it is nothing that a director could inculcate or another actress imitate. It is all part of an immense tact, of a total femininity both physical and metaphysical, and it must, in the last analysis, stem from the unconscious. It is beautiful, ennobling. Strained through Anouk Aimée's being, the ordinary becomes aristocratic. And a good thing, too, in this case, for Claude Lelouch's film is aggressively ordinary. Except, to be sure, in its colors.

We have by now become quite used to director's cinema, both in its bad, or Godardian, aspect, and in its (usually) good, or Truffautian manifestation. But what Lelouch offers us is cameraman's cinema, in which the director is his own director of cinematography and does not so much write with his camera as allow the camera to write for him. Time and again in *A Man and a Woman* I had the feeling that it was the camera that wanted to zoom in or out on a particular scene, to pan panegyrically with a car cavorting along a beach, to be fed monochrome instead of color film by way of a balanced diet—and though the cinematographic effects are often exhilarating and almost always exquisite, I felt that by indulging his camera (even to the point of arbitrarily switching from color to monochrome blue or ochre sequences) Lelouch has spoiled his film.

The colors are, in their nature, juxtaposition, and consecution, quietly spellbinding. Always understated, tawny or hazy, they force the eye to make fine distinctions, to hear, as it were, the quarter tones of the color scale. This makes *A Man and a Woman* the most beautiful color spectacle since Antonioni's *Red Desert,* and less *recherché* in its effects. Whether it is trees racing past a setting sun as seen from a speeding car, or a motley boat gliding past intricate wooden balusters of a greyish green, or a silvery-bluish shimmer of sea framed by the silhouetted, unfocused heads of kissing lovers (between touching lips and chests a lozenge of frizzled silver), or even just a reddish fur collar whose windblown hairs ripple along the heroine's face, movement is wedded to color. Color, far from striking gorgeous but static poses, continually unfolds before us: the camera has become a kaleidoscope, and the whole world but the colored particles in it.

Where, however, does this leave the plot? The chief characters of the film are not people but automobiles. The hero is a racing driver, and when he is not racing, he is driving about in his car, either with the heroine or in pursuit of her. For some sequences, Lelouch strapped himself and his camera to a car, and, it would seem, never got quite untied. The nonmotorized sequences seem scarcely more than interludes for all their fleeting charm. And even there, kinetics carries the day. If the hero embraces the heroine on a bench, he whirls around with her and the camera whirls with both of them, and next, in a visual echo, a dog is gamboling about describing unleashed parabolas in the sand. But where, I ask, is the plot? Nowhere. A nebulous husband of the heroine and shadowy wife of the hero are evoked only to be preposterously killed off; the rest is merely a routine romance blossoming on the front seat of a Ford Mustang shuttling between Deauville and Paris, as two hearts beat in tune to the ever-busy windshieldwiper turned metronome. (It rained a lot while he was shooting, Lelouch explains.) Everything is done in the car, from shaving to planning one's amatory strategy. Only the consummation is relegated to a bed, the locale being France, not the U.S.

Visual details are handled with imagination. A man's hand and a woman's almost meet on a child's black fur collar, but shy away from contact; the heroine's figure floats, like a dream vision, in front of the cityscape of Paris—only much later do we realize that she was sitting in front of the window of a bus. Cross-cutting is handled inventively: Camels seem to be watching the hero's car race through France, until it is revealed, gradually, that they are appearing in a film on which the heroine is working, and that we are merely witnessing the parallel lives of hero and heroine in apparent fusion. But the characters—what of them? They remain ordinary and largely subliminal. And the dialogue? Generally improvised by the actors; and in an age when writers can hardly write, what can we expect from actors? Besides, at a crucial moment when characters and speech have a chance of coming alive, Lelouch cuts the dialogue in and out of a silly song on the soundtrack. Effective in a way, but scarcely illuminating.

What is clear from all this is that to the young director technology is far more interesting than man—who matters mainly insofar as he provides data with which the camera-computer's hunger can be stilled. Does that mean that the machine is getting more alive and man less so? Since we can see the machine only as man interprets it, the man only as the clever mechanics of the finished film reflect him, we must conclude that we are faced with an elaborate symbiosis in which one cannot tell the players even with a program. *A Man and a Woman* is really about a man and a machine, and by that kind of love story I find it rather hard to be moved.

A much more human film is *It Happened Here*—human, that is, not merely in detail, but in its general orientation and concern. To show what would have happened if England had been occupied by Nazi Germany is a good, though not extraordinary, idea. After all, other countries have been thus occupied, and we know what happened in them. But the attempt to dent the British stiff upper lip in a serious, not-beyond-the-fringe way is a worthy undertaking, particularly when it had to be done by two young men, Kevin Brownlow and Andrew Mollo, on no money whatever, with amateurs giving freely of their time, and the whole dogged operation spread over several years. Brownlow, evidently, has a genius for making one tank and twenty men look like a whole German army of occupation, and there are many directorial touches that, in their occasional raw effectiveness and general somewhat slapdash, hit-or-miss quality, remind me of the young Stanley Kubrick's *Fear and Desire*. Actually this film is considerably better, despite thematic disjointedness, uneven performances, and sketchy characterization.

There are those little touches that augur well. A pair of forlorn, very white woman's hands disconsolately dropped into a lap swathed in a black fascist skirt; a partisan ambush in which half of a German officer's face is volcanically blown off; a jovial indoctrination speech by an English *gauleiter*, full of the most blatant racism expressed in sweetly reasonable tones, more in sorrow than in anger; and one or two other moments in which the monstrous assumes the mask of mere drab routine. This, to me, is a much more effective way dramatizing man's inhumanity than Lionel Rogosin's protracted, repetitious, heavy-handed irony in *Good Times, Wonderful Times,* in which documentary footage of war's horrors is contrasted with idle and reactionary cocktail-party chatter.

One of the troubles with Rogosin's film, as with *A Man and a Woman,* is the reliance on improvisation and *cinéma-vérité.* There is a lunch scene in the latter film, in which Miss Aimée and Jean-Louis Trintignant, out of sheer enforced spontaneity, end up acquiring the same unnaturalness, whether real or merely apparent, that people in *cinéma-vérité,* paradoxically, are almost never without. The sooner we realize that improvisation is useful only in very small doses—and then, usually, with children, psychotics, or geniuses—the sooner, in other words, we fathom that dialogue, to be a work of art, must preponderantly be *written,* the better. For a grain of artistic truth, we can forgive even the grainy photography and wavering sound with which part of *It Happened Here* is afflicted. Going to see it is a little like a donation to charity, but, in this case, the donor may turn out to be the beneficiary.

NOT 'ALF BLEEDIN' WONDERFUL

The best comedy and the best serious film seen in New York so far this year happen to be one and the same: they are called *Alfie,* and they should please everyone but the most rabid avantgardists to whom anything with plot, character, and resemblance to life is anathema. *Alfie* proves that the systematic but loving examination of a contemporary individual—or type—never ceases to be of artistic interest, provided that the observation does not skimp on detail or try to know more than there is to know. Or less.

Alfie, the eponymous hero of the film, is a Cockney hedonist in his middle thirties; he has made use of the upward mobility of English society to the modest degree of

progressing from truck-driving to the chauffeuring of lim-
ousines, snazzy dressing, and the extending of his real
vocation, seduction, to the happy hunting grounds of the
middle class. Although the film is chiefly concerned with
the amatory conquests and occasional setbacks of its hero,
this does not reduce it to a mere catalogue of picaresque
exploits. The typical picaresque hero is either a good guy
forced to resort to shrewdness to outwit a hostile world, or
a heel who, nonetheless, has a redeeming feature or two.
Alfie is not quite either of these. He is someone in whom
good and bad are so thoroughly intermingled that moral
values lose all meaning.

He is a complete egoist, but he would genuinely like to
see everybody happy, including the husbands whose wives
he dabbles in. He is an abject coward, yet when it comes
to subverting another, tougher man's girl under hazardous
conditions, he rises to the occasion like any *chevalier sans
peur et sans reproche*—self-reproach, that is. He is a cheat
and petty crook, but his two recurrent dictums are
"Nobody don't 'elp you in this life—you gotta learn to
'elp yourself," and "If they don't get you one way, they get
you another," and he wrests such juicy variations from
these two verities, and believes them with such moral fer-
vor, that you would find it hard to dispute him. Particularly since at least half the time he is proved right. And
in a world of half-truths, isn't that close to being wholly
right?

Alfie calls women birds or bints, and the only pronoun
they rate is "it." He tells Annie, a girl he has picked up on
the road and who has moved in with him and slaves away
for him—largely, to be sure, to forget another man—that
she will ruin her hands by ceaseless scrubbing. "They
don't matter," says she. "They might not to you, gal, but
they do to me. Nothin' puts me off more'n a woman get-
tin' 'old of me with 'ard, 'orny mitts." And watching her
persist in her toiling, he muses, "Sometimes it gets a dead
ghostified look come over its little face, as if it was all sick
inside with love or summink, an' its poor bleedin' mind
was stumblin' abaht lookin' for a corner to rest in." "You

can never know with a bird where it's bin, nor wot it's done," he tells a husband confined to a hospital bed. "Would you mind saying 'she,' " the fellow retorts, "you're talking about my missis." "She or it," Alfie obliges, "they're all birds. You don't know wot it or she is doin' this minute . . ." Alfie has his brand of magnanimity, to be sure. Of one girl he says approvingly, "She's a standby and she knows it, and any bird wot knows its place in this life can be quite content." For what birds "don't realize is that men are more sensitive than women"; although, at times, Alfie can be surprised: "Alfie, I says to myself, she's as 'uman as you are."

In fact, Alfie would like to be good. Thus, after relating a particularly nasty nightmare, he comments, "Alfie, I says to myself, if only you could get yourself to do summink good in your dreams, it wouldn't cost you nothink, an' you would get quite a bit of satisfaction out of it. 'Course it only goes to show—if they ain't got you when you're awake, they get you when you're ableedin' sleep." And when he walks out on a friend's wife who is about to have an abortion—the baby, of course, would have been Alfie's—he explains, "I know it don't look nice—but wot do look nice when you get close up to it?"

Bill Naughton, who adapted *Alfie* from his own play, knows the milieu and the men in it well; he was himself once a truck driver. More importantly, he was and is a human being, as every line of his play and film testifies. Only out of love could a small scrounger and mini-skirt chaser be made to seem so insidiously universal, neither bigger nor better than he is, but, as it were, truer than the truth, more essential, more incontrovertible. And the various birds around him, however briefly we follow their flutterings, emerge as more than the usual smart stereotypes; something of Naughton's enormous susceptibility to life and all its carriers makes every being he comes in contact with infectiously alive. Not only is nothing human alien to him, none of it can ever be too familiar, either; in the most trivial and obvious he discovers the freshness, the mystery.

And there is here, as in all good comedies, a very genuine seriousness, even sadness, behind it all, as Alfie keeps acting out his compulsive pattern and, though accepting defeats almost as cheerily as victories, wondering what his life really comes to. In his addresses to the audience (and he is inexhaustibly talking at us—even, gulpingly, out of embraces that are about to engulf him), he makes a refrain out of the laconic, confidential, complicity-making phrase "Know wot I mean?" But when, at film's end, he remarks, "Wot's it all about?" and adds his usual breezy "Know wot I mean?" the words elicit from us, without the actor's having to do anything special with them, a great, tender, grieving sense of kinship.

The play had two advantages over the movie. It included some racy bits of dialogue that have been suppressed—though much that is almost as racy is still there, and not a little that is quite tart has been added. And there was in the play a trifle less moralizing. Less heavy weather was made of the abortion, and there was not, in the end, the implication that Alfie may be losing his grip. In the movie, Alfie finds himself sharing Ruby's opulently middle-aged favors with a guitar-strumming mod; challenged, Ruby explains that the chap is younger. Alfie leaves her and runs into Siddie on the Embankment, but whether she will resume her dalliance with him is left an open question. The film ends with Alfie's puzzled monologue about the inscrutability of it all. In the play, Ruby is two-timing him with Lofty, the truck driver from whom he stole Annie, and both Lofty and Ruby invite Alfie to a bit of *ménage à trois*, from which he flees horrified. The existentially troubled soliloquy follows next, and the play concludes with Siddie, the adulterous wife from the parked car in the beginning, popping back into Alfie's car.

Thus, in the play, Alfie emerges ultimately as a bit of a puritan (an amusing and profound insight), and the story ends with the adultery with which it began. Alfie has learned nothing, and therein lies the comedy or tragedy of his existence. In the film, aging, replaceability and bewil-

derment begin to cast their retributive shadows on Alfie—by way of that divine justice which, not visible in our
lives, the movies take it upon themselves to dispense. Yet
even as it is, the film very nearly ran into censorship troubles.

But the movie version also has several advantages over the
play. It is able to take Alfie to the locales of his various
deeds, and thus show him more immersed in action as well
as illumine his relationship to his natural habitat. It can
also demonstrate and delight in encounters that the play
could merely allude to, and it finds time for the introduction of a few lively new episodes, all of which work
handsomely, except for a barroom brawl that is both
cliché-ridden and out of keeping with the tone of the rest.
Alfie's continuous, and continually interrupted, confidences to the audience work even better than on the
stage, partly because the director, Lewis Gilbert, is able to
alternate them with off-screen narration (also by Alfie,
and neatly flowing into his on-screen commentary), and
partly because Gilbert finds ever new ways of staging and
photographing Alfie's stream of asides. Last, and anything
but least, there is Michael Caine.

Caine's Alfie is more than a performance: an am-
buscade for all critical reservations. It is as if a lifetime of
apprehending and comprehending had gone into this creation. Caine has done nothing of real significance before
this; after this, he does not need to. Every ingenuous or
disingenuous look of that slightly bent face of his, every
lustily sucked-on jujube or condescendingly tossed-off
crumb of an utterance, every piece of braggadocio or
deflation in his entire bearing, reveals the master. Nothing
is thrown away, nothing clutched or brandished. The acting is total, in that each line is delivered also by the face
and body, and each glance and gesture leads into, out of,
and beyond the corresponding words. It is a definitive performance, whose ultimate virtue is the beautiful sonorous
compromise it brings about between Cockney speech and
the next linguistic set up—and what jazzy, cajoling and

jolting, cadences and turns of phrase that gives rise to!

The others in the cast are all uncannily faultless, and most of the women have, as an extra gift, that wonderfully honest homeliness that only British actresses seem to have, and that, without major sacrifice of feminine appeal, stamps the characters with a painful veracity. Lewis Gilbert's direction, except for an occasional lapse into platitude, is forthright and blessed with a perky resourcefulness (*mirabile visu,* even Shelley Winters is kept under relative control), and Otto Heller's color photography knows when to court vulgar lushness to good effect, and when to remain homey and sober.

The captious can find weaknesses in *Alfie,* some of them real enough, but none important. That the movie is not daringly, path-blazingly cinematic pales before the fact that there is hardly a moment in it without its scraggy but resilient corporeality, its peculiarly buttonholing charm.

A FAIR FOURTH

New York's Fourth Film Festival represents a marked improvement over last year's pitiful gallimaufry. It may be that this is due to the infusion of new blood into the selection committee, whose numbers were raised from two to four; there may, after all, be truth in the old German saying that four eyes see more than two. Perhaps also this was a better, or less bad, year for film. Whatever the reason, there were fewer absolute nullities among the feature films, and there was a decent proportion of pictures that could be watched with interest.

The outstanding event of the Festival was Peter Watkins' *The War Game,* a 47-minute proto-documentary of what atomic warfare would be like if it hit Great Britain. The cataclysm is seen chiefly from the point of view of a part of Kent on which, accidentally, an atom bomb is dropped by the enemy. Far from contenting itself with recording superlatively the biological horrors entailed, the film also probes the far-reaching social, political, and moral consequences that sinisterly mushroom from this disaster. Watkins further examines, by intelligent intercutting, the ignorance of the public before the event, as it answers questions with pathetic unawareness; and he reenacts actual statements by government officials, scientists, and clerics in all their grueling fatuity. Thus the film contains elements of black humor as well as tragic blackness.

One is aware throughout of horror being faced squarely without hysteria and even—a much greater achievement—without allowing righteous indignation to get out of hand. Perhaps the most shattering scene of all, one in which the documentary transcends itself into art, shows an interview with a group of postbombardment school children. One after the other, these boys, physically relatively unharmed but their blotted-out facial expressions bespeaking a deeper marring, answer the single question. "What do you want to be when you grow up?" with the same blankly intoned, "I don't want to be nothing when I grow up." That is one of those ultimate statements in which (to emend myself) even art transcends itself into self-effacement before the ineffable. The BBC sponsored this film, then refused to televise it. It has, so far, found no distributor in this country. If it is not to be released, the loss will be immeasurable.

Several pictures can be classed as meritorious near misses. There was Kon Ichikawa's dignifiedly humane war film, *The Burmese Harp* (made ten years ago), about a young Japanese soldier upon whom, at war's end, the dreadfulness of it all weighs so heavily that he becomes a monk in Burma, goes about interring the unburied dead and lets his regiment return without him. I have heard a critic I respect compare this film to the Joe Pasternak sentimental outpourings of the 1940's, and there are two scenes that are a bit sticky, largely because they are overlong. But the relationships between the soldier and his captain, between the soldier and his buddies, and, indeed, the interaction of various military and civilian persons, are portrayed with such quietly respectful sympathy; there is such reverence for the ultimate mysteries of motivation—which does not mean that, as in Godard and Bresson, the highly improbable becomes the order of the day; that if I am reminded of anything by *The Burmese Harp,* it is of Renoir's *The Grand Illusion.*

The intimate role a musical instrument can play in the psychic development of a man, and how this can extend even to his fellow-soldiers, is delicately apprehended. If Ichikawa had done nothing more than capture this elusive theme with such lyrical finesse, he would already deserve our thanks. It is, however, true of this as of many another Japanese film that it has a beginning, a middle, and at least three endings.

The Hunt, from Spain, is a remarkably courageous and intelligent work—if only it could have had commensurate artistry! Carlos Saura's film concerns three friends who once fought with Franco and are now big businessmen of varying degrees of success, and a fourth, a young man, the son of another old ex-Falangist friend of theirs. The four go rabbit-hunting together on land belonging to one of them. In the course of what starts out to be a carefree hunting party under a hot sun, old rivalries and resentments, exacerbated by new feudalism and materialism, reach such a pitch of fulminant hatred, that the three older men kill one another off to the helpless consternation of the younger one.

The action moves on three planes. There is the sheer voluptuous brutality with which the rabbits are exterminated (clearly the poor beasts are symbols for the populace). There is, parallelly, the genteel, patronizing inhumanity with which the overseer of the land, his mother, and daughter are all treated by the older huntsmen. Lastly, there is the contempt or envy with which the three supposed friends regard one another, until, no longer containable, the feelings erupt into massacre. All this is told patiently, painstakingly, with a nice

sense of detail and atmosphere. Success and failure, riches
and poverty, confront each other with all the poignance of
the contrast, but without lapses into sentimentality or
cliché. Some (but only some) of the incidents have genuine bite reminiscent of Buñuel's, and the dialogue has
its moments, too, as when the youth asks, upon hearing
his elders mention the war that raged in this area, "Which
war?"—as if it could be something from the days of
Napoleon or Ferdinand and Isabella. But the recording
of subtly mounting violence needs consistently good
dialogue, better pacing (the rhythm here is too slow for
too long, then suddenly too fast—a deliberate device,
but unsuccessful), and probably, more ingenious cinematography. Even so, Saura's film is considerable in
itself and promising for its maker's future.

Buñuel, Saura's apparent mentor, was represented by a
fine short film, *Simon of the Desert*. While this 44-minute
satire makes fun of the church and the laity as they im-
portune the stylite in their various ways; of the devil as he
tempts the saint in sundry, mostly feminine, disguises;
and, in a gentler way, of the saint himself; it is Buñuel at
his best: stylite and stylist face each other from their
respective pedestals. But there is a gratuitous ending,
possibly tacked on to get the film over with quickly when
financing ran out, which leaves us with a bad taste in the
mind.

The provocative Italian novelist and film-maker Pier
Paolo Pasolini was represented by two films. The vintage
1961 *Accattone* (for some reason, it was nowhere made
clear that the title means "beggar") now seems fairly
uninteresting. It is an extension of neorealism to essentially obnoxious, or, at least, opprobrious characters,
mostly pimps and whores; it is discontinuous, lacka-
daisical, sometimes improbable, almost always superficial.
But Pasolini's new film, *The Hawks and the Sparrows*, is
something else again. It is a fantasy, mixing in equal
measure frivolity and satire, and for the first half it works
well enough or better. A man and his son undertake a

symbolic journey to the city, and are joined by a Communist crow. The episode in which the crow transmutes its human traveling companions into two monks around St. Francis of Assisi, whom the saint orders to convert the hawks and the sparrows, is beautifully conceived, written, directed, and photographed. But in the second half of the film the satire becomes either slapstick or so far-fetched as to seem pointless, and though an occasional comic touch still registers effectively, the sophomorically desperate straining to get in a potshot at everything, as well as the obtrusion of effects for effects' sake, manage to undo much of the good of the first half.

A more upsetting, but still highly imposing, miscalculation is Vittorio de Seta's *Almost a Man*. De Seta, who made that overwhelming film unjustly condemned to speedy disappearance, *Bandits of Orgosolo,* here examines the circumstances that turned an intelligent young man into an unhappy, self-destructive voyeur. The script is a rather ordinary psychiatric case history, undistinguished in the writing, and finally commonplace and unilluminating. But acting, direction, and photography combine to make *Almost a Man* visually commanding from start to finish. It can honestly be said that de Seta and his cinematographer, Dario di Palma, have succeeded in making a film of which every frame is worthy of framing, a film you would prefer to see, not on a theatre screen, but hanging, image by image, on your wall.

For example, a writer struggling for inspiration at his typewriter has become a filmic platitude. Here, however, the oppressive lighting, the expressive face of that flawless actor, Jacques Perrin, and the impressive camera angles merge to make the conventional motif a profound experience. The way in which the white sheet in the typewriter creeps up between us and the hero's face, obliterating more and more of it, and then, with a shift of the carriage, starts its unholy march over again; the manner in which a page of manuscript is being belabored by a thick, severely excising pencil until almost all traces of writing are obliterated; a view, suddenly, of the writer's face from below, through the typewriter keys, which are now projected, like some horrible rash, onto that grappling face; the final explosive gesture with which everything is swept to the floor, the camera hurtling along—all this is cinematographic art of the first order.

So, too, is a pheasant hunt, made unbearable in its sad cruelty through striking use of repetition, yet, again, by ingenious camera work, auditory effects, and montage, turned into nightmarish beauty. Or there is a series of shots in which the hero is losing a girl to his brother now dancing with her. I have never seen triple close-ups, two happy faces and one wretched one, maneuvered with such choreographic imaginativeness across the screen. Just three large faces, joining, separating, evolving: the two radiant ones now obscuring the third, now parting to reveal it in its full agony. If the screenplay could have lived up to the rest of the film, *Almost a Man* would have been a triumph.

Much can be said, too, for an insinuating little charmer from Czechoslovakia, *Intimate Lighting*. Ivan Passer's film tells of a small-town music teacher's entertaining for a couple of days a former fellow student from the Prague Conservatory. The friend is to be guest soloist with the local orchestra, and he brings with him a pretty and playful mistress. The host, an *homme moyen sensuel,* lives with his amiably dumpy wife, two small children, and two charmingly eccentric parents. There are several scenes that are gems of spontaneous, offhanded, rather microscopic humor, none the less fraught with total humane sympathy. Best of all are a much-interrupted string-quartet session, where a little night music results in much funny mutual scraping on nerves; and a nocturnal drinking bout for the two friends in which bumbling conviviality and melancholy longings for the greenness in the other man's yard blend into the very texture of human confusion. There are unforgettable lines, as when, after the friends have listened to a symphony of snores from various rustic sleepers, the guest leads the host to the door of the bedroom where his mistress is sleeping, and asks with a mixture of Candaules-like pride, amusement, mild resentment (she is a rather childish creature), and even a trace of cosmic sadness, "Have you ever heard a *lovely* woman snore?"

Milos Forman was represented by *Loves of a Blonde,* likewise in the tradition of recent Czech films: small people, everyday incidents, and sympathetic scrutiny not untinged by a sense of the absurd. But this film seemed to me less pleasing than Forman's previous *Black Peter,* for reasons that are hard to pin down. Perhaps it is that in the earlier work Forman brought out more mischievously the surreal inherent in reality; now an overgenerous dose of ordinariness gets the better of a nice touch here, a moving insight there. *Loves of a Blonde* accentuates Forman's tendency to stretch slenderness beyond the breaking point.

The Yugoslav film, *Three,* offers a trio of diverse but equally harrowing episodes from World War II. It is based on short stories by a notable experimental fictionist, Antonije Isakovic, who collaborated on the script with Aleksandar Petrovic, the director. The first sequence relates an incident during the initial panic of the German invasion: a man is killed as a fifth columnist by ignorant soldiers abetted by the mob merely because he cannot pronounce his r's correctly. The episode effectively evokes the forlornness of a small nation caught in a huge war, and the petty meanness of crowds in the grip of fear. The second episode is a more or less conventional hunt of a Partisan and a regular Army man by Nazi soldiers, dogs, and planes, but the relationship between the two men, one absolutely brave, the other slowly emerging from cowardice, is not unmoving, though portrayed somewhat sketchily. The last sequence, about the execution of an attractive girl collaborationist and its effect on a sensitive Partisan officer, is rather primitively written and filmed. *Three* is structurally and otherwise indebted to *Paisan,* though it lacks the power of Rossellini's film.

Several rungs lower was Hungary's *The Roundup,* a study of nineteenth-century police brutality, both psychological and physical. Miklós Jancsó's film is jerkily told, full of obscurities and loose ends as well as sheer improbability, but there are good scenes in it and also a feeling for composition and the use of sets nicely learned from Antonioni. France's *The Shameless Old Lady,* based on a Brecht short story and showing the strain of drawing out a vignette to feature size, tells of an old woman who, widowed, suddenly changes from drudge to Sybarite, much to her family's dismay and her own satisfaction. René Allio's film is quite amateurish, but that superb actress, Sylvie, invests the protagonist with a sly vitality that makes one oblivious to the surrounding ricketiness.

An all-Scandinavian coproduction brought to the screen Knut Hamsun's *Hunger,* and Henning Carlsen's film did have a good period atmosphere, pleasing performances, and one job of pure bravura by Per Oscarsson as the autobiographical hero. But the gloom and sordidness of the film are so unrelieved, the pride of its hero is so monotonously fanatical, that first the mind, and gradually even the heart, ceased to be engaged. Also worth a pat is *Wholly Communion,* a 47-minute record of American beat and British quasi-beat poets disporting themselves amusingly before a scarcely less amusing audience in London's Albert Hall.

The rest was disappointing or downright bad. Of Resnais' *La Guerre est finie* I shall probably write when it opens commercially; perhaps also of Godard's two new, and customarily offensive, films, *Pierrot le fou* and *Masculine Feminine.* Bresson's *Balthazar* carries that filmmaker's perverse aridity and maniacal pseudo-mysticism a depressing step farther, and Agnes Varda's *Les Créatures* is the last word in distastefully pointless, pretentious mumbo-jumbo. A Czech episodic film, and a Russian and a Belgian entry might as well be passed over in silence, as should campy revivals of old Garbo and De Mille claptrap. A splicing together of three unrelated but equally ineffectual documentaries, *The Scene,* was boring, as was Bernardo Bertolucci's maiden effort, *The Grim Reaper* (preferable, at that, to his later, fulsomely overpraised *Before the Revolution*). But a word must be emphatically said about Torre Nilsson's latest compilation of bogus pyschology and politics with pretentious *frissons* thrown in, *The Eavesdropper*. The word is: Desist!

NO THANKS

Not much a moviegoer can give thanks for this Thanksgiving. Turkeys, to be sure, are plentiful, foremost among them Jules Dassin's *10:30 P.M. Summer*. A script by Dassin and Marguerite Duras based on one of her antinovels—two others, *This Angry Age* and *Moderato Cantabile* have already yielded rich flops—is bad enough. Add to this ostentatious sexual display, *faisandé* photography, bathetic dialogue ("I think I can fight against everything except this fatigue! It's a fatigue that comes from way back, made up of everything!"), and pretentious direction that insists on rubbing *our* noses in the messes *it* has perpetrated, and all combine to make a worthy sequel to Dassin's unfortunately unforgettable *Phaedra*.

The cinematography of Gabriel Pogany strives determinedly to equal Goya or, at least, the Picasso of the blue period, and thus achieves a hammy impact or two. Typical is a sequence in which the dipsomaniac wife is seen in close-up with the Morandiesque shadow of a bottle looming on the wall behind her; or, another one in a Madrid flamenco joint where technicolor is used to film people rigorously clad in black and white, except for one red flower pinned to a dress that becomes the bloody center of a zebraed whirligig.

Melina Mercouri would have to get away from Dassin before we could tell whether she can still act (once, very long ago, she seemed able to); the paltry Romy Schneider has increased her stature only in the area of the bosom, which has grown noticeably since its last exposure in *Boc-*

caccio 70. But Peter Finch deserves a tribute and a lament. This intelligent, elegant, and, above all, clean actor—he is the most eloquent underplayer since Ralph Richardson, and far less studied—has been consistently undervalued and maltreated by the movies. Whenever given half a chance, he turns in a performance of Brancusi-like streamlining and simplicity; but more often, as here, he is given no chance at all.

The bulkiest disappointment of the month, however, is René Clément's *Is Paris Burning?* The maker of that masterpiece, *Forbidden Games,* and of the excellent *Bataille du rail,* has been steadily declining of late, but I hoped that he might here do for World War II what David Lean did for Lawrence's desert warfare, or Kubrick for Spartacus' uprising. Instead, *Is Paris Burning?,* like its protagonist, never catches fire, and merely follows in the mammoth footsteps of *The Longest Day* or *Battle of the Bulge.* It lacks both clarity and suspense, and features the usual stars in bit parts for which, trading on their glamor, they do less than bit players would. The script, chiefly the work of Gore Vidal, though three other scenarists are variously credited, was hardly worth Vidal's fight for top billing; in it, the customary action sequences alternate with the obligatory repartee, to which Vidal is merely able to add a touch of feyness, as when a surrendering German officer observes that he will at last have time to read *War and Peace.* Too bad those who made this film didn't.

Saddening, too, is the score by Maurice Jarre, who is rapidly becoming the most schizophrenic composer in the cinema. For small films he is capable of composing or arranging pointedly imaginative scores; for spectacles, he erects musical towers of Babel. From behind the obvious and unpleasant dubbing, as through ill-fitting dentures, two performances come close to registering: Gert Fröbe's General von Choltitz and Pierre Vaneck's liaison man from the FFI to the Allies—but, then, these are the only parts whose bare bones display anything like a speck of meat.

Georgy Girl is an attempt to blend the romantic

realism of *Room at the Top* with the lowbrow avant-gardism of Beatles farce, and the result is a hodge-podge of the spuriously sentimental, the simple mindedly absurdist, and the genuinely tasteless. As the oafish Cinderella of the title, Lynn Redgrave (a girl who carries unattractiveness to heroic proportions) gives a performance that is so artfully natural, cloyingly tomboyish, and aggressively charmless that it could not fail to elicit the enthusiasm of most reviewers. As for *The Fortune Cookie,* it conforms to the by now firmly established Billy Wilder formula: sophomoric misanthropy; machine-made cynicism; gags, gags, and more gags (two or three of them funny, the rest tripping over their own floor-length beards); and a cop-out as big and factitious as all Movieland. Wilder's goody-goody endings would be sticky in any context; following on the pseudotoughness that goes before, they are the essence of nausea. Walter Matthau, an actor who looks like a half-melted rubber bulldog, delivers the wisecracks for whatever they are worth.

A more painful letdown is Roman Polanski's *Cul-de-sac.* Already in his previous film, *Repulsion,* it was hard to recognize the master of *Knife in the Water* and two or three brilliant shorts, all made in Poland; here, except for some clever nastiness, generally quite gratuitous, no artistry survives. A film in which all characters are perverted or feeble-minded or both is possible if it adds up to an oblique comment on something: here almost all behavior is unmotivated or pointless, neither really funny nor exciting, only mildly distasteful, with whatever shock value mild distastefulness has. Of sympathy for anyone there can be no question, least of all for Polanski, who coauthored this script with Gerard Brach, his collaborator on *Repulsion.* I shall spare you the idiocies of the plot.

As for the actors, Françoise Dorléac continues to strike me as a shrunken head bordered on one side by a waterfall of hair, on the other by an undulating landscape of body, and on none by talent. Donald Pleasence merely repeats his customary performance, which, like the Reverend Chasuble's sermon on the meaning of the manna in the wilderness can be adapted to almost any occasion, joyful or, as in the present case, distressing. Lionel Stander plays a serio-comic thug in much the same way he always has, and various others manage to be as undistinguished as the script will allow, which is plenty. As another gangster, Jack MacGowran is pretty good imitation Guiness, but that is what Sir Alec is these days even more convincingly.

Krzysztof Komeda's bitingly suggestive jazz score is probably the only salvageable feature, and, significantly, Komeda is the only other Pole creatively involved in this English-made film. Poland was a blessing for the Paris-born Polanski: the constraints of socialist realism were the bars of a cage through which he performed dazzling escapes. Set free, his talents are promiscuously dispersed.

But the worst current shock is François Truffaut's latest, *Fahrenheit 451*. Ray Bradbury's book was a shaky basis for a work of art, but I had hoped that, by ignoring Bradbury's dialogue and other weaknesses, the film might come to something. The trouble is that Truffaut clearly likes the novel: though *1984* has already been turned into an inferior film, other tales of future fascism were still available—Huxley's *Brave New World*, for example, or Henry Green's *Concluding,* both more accomplished and rewarding.

Fahrenehit 451 tells of a future Fire Brigade whose job, houses being fireproof, is to burn books; these are deemed inflammatory by the State and are still inflammable. Montag, an exemplary fireman, is tireless at unearthing and destroying books that rebellious spirits have ingeniously concealed. His wife, Linda, is typical of the new anesthetized society, in which most people are happy with comic strips and wall-sized TV into which viewers can become incorporated. Some few people still play with their breasts or fur collars to maintain some semblance of feeling; others even harbor books, considered to be the root of evil untogetherness.

Riding home on the monorail, Montag meets Clarisse, a

young woman who still reads and feels. Gradually she
wins him over to these noble activities; his conversion is
accelerated by witnessing an older woman's choosing to be
burned alive with her books. Finally, both Clarisse and
Montag, who has been turned in by his own wife, escape
to the woods, where the Book People lead a kind of
aboriginal life. (Their survival is not made at all convincing.)

These good folk commit a book apiece to memory, and
are named after their books: Machiavelli's The Prince,
Stevenson's Weir of Hermiston, or Ray Bradbury's Mar-
tian Chronicles (Western civilization, it seems, has some
pretty slender underpinnings). These books and names
they pass on to their children, until some day culture and
decency return. Clarisse becomes The Memoirs of Saint-
Simon, which Julie Christie mouths in execrable French
and Montag turns into Poe's Tales of Mystery and
Imagination which Oskar Werner mangles with his
awkward English. I have, incidentally, serious doubts
about Poe and Saint-Simon being able, as the film implies,
to live together happily ever after.

Had the budget been bigger, the set and costume design
could at least have avoided the clumsy coupling of the
futuristic with the contemporary, sometimes almost as
ludicrous as in *Alphaville*. But it is less the visual im-
probabilities than the aural and intellectual impossibilities
that matter. In vain does Truffaut come up with impressive devices: closing in, with tiny jump-cuts, on a terrified face; blacking out half the screen to hem in a
harassed victim; showing the hero simultaneously in close-
up and medium shot with slightly different expressions;
dissolving almost imperceptibly from the hero's sleepless
face into the heroine's equally sleepless one. The fact remains that Bradbury's vision is not on the level of those
gloriously dangerous books, but on that of the state-
promulgated comic strips.

The performers work competently, except for the
plainly sleep-walking Werner; Nick Roeg's photography

achieves some tricky coloristic effects; and Bernard Herrmann's score, though ostentatious, is preferable to the dialogue.

ART TAINT AND ART ATTAINED

The National Student Film Awards for 1966 made a poor showing. It may be that the writing, painting, or composing of college students would have been no better, but, on the other hand, neither would it have been displayed at Lincoln Center, excerpted for TV presentation, and lauded by the *New York Times*. (Come to think of it, I can't guarantee the last item.) What was particularly dispiriting was that some of the losers were better than the winners, but I wish to dwell here on two points only.

First, that there was a category called "Experimental Film." The obnoxious claptrap it proffered must be blamed largely on the organizers and judges. It is a colossal piece of stupidity to institute such a category when you already have "Documentary," "Dramatic" and "Animated" categories. For this means either that, in the latter three, films are expected to be old hat, or that to qualify as "Experimental" is an end in itself. Typically, the winner in this class was something called *Metanomen*, a bunch of boring tricks meaninglessly strung together. The title, I suppose, is meant to be translated as "The Unnamable." It was, in fact, unspeakable.

A category like that, I am afraid, invites the worst. And, significantly, it is only in the area of film that such madness prevails. There are, glory be, no awards for experimental novels or paintings or music (not even at Donaueschingen), which, needless to say, does not prevent works in various competitions from being radical and winning prizes. But in film there is even a festival of ex-

perimental films—and, of all places, in Belgium, where
they haven't been able to make a decent rear-guard film
yet. Those who are still unconvinced of the worthlessness
of labels like "Avant-garde" or "Experimental," I
earnestly urge to read Hans Magnus Enzensberger's essay,
"The Aporias of the Avant-garde," reprinted in Philip
Rahv's *Modern Occasions*.

My second strong objection is not unrelated to the first.
The grand prize for the "Dramatic" film went to an abortion called *The Little Match Girl* by someone from Boston
University who, when in New York, obviously camps out
with Andy Warhol and Company. This sophormoric concoction featured an unattractive and untalented girl (and,
by the looks of it, quite possibly lobotomized as well) who
kept explaining why she likes to light matches—and lit
them continually—while Warhol, in whose studio the
inaction took place, went about his monkey business, and
his aide-de-camp, Gerard Malanga, did the frug all by
himself. An off-screen voice read snatches of Andersen's
tale.

The platonic pyromaniac then went home, where she
lounged about in a bra and panties. Next she dressed up
nattily and warmly, went out to nocturnal Fifth Avenue
carrying a container of those foot-long fancy party
matches, which she occasionally wanly held out to a puzzled passer-by. There was more off-screen desecration of
Andersen. And that was all. A large segment of the hip,
mostly student audience in Philharmonic Hall booed and
hissed. Even they! But, next morning, Bosley Crowther
loved it: it could have easily been stretched, he wrote in
his *Times* column, to a fine full-length film. If only some
reviewers could be stretched into full-length human
beings.

Well, Andy Warhol's *The Chelsea Girls* is full-length
with a vengeance. It goes on for about 3½ hours on two
separate but equally dismal screens, thus really lasting
seven hours. But because a minute of Warhol's brand of
boredom is easily the equivalent of an hour of the Hollywood kind, the actual duration is 17½ days.

Ostensibly intending to show how the decadent tenants of the Hotel Chelsea live, Warhol has merely invited his various friends, followers, and freaks to disport themselves *ad libitum* and *ad nauseam,* while his no less freakish camera either just lies there chewing the crud [sic], or jiggles around as if palsied, or zooms in and out compulsively, for no reason except that the zoom lens is a gadget, and Warhol's birdbrain is enamorated of gadgets. Indeed, I think it *is* one. We get narcissists, pederasts, lesbians, transvestites, drug addicts, sadists, hustlers supposedly revealing the shabbiness of it all, but actually reveling in the exhibitionism of it. If, for example, Nico, who is a genuine narcissist all right, primps and preens for the camera for a minor eternity, that still does not yield any revelation. Either the girl or the camera would have to be a little more than an idiot. As it is, no comment on narcissism emerges, no point of view, not even anything like the beginning of a conspectus. And when the subject is more ticklish, say, homosexuality or sadism, the "exposé" becomes even more coyly truncated: suggestions, titters, token gestures. Not even the courage of scabrous convictions.

One character, the self-styled Pope of Greenwich Village, does reel off a few funny remarks along with endless trashy farrago. But it is all too stagey to be *cinéma-vérité,* too stupid to be cinema. *The Chelsea Girls* is a testimonial to what happens when a camera falls into the hands of an aesthetic, moral, and intellectual bankrupt.

I turn with relief to *A Man for All Seasons,* which may not be a film for all seasons, but certainly is a godsend in this particularly impoverished one. I have written a good deal elsewhere *(The Hudson Review, Theatre Arts)* about this commendable but somewhat less than considerable play; in adapting his work for the screen, Robert Bolt once again both idealized and oversimplified Thomas More, who was, at times, both more religiously fanatical and broadly facetious than Bolt's protagonist. By giving us such a flawless man, Bolt gives us a flawed play and film.

From the film, moreover, some of the play's strongest or wittiest lines have been excised.

Some of these lines may have seemed too epigrammatic or erudite or philosophical for the larger public (but will the larger public take to this film in any case?); other changes I cannot for the life of me comprehend. Thus it is unfathomable why the immensely moving bit of dialogue when More sees his wife for the last time: "*More:* That's a nice dress you have on. *Alice:* It's my cooking dress. *More:* It's very nice anyway. Nice color . . ." should have been reduced to: "*More:* That's a nice dress you have on. (*Pause.*) A nice color, anyway." Most of the lovely, understated pathos is unhappily lost thereby.

On the other hand, it is all too painfully clear why More's answer to the jailer who tries to justify his carrying out of heartless orders by explaining that he is a plain, simple man—"Oh, sweet Jesus! These plain, simple men!"—has been cut. Movie audiences, after all, are plain, simple men (and women), and God forbid that they should take offense! Not only that, but producers, too, are plain, simple men. Like Samuel Z. Arkoff, for instance, the cigar-smoking executive vice-president of American International Pictures, who had this to say recently about A.I.P.'s *The Wild Angels:* "No one was more surprised than we were when the film was chosen to be shown at Venice. However, it did give the film a sort of art taint, which is important in Europe." Now why should the Arkoffs of this world, who surely would not have permitted the beheading of a saint, be insulted?

But I digress. *A Man for All Seasons* suffers from the usual ills that plague a play adapted to the screen. Neither Bolt, nor his director, Fred Zinnemann, was able to do much about that. The outdoor scenes always have that feel of, "Oh, yes, that was thrown in to make it more of a movie!" about them, and Zinnemann's direction is decent but plodding. When, in the trial scene, the camera shuttles swiftly across the faces of the spectators, it seems rather as if Zinnemann had suddenly remembered that he had forgotten to put the art taint in. One device, though, is effective. A bird in a tree sings against a delicate pale blue sky. Cut to More and the headsman on the scaffold, against the same sky. But one bird does not make a summer, to say nothing of all seasons.

Ted Moore's color photography is consistently appealing, and production and costume design are, on the whole, more graceful and flowing than the sometimes jagged continuity of the script. Georges Delerue is uncomfortable with antiquarian scores, as his music for the Comédie Française's recent *L'Avare* also demonstrated. The male supporting cast could not be improved on; even Orson Welles as Wolsey is, for a change, controlled and effective (his Swedish consul in *Is Paris Burning?* was an outrageously dishonest performance), and Robert Shaw's Henry VIII is a small masterpiece. But Wendy Hiller's Wife to More is unexpectedly unmoving, and Susannah York's Daughter is expectedly so.

What makes this film required viewing, however, is Paul Scofield's More. In the theatre you could not get close enough to that subtly overpowering face. Now, with close-ups, you can. This countenance seems almost immobile—even as the voice appears never to be raised. But, within that deliberately narrowed range, the expressions, like the inflections, are a perfect, filigree variety, and as scrupulously precise as the illuminations of a precious medieval manuscript. It is all there: the pity, the pride, the just contempt, the righteous but controlled anger, the infinite compassion. And, above all, the sad, wise, ironic patience. When, in the final self-defense, that patience is cast away, it is as if you saw the soul, unbearably luminous, shooting out of the body into heaven.

A BIT OVERBLOWN

Michelangelo Antonioni's *Blow-Up,* ignoring the precept
of Archibald MacLeish, means more than it is. A film, I
feel, should *be* before it means, should have a reality of its
own before making metaphysical pronouncements. The
metaphysics of *Blow-Up* are in limbo, which may not be a
bad place for metaphysics, but is no place for people.
Even if people are lost souls, as those in the film certainly
are, their relationships to one another, to their surround-
ings, to the work of art in which they figure, should be
firmly apprehended and made convincing.

A synopsis of the wispy plot is unfortunately una-
voidable. Dawn in London: A noisy rag-party of students
with their faces painted white rides in a jeep into a building complex; a bunch of ragged men emerge from a
flophouse. One of the latter gets into a Rolls-Royce; he is
a highly successful photographer who has spent the night
taking pictures for his forthcoming book of photographs.
The mimes start collecting money for some cause or other
and touch him for a bill. He drives back to his large studio
cum apartment in a charming mews. A battery of models
and personnel awaits him. In his filthy bum's attire, he
rushes to his work, photographing first a sexy model
(played by Verouchka, a sexy model) in a series of extremely erotic, scantily clad poses. He washes and changes,
and proceeds to shoot a group of fashion models in suggestive mod clothes and weird groupings. He saunters over
to a neighboring studio where an artist friend refuses to sell
him one of his abstractions. He casts some yearning
glances at the artist's wife, and returns to his own studio
where two silly, pushy teenyboppers intrude on him in the
hope he will photograph them. He gets rid of them and

drives off to an out-of-the-way antique shop he wants to
buy.

The shop owner is out, and the photographer wanders
into a neighborhood park, taking pictures of pigeons and
such, until he comes upon a couple, a young girl and a
middle-aged man, in a rather quaint love-ballet and starts
avidly photographing them. The girl has a curious way of
both leading the man on and dancing away from him. As
the photographer is about to leave, the girl, who has just
caught on, runs after him and tries to beg, buy, or wrest
the film from him. He refuses, takes some shots of her
running away, and returns to the antique shop. He haggles
with the owner, a young girl who is tired of the business
and wants to travel (everyone wants what he hasn't got),
and buys from her an old-fashioned airplane propeller.
Then he drives to a lunch appointment with a literary
friend who is writing the text for his picture book. He tells
the writer that the idyllic shots of the lovers in the park
will be a perfect conclusion for an otherwise violent book.
Through the plate-glass window someone has been spying
on them, but disappears when followed. As our hero
drives home, a peace demonstrator sticks a sign into his
car, but the sign is presently blown out of the convertible.

Back at the studio, the photographer is met by the girl
from the park. She must have those negatives; she has
been tailing him, and will tail him into bed to get them. A
dalliance begins that might lead to a little more than a
quick sex bout, when they are interrupted by the delivery
of the propeller. The staging and editing do not make clear
whether intercourse occurs, but the girl leaves, having
received a roll of film. The film is a phoney, as is the
phone number the girl gives the aroused photographer. He
now proceeds to develop the real film, and, in studying the
blow-ups carefully, notices something fishy. After a series
of hectic magnifications, detections, further magnifications, it emerges that a man with a gun was hiding in the
bushes. Apparently he killed the man in the tryst, for
something like a body appears in the shrubbery in the pictures of the girl running away.

Our hero calls his writer friend with the startling revelation, but his story is not believed. He is interrupted by the return of the mini-skirted would-be models, drifts into a mini-orgy with them, packs them off, and goes back to the by now nocturnal park. The man's body is indeed there. A noise, as of a camera clicking, frightens the photographer and he drives away. He wanders into the apartment of his painter friend and finds the couple copulating. The wife looks at him longingly even as she is being made love to by her husband. Our hero returns to his studio and finds it ransacked, his photographic evidence of a crime stolen or destroyed. He is visited by the painter's wife who tells him she can't leave her husband for him. She wants to talk to him about her problem, while he can go on only about the body in the park. Neither can help the other.

The photographer is driving to a party where his writer friend is, but, en route, he glimpses the mystery girl. He thinks she has ducked into a rock'n'roll club, and looks for her there in vain. All that happens is that one of the performers, angered, stomps his electric guitar to bits, a melee ensues as the kids fight over the pieces, and our hero somehow ends up with the biggest chunk, runs out with it, and promptly discards it.

He finds the writer at what proves to be a marijuana party, and urges him to come inspect and photograph the body with him. The friend, high on the stuff, refuses; the exhausted photographer falls asleep. He gets back to the park at dawn, but the body is gone. Now the mimes from the previous morning arrive in the park, and two of them proceed to mime a tennis game, while the rest mime engrossed spectators. Our hero finds himself caught up in the imaginary game. When the imaginary ball is hit out into the park, he actually mimes picking it up and tossing it back onto the court. Suddenly he begins to hear the nonexisting ball: its puck-puck grows louder as the camera comes in for an overhead shot of the bemused photographer, forlornly heading for home.

The essential point of the film is Pirandellian: the real and the imaginary encroach upon each other and become, finally, inseparable. Most obviously so at film's end: the corpse has vanished as has all evidence of the murder— the very real killing has been rendered nonexistent; conversely the illusory tennis game has been willed, believed into existence. Related to this notion is that of the interpenetration of opposites, whereby the grave and the trivial, the earnest pursuit and the game, become interchangeable. We see this at the very beginning: The idle, roisterous mimes turn out to be collecting for some "worthy" cause, while the grim, shabby young man emerging from the flophouse with nothing but a small, grimy parcel unwraps an expensive camera from it and gets into his luxury car.

Or take the session when the young man photographs his luscious model. The foolish business of taking suggestive pictures is converted into, indeed usurps the place of, sexual fulfillment. He gets closer and closer to her as he photographs away, and disarranges and disarrays her more and more. Occasionally there is even a piddling, nibbling proto-kiss. The girl finally sinks back supine and the man straddles her as he and his camera swoop down for a clicking climax. All along, he rattles off clucking, hectoring, spasmodic verbiage, which, in its accelerandos and crescendos as well as in its ambiguity, is the very deverbalized language of intercourse: "Lurch, lurch more . . . That's great! . . . Now give it to me! More of that, as fast as you can . . . Very good, marvelous, great! Much more, much more! . . . Now really give it! . . . Go, go, and again! Lovely, make it come, luv, for me, for me! Yeah, yeah, yes!" The girl now falls back on the floor and feebly stirs her limbs to relax them; she is deliciously, narcissistically satisfied. Our hero, all pseudopassion spent, collapses on a near-by sofa.

Amid all this a twinge of real jealousy occurs: "Whom the hell were you with last night?" the photographer at one point asks the girl whom he has himself just kept waiting an hour; she merely smiles, mysteriously, bitchily. She tells him she's off to Paris. Later, he meets her at the pot party and exclaims, "I thought you were in Paris!" She drawls, "I *am* in Paris." Shades of des Esseintes, who sets out for England but, on a rainy night in Calais, as he dines on mutton chops at an English-looking inn, concludes that he has had the English experience. But Huysmans' dilettante still had to dislodge himself a bit; today's trips, in a cigarette or sugar cube, come to us. And for those to whom Paris is a drug-orgy, why shouldn't a drug-orgy be Paris?

As one's husband makes love to one, one's face clutches that of a lover; illusion and reality, seriousness and play have become identical; all things end by floating into one another. So when our hero looks at his blow-ups of the park scene, the soundtrack rustles with wind-stirred leaves; when he is out inspecting the cadaver, he is frightened by what sounds like the click of a shutter—he may have been transferred to someone else's incriminating film. In the studio, strange photographs have their strident aliveness; while people, grotesquely costumed and environed, seen in reflections or through semitransparencies, become dehumanized and reified before our eyes.

Fusing—or confusing—similitudes suffuse the whole work. When the girl from the peace march sticks her "GO AWAY" placard into a Rolls convertible, she thinks she has planted her banner on the enemy's stronghold; but our callous hero, whose car it is, is just as indifferent then as a bit later, when the placard is swept out of his fast-moving car. Similarly, when the neck of a guitar over which teenagers fought like ravening beasts ends up in the hero's possession, he can only throw it away; even the typical mod passers-by, who next pick it up, discard it with utmost indifference. Those who march for peace and those who disturb it are, ultimately, equally disoriented, their sacred symbols equally inefficacious.

Even more striking is the echo of colors. When the hero is photographing his model, he is dressed in pale colors (blue, beige), she in a black quasi-nightgown, and the flat backdrops are of a dark, brooding blue-green (this device of surrounding characters with a large, flat, monochrome expanse was well used by Antonioni before: the white hospital walls for the demented girl in *La Notte*; the red interior of the shack for the "siesta" in *Red Desert*.) Against this lowering viridescence, the pseudosexuality of the photography session takes on an even more stylized, artificial look. But when the hero is in the park, shooting the temptress and her victim, his own attire echoes all the colors from the studio session (black jacket, blueish shirt, white trousers), while the surrounding vegetation repeats the same, somewhat lurid, blue-green coloration of the backdrop. Antonioni, we learn, actually had the grass dyed for this sequence. The cold colors thus juxtaposed create the same kind of elegant detachment in the studio as in the park, and help suggest that both photography as lovemaking, and lovemaking as a subject for shooting (with camera or gun!) are rather alike: unnatural and un-wholesome.

So, too, when the hero visits the painter, he admires an abstraction of his which, to quote Francis Wyndham, has "colored dots arranged to give an effect of explosion." When the hero discovers the painter and his wife during intercourse, the camera pans to those explosive dots again—rather like the colored lights Tennessee Williams' Stella says she sees when her husband makes love to her. And when the painter s wife comes to see the pho-tographer and looks at the one remaining blow-up that the ransackers neglected to destroy—possibly because the corpse, in desperate magnification, shows only as a vague blur of dots—she exclaims, "Looks like one of those paintings!" There you have it: sex, murder, artistic crea-tion—nothing but the same swirling shapes and colors slightly rearranged. It is almost Baudelaire's forests of symbols where "*les parfums, les couleurs et les sons se répondent,*" except that here nature is not a temple; or, if so, the temple of a god who is malign, oblivious, or dead.

Characteristically, in a world where sensations, colors, sounds, and the perfume of available (which is to say all) flesh take on the functions of ratiocination and discourse, the word becomes debased and obsolete as a caudal appendage. Dialogue becomes a perfunctory caress or a sudden blow. When a group of absurd models in bizarre get-ups, posing among square transparent screens inside a ghostly white parallelipiped—the whole thing looking like a cubist-surrealist hallucination—fail to achieve the desired expression of breathless hebetude, the photographer barks at them, "Start again! Rethink it!" These fruging gum-chewers rethink? Or even think? But the angry tone tells all. Quite consistently, the film depends to an unprecedented degree on noises, and may be the first in which the climactic revelation is a sound: the dull but loud and persistent whacking of a nonexistent tennis ball. So, too, the lines spoken by the actors—the ably devious Vanessa Redgrave, the suitably subliminal Sarah Miles, and the (regrettably) charmless David Hemmings—are mostly balls of caprice batted about by backhanded drives.

The two basic statements of the film seem to be the painter's comment on his works, "They don't mean anything when I do them, just a mess. Afterward I find something to hang onto, like that leg. Then it all sorts itself out; it's like finding a clue in a detective story"; and the photographer's praise of his undeveloped park pictures, "very peaceful, very still," with which he wants to end his violent book to make it "ring truer." Life, like art, Antonioni appears to say, can be figured out only *a posteriori;* but we are in for some nasty surprises: the final truth does not ring true, or, rather, what rings true isn't the truth. (The film, by the way, is based on a story by Julio Cortázar, of whose novel, *Hopscotch,* it has been said that it must be read twice to be read at all; and the English adaptation is by Edward Bond, whose play, *Saved,* is a notable contribution to the theatre of cruelty.)

An essentially ironic relation between illusion and reality, why not? I believed Pirandello, and I am prepared to believe Antonioni, particularly since his photography, design, and direction are all spectacular. But there is a hitch. The grand philosophic stance is not, as in Pirandello, attached to characters and plots that have a life of their own.

It is the real that has to become illusory, after all, and the illusory real. When everything is evanescent, wraith-like, superficial—even the genuinely fleshly orgy with the mini-skirters is finally unreal because locomotion is substituted for emotion—only nebulae whirl into other nebulae, atoms into other configurations of atoms. There is nothing for me to make human contact with and become genuinely drawn to. It may all sort itself out in the end, but just what is that initial "it"? Unlike in a detective story, I haven't a clue.

SEVEN

GODARD AND THE GODARDIANS:

A Study in the New Sensibility

In the phrase "the new sensibility"—it may or may not have been coined by Susan Sontag—the operative word is, of course, *new,* not *sensibility.* It is nevertheless true that the word *sensibility* has never before been thrown, batted, kicked about as it has been of late, and not the least by Miss Sontag. That in itself raises two questions. First, cannot any word by which we are constantly bombarded, including the word *sensibility,* batter us into insensibility? May not the very thing it stands or is supposed to stand for become hateful to us? And secondly, are the people who indulge in such assiduous and militant sensibility-mongering perhaps doing so out of a lack of that quality—as it were, protesting too much?

However that may be, let us get back to the concept of "the new sensibility," which is supposed to account for the revolution in the arts—for things like aleatory and electronic music, or indeed, measured silence in place of music; for action painting, pop and op art, junk sculpture, and the like; for rock 'n' roll and its sundry derivatives in popular music; for happenings, events, environments, and other "mixed media," including psychedelic projections; and for a realm of film-making whose summit is Godard and bottom the "underground movies" or "New American Cinema," as, in its newly sensible way, it likes to call itself. These and many more the Pandora's box of contemporary pseudo-art has unleashed upon us: every kind of plague in fact, excepting only hope.

Who was the Pandora who actually opened the lid? As far as film is concerned, I would locate the moment of disaster—inasmuch as this can be done at all, and it can be done only approximately—in a seemingly innocent scene of Jean-Luc Godard's *Breathless*. In 1959, when it came out, that film looked rather good to me, as it did to most of us; today, though one can still see merit in it, it seems a considerably less satisfactory work. In this particular scene I'm talking of, the lovers have gone to the movies and are watching an American, or American-style, western, complete with thundering hooves and guns. But suddenly, we hear from the soundtrack two idiot voices reciting at each other Apollinaire's beautiful poem, *"Cors de chasse"*: *"Notre histoire est noble et tragique/ Comme le masque d'un tyran. . . ."* Now this is obviously nonsense: What business have the characters in a vulgar American western reciting one of France's finest twentieth-century lyrics at each other—and antiphonally, at that, as though it were dialogue that they were improvising?

Godard was doing one of three things here. He may have been trying to make fun of Apollinaire's poem by introducing it into a ridiculous context, or he may have been hoping to elevate the western to the stature of genuine art. Most likely, though, he was merely tossing a poem he had just stumbled on into an antithetical environment to create a comic shock effect. But whatever the intention, the "sensibility" that will indulge in this kind of effect is unmistakable. It is cynical, pretentious, and disaffected. Cynical, because it is willing to make a value judgment in the most casual, indeed backhanded, way; pretentious, be-

cause it will allude without justification to something that
is supposed to confer intellectual prestige on the film-
maker himself; disaffected, because it does not care what
the cost as long as it gets its kicks. When Truffaut introduces the story of Apollinaire and a young woman he
met on a train (a piece of fairly well-known literary
biography) into *Jules et Jim,* he explains what he is doing
and tries to justify it, whether or not to our full satisfaction is irrelevant. We are not left, as in the case of
Breathless, with something that strikes us as sensationalism and showing off.

It is in this direction that Godard has proceeded. One
watched with horror the gratuitous but arrogant devices
multiply, the idea being to jolt us, if possible continuously.
Baudelaire had already demanded of art that it surprise
us, but there is a considerable difference between the surprise and the jolt. A surprise may dilate our organs of perception and our understanding; it may deepen our
awareness of something we vaguely sensed; it may be an
old thing put in a new and more vital form. It is not a
mere shock, a titillation, a disturbance or reversal of the
established order. A surprise makes us expand and,
perhaps, exclaim; a jolt makes us contract and, most
likely, gasp. A surprise surpasses the expected, a jolt
merely bypasses it. In no case would Baudelaire, to say
nothing of Eliot, have subscribed to a statement Godard
attributes to Eliot in *Band of Outsiders:* "Everything that
is new is automatically traditional." (For "traditional,"
we are, of course, to read "accepted, acceptable, good.")
In art nothing is automatic; in Godard, just about everything.

What are the Godardian devices? To list a few at random: in-jokes, usually verbal or visual references to New
Wave films, often one's own; allowing actors to improvise
at length while the camera holds their faces in a close-up;
using stop-shots on the slightest excuse (usually while
someone is photographing somebody) or on none; panning
back and forth *ad nauseam* between the faces of two
talkers, often with an object in between them; using a

hand-held camera on the least provocation; making points by means of posters, signs, inscriptions behind the faces of characters—the whole inscription may be used or just a portion—for example, in *The Married Woman,* a sign reads "DANGER," and in the next shot the camera picks out the middle part of the word, to read: "ANGE." And further: the division of a film into episodes to each of which there is affixed a pretentious summary, often with some quotation for epigraph; the encouraging of actors to jump about (usually in gun duels) in a sort of unplanned, campy pseudo-ballet; the introduction of quick, short scenes, generally violent, which have no discernible connection with anything; references to literary or philosophical works either made by the camera picking them up on a shelf or in someone's hands, or by a character's quoting or mentioning them (these references are often wholly gratuitous); sudden deaths, often at the end of a film, where they are tacked on for no good reason except to provide an ending and a semblance of dramatic impact; stopping the music on the soundtrack for a few moments, and then resuming where it left off, all without motivation; a pontificating, pseudopoetic, pseudoprofound off-screen narration accompanying the most mundane occurrences on-screen; a character winking out at the audience and addressing them directly.

Devices such as these, and many kindred ones, are not necessarily bad—they may even be good—but when used promiscuously, repititiously, excessively, with the notion that they are *ipso facto* good, they become distasteful and ultimately dull. Godard's "new" rapidly turns into something other, and less, than the traditional: it becomes instant antique. Why do these innovations age so swiftly? Because, having nothing but them to lean on, Godard has to work them into the ground; because behind the devices there is nothing. Yet to a critic like Susan Sontag—a critic, by the way, who is "against interpretation," which is rather like being against criticism—this very affectless emptiness is a virtue. Of *Vivre sa Vie,* she writes, "We don't know

Nana's motives except at a distance, by inference. The film eschews all psychology; there is no probing of states of feeling, or inner anguish." And further, we read that *Vivre sa Vie,* like Godard's other movies, is "proof, rather than analysis. . . . It shows that something happened, not why it happened. It exposes the inexorability of an event."

Now all this is manifestly absurd. Obviously if the film eschews *all* psychology, we cannot even infer what Nana's motives are: Her actions are completely arbitrary, and we see them from such a distance that, unable to infer, we merely attribute whatever suits or pleases us. Yet we are told this is "proof" and "exposes the inexorability of an event." It does nothing of the kind. Miss Sontag confuses—I suspect, deliberately—an action with the portrayal of that action. That Godard has his heroine become a prostitute makes the event inevitable qua film, but it does not begin to make it inevitable or even plausible as an event, as a human action that the film is supposed to be portraying. The very word "proof" is tendentious and dishonest here. Art can only suggest, persuade, or at the utmost, demonstrate; it cannot prove. But irresponsible or downright bad artists and critics love to invoke the notions of proof, inevitability, the inexorable. These are generally elegant euphemisms for the arbitrary, the sloppy, the mindless. A piece of film has happened, and that is supposed to be its justification. It is because it is; it is like this because it is like this.

Or in other words, has the emperor no clothes? How marvelous! Who wants clothes anyway? There is more enterprise in walking naked. Nudity is so much more daring and more real. Well, that may be so in the case of avowed nudity, in nudity for a purpose, say, to show off a glorious body. But Godard's films pretend to clothes, they pretend to be constructs, artifacts, demonstrations of human action; in fact, however, they are nothing: not even nudity, only skeletons, and even those artificial, made of cardboard. Consider the dialogue even: here are two passages from *Contempt.* "Why do you assume this thoughtful air?—Because I am thinking of something, would you believe it?—Of what?—Of an idea." And again: "Why don't you love me any more?—That's life.—Why do you despise me?—That I will never tell you, not even if I were on the point of death." How pretentiously pseudomeaningful these utterances are, yet even a slightly closer look reveals them to be trite and hollow. Nor will it do to say that in Godard the words are unimportant. In his films, as he himself has proclaimed, "you have to listen to the people talking."

Miss Sontag goes so far as to take seriously a long speech of Nana's, from which she quotes and comments on the following: "I am responsible. I turn my head, I am responsible, I lift my hand, I am responsible." And further: "A plate is a plate. A man is a man. Life is . . . life." What began as a tipsy schoolboy's parody of Sartre ends with a grand revelation of mystical irreducibles, which, once again, prove merely the ultimate in platitudes, the quintessential truism. Yet Miss Sontag can assert thereupon, "Godard is perhaps the only director today who is interested in 'philosophical films' and possesses an intelligence and discretion equal to the task." If you are interested in learning how such philosophical film-makers come into being, here is an example. Miss Sontag interprets: "The twelve episodes of *Vivre sa Vie* are Nana's twelve stations of the cross. But in Godard's film the values of sanctity and martyrdom are transposed to a totally secular plane." (There are, actually, fourteen stations of the cross, but such details probably do not matter if you are against interpretation.) Questioned about the meaning of the twelve tableaus, Godard replied, "Why twelve? I don't know." But, to be sure, he had to add that the tableaus themselves "accentuate the theatrical aspect, the Brechtian side," as if using one measly device that Brecht also happened to use, and in a different medium at that, gave Godard's film a "Brechtian side."

But let us now approach Godard through a very different critic, Pauline Kael, that curious combination of lively shrewdness, sentimental-hysterical self-indulgence, and dependably plebeian tastes, who might be expected to be suspicious of Godard. Her hearty review of *Breathless* is rather too favorable—calling, for example, Jean Seberg's adequate, type-cast playing "exquisite"—but *Breathless* was, for its time and barring some lapses, a good enough film. About the ending of *Vivre sa Vie* she is duly skeptical, wondering why "the heroine [is] shot, rather than the pimp that the rival gang is presumably gunning for? Is she just a victim of bad marksmanship? If we express perplexity, we are likely to be told that we are missing the existentialist point: it's simply fate, she had to die. But a cross-eyed fate?" Well, that is properly doubtful, but by the time of *Band of Outsiders* Miss Kael is becoming reconverted to Godard.

Band of Outsiders is for Miss Kael "as if a French poet took an ordinary banal American crime novel and told it to us in terms of the romance and beauty he read between the lines"—can you imagine Valéry, Eluard, or Reverdy composing his poems in between the lines of Erle Stanley Gardner or Mickey Spillane? Not even André Breton or Raymond Queneau would have perpetiated such a thing, though it is true that Truffaut has done something like it in *Shoot the Piano Player*. Only there, for "French poet" you would have to read "French humorist." Miss Kael proceeds to defend the alienness of Godard's world of amateurish, infantile would-be gangsters by pointing to the alienness of American gangster movies that have "fed our imaginations and have now become part of us. And don't we—as children and perhaps even later—romanticize cheap movie stereotypes . . . ?" she asks, and that "perhaps even later" gives the show away. Certainly: Those who as adults can still wax dewy-eyed over the Cagney-Bogart-Robinson figure may relish Godard's overgrown pigmies who play at robbery and murder as they do at phrase-making and sex. On the other hand, even such moviegoers may prefer their hokum straight.

Apparently, it devolves to Godard's credit that "it is as if the artist himself were deprecating any large intentions and just playing around in the medium," which is peculiar praise at best, but particularly misapplied to a film that purports to examine cogently and even poetically the disaffected young. But, it seems, playing around with one's medium is, for Miss Kael as for Godard, poetry. She writes: "If I may be deliberately fancy: he aims for the poetry of reality and the reality of poetry. I have put it that way to be either irritatingly pretentious or lyrical—depending on your mood and frame of reference, in order to provide a critical equivalent for Godard's phrases." Unfortunately Miss Kael's little inversions have nothing whatever to do with the "lyrical," though if one's frame of reference happens not to include a single volume of decent poetry, Godard's and her maneuvers may indeed pass for lyricism.

Miss Kael continues: "When the narrator in *Band of Outsiders* says, 'Franz did not know whether the world was becoming a dream or a dream becoming the world' we may think that that's too self-consciously loaded with mythic fringe benefits and too rich an echo of the narrators of *Orphée* and *Les Enfants Terribles,* or we may catch our breath at the beauty of it." I cannot imagine anyone short of a sufferer from acute asthma catching his breath at that; but it *is* arresting that Miss Kael does not quote the full statement which runs, "*Franz pense à tout et à rien. Il se demande si c'est le monde . . .* [etc.]." Thinking about everything and nothing, apart from being a pretentious commonplace, unfortunately also happens to be the perfect description of Godard's *modus operandi.* Miss Kael then proceeds to argue that "those most responsive to Godard [whatever that means: connoisseurs? cultists? the happy few? imbeciles?] probably do both simultaneously," that is, object and gasp at the beauty of it. Well, why not? When one aims for the poetry of reality and the reality of poetry by wondering whether the world is becoming a dream or a dream becoming the world (while thinking about everything and nothing), it is only natural that he should leave us overcome by his Muse and musing about what's come over him.

But Miss Kael does not stop here. It seems that we have a similar dual reaction when we read Cervantes, and that

Godard's heroes "dreaming away at American movies, seeing life in terms of cops and robbers" are descended from Don Quixote "confused by tales of Knight Errantry, going out to do battle with imaginary villains." The comparison of Godard to Cervantes is so ludicrous that, if I bother to refute it, I run the risk of seeming as quixotic as the Don and as absurd as Godard. But let me at least point out that the Don stands for chivalry in an age that has become mercantile and practical, which makes him both noble and risible because he champions the right in an obsolete and, therefore, wrong way. Godard's heroes, however, want to be reckless and wicked in a manner that is unreal and inept, so that, instead of being at least wrong in the right way, they are, in fact, wrong in the wrong way. Don Quixote is heroic, comical, and pathetic. Godard's heroes are deluded squirts, amateurish hoodlums. There are no tragic contradictions in them—nothing to engage our feeling of pity or our sense of beauty.

"At times," writes Miss Kael, "it seems as if the movie had no points of reference outside itself. When this imagined world is as exquisite as in *Band of Outsiders* we may begin to feel that this indifference or inability to connect with other worlds is a kind of aesthetic expression and a preference." No points of reference outside the movie itself; an exquisite imaginary world—this applies at least as much to *Last Year at Marienbad,* which Miss Kael, quite rightly, rejects, as to *Band of Outsiders,* which she touts. The same criteria can be made to denigrate or vindicate, as Miss Kael's whims would have it. "The sadness that pervades the work is romantic regret that you can no longer believe in the kind of movie you once wanted to be enfolded in . . ." So there you have it: Regret for the unreality of the world of Bogie and Jimmie Cagney is, it would seem, a valid artistic and philosophical concern. Miss Kael concedes that "Godard may . . . share some of his characters' delusions." That "may" is sublime! Godard is the essence of immature, escapist nostalgia under a thin veneer of sophisticated irony, and it *may* be that because Miss Kael shares some of his attitudes his films become so attractive to her.

About *Masculine Feminine* her enthusiasm is almost
unlimited. As might be expected, the self-contradictions
now ring out as intemperately and incongruously as a
defective fire alarm. The style of the disaffected kids in
the film "is made up of everything adults attack as the
worst and shoddiest forms of Americanization and
dehumanization. It is the variety of forms of 'Coca
Cola'—the synthetic life they were born to and which they
love, and which they make human, and more beautiful
and more 'real' than the old just-barely-hanging-on adult
culture." These kids, it appears, "have the beauty of youth
which can endow Pop with poetry . . ." This, I fear, is so
much sentimental nonsense. How can Pop, which is, and
boasts of being, anti-poetry, possibly be endowed with
poetry? If a great actor were to recite the telephone book,
it still would not, despite the stock hyperbole of daily reviewers, become art. At best, the actor's voice production
and demeanor might be artistic; the telephone book would
remain the telephone book. It may be that to a critical
malcontent with a strong anti-intellectual streak the excesses of fruging and fornication, rock 'n' roll and af-
fectlessness begin to take on the colors of Utopia; but how
a combination of violence, heedlessness, narcissism, aimless locomotion, banal chatter can possibly be made
more real and beautiful than any culture, whether flour-
ishing or merely hanging on, is incomprehensible to me.
Except, of course, from the point of view of the yé-yé
world, which is doubly looking-glass country: in its reversal of reality, and in its narcissistic mirror-gazing.

My point is that youth, merely by doing something, cannot make that thing more beautiful or more real; perhaps
real (though not more real), simply because it is happening, but surely not beautiful. Botticelli's *Venus,* if she
stood there picking her nose, might still be beautiful, but
she could not turn nose-picking into a thing of beauty and
a joy forever. Nor is a culture, merely because it is
beleaguered, to be made mock of by a critic wishing to
prove how youthful and "with it" she is.

But Pauline Kael becomes even more preposterous. She says that these young people "have their feeling for each other," but when she describes the heroine of the film, the words she uses are "nothing," "empty," "thin," "reedy," and "soulless." The hero "can have her and have her and she is never his." What kind of feeling for each other is that, I ask? I consider it infinitely more real and more beautiful to keep faith with a Western culture that produced great works of art and science, however barely-hanging-on it may be, then to latch on to the body and values of a self-absorbed little rock 'n' roll zombie in all her resplendent emptiness, thinness, soullessness, and nothingness.

Masculine Feminine is blessed, along with numerous other deficiencies, with a veritable school of red herrings swimming across the screen. For no visible reason at all, a whole sequence will echo *The Zoo Story* or *Dutchman* by way of incongruous *hommages* to Albee and, of all incompetents, LeRoi Jones. Or there will be a scene in which a stage director, Antoine Bourseiller, coaches Brigitte Bardot in a part in Jean Vauthier's *Les Prodiges*. Andrew Sarris, who (with some justification) hasn't the faintest idea of what is going on here, makes up the following interpretation: "Even Brigitte Bardot is recruited to assist in a parody of playwrights who seek to control every intonation of an actor's reading, but this sequence, like so many others, ends on a note of detached lyricism." What actually happens is that the hero, sitting in a café, sees at another table Bourseiller coaching Bardot. The advice he is giving her is perfectly sensible, if we allow for the fact that Vauthier is a dreary playwright and *Les Prodiges* a lamentable play. But, clearly, Godard admires it—as he admires *Dutchman*—and after Bourseiller's explanations, poor, stupid Bardot begins to mouth the lines as she has been instructed to do. There is no parody here, and even less "detached lyricism"—a contradiction in terms, in any case—only another boring tribute. But he would be a poor "hip" critic indeed who would allow a little simple ignorance to stand in his way.

Kael's method with these Godardian *non sequiturs* is more sophisticated: Tertullian's *credo quia absurdum*. Thus she writes: "The rhythms, and the general sense, and the emotion that builds up can carry you past what you don't understand: you don't need to understand every detail in order to experience the beauty of the work as it's going on." It is scarcely surprising that in his defense of Vauthier's dramaturgy, the critic Robert Abirached should write in much the same vein: "The word . . . no longer seeks to signify something, but only to express a feeling or situation musically. . . . Speech may be limited to a mere sonorous backdrop, intended rather to be taken note of than to be understood." But what, to return to Miss Kael, is the value—in rhythm, general sense, or emotional build-up—of having the hero sit in a café and suddenly observe a marital quarrel flare up, the wife shoot the husband, and not a soul batting an eyelash? Or having the hero riding the subway and watching fascinated as a white woman slowly prepares to shoot two Negroes she is arguing with? Of a man in a pinball parlor chasing the hero into the street with a knife, and then, without a word, disemboweling himself? All three episodes, to add to the improbability, occur within a short period of time; and not much later, a man in the street borrows the hero's matches and sets himself on fire with them, by way of political protest.

But ours, apparently, not to reason why. "An Elizabethan love song," Miss Kael informs us, "is no less beautiful because we don't catch all the words . . ." The analogy is cockeyed. In the song, the melody is surely accessible, as is the over-all meaning of the words, which is always very simple. In *Masculine Feminine,* however, there is no discernible underlying structure, and whole scenes are tossed in for the sheer hell of it; meanings are not obscured by the passage of time—they just don't exist.

Godard's adulators will stop at nothing, which is, of course, in keeping with Godard's own procedure. Thus Andrew Sarris declares: "Godard's allegedly revolutionary position is comparable to the positions of

Stravinsky, Picasso, Joyce and Eliot." About the only place where Godard's position might be comparable to that of the other four is on the toilet seat. But Godard, alas, also expels his works from that position. Typical of Sarris's godardliness (which, in style, is next to uncleanliness) is a statement such as, "Where *Breathless* achieves the suspense of poetic gratuitousness, *My Life to Live* is dictated by the logic of poetic necessity." Leaving aside that "where" for "whereas," I would wager that only Marshall McLuhan could stuff as much absurdity into one short sentence. How does gratuitousness get to be poetic? And if it is gratuitous, why should it be suspenseful? How does necessity get to be poetic? And if necessity is poetic, how come gratuitousness, its opposite, is poetic, too? And if the two extremes, gratuitousness and necessity, are both poetic, may we not safely assume that everything is poetic—or, rather, that nothing is, for by now all meaning has been syphoned out of the concept.

The fuzzy thinking and writing of the Godard enthusiast is ubiquitous in Sarris's encomia to the idol of the new sensibility. "Tragedy and comedy float in such free orbits in Godard's sensibility that we often seem to be stuck in a steady stew of tromedy. Catherine's put-down of Robert [in *Masculine Feminine*] is perhaps the most excruciatingly moving scene of a male Waterloo on the field of femaleness in all the history of dramatic and cinematic art . . ." Consider, first, the distressing diction. Why do we need the barbarism "tromedy," when we have the perfectly good word "tragicomedy"? What is a "steady stew"? Sarris is obviously trying to improve on "steady stream," which, at least, makes sense, whereas "steady stew" is either nonsense or rank pleonasm. As for "a male Waterloo on the field of femaleness," it is a superb specimen of catachresis. If we now proceed to the meaning of all this, it would appear that because Godard recklessly mingles the brutal and the facetious, which Sarris chooses to dignify with the terms "tragedy" and "comedy," he is to be credited with the invention of a new genre, "tromedy." And it further appears that a seemingly improvised scene in which a dull girl tells an oafish young man in clumsy and trivial words that she won't go out with him is not only one of the summits of cinematic art, but also one of the triumphs of world drama. This would be merely comic if it were not for the fact that such movies, and such movie criticism, are taken seriously by large numbers of viewers and readers, which makes it all rather tromic.

What the chorus of praise for Godard tends to come down to is a paean to inventiveness and manifoldness. "The most dazzlingly inventive and audacious artist in movies today," writes Pauline Kael; and John Thomas, discussing *The Married Woman* in *Film Society Review* (October, 1966), alleges that "With Godard's film . . . we are challenged to split our attention; at the same time really see, really hear, what's happening on the screen. Not only does Godard brilliantly evoke the modern world with its constant and conflicting sensory impressions, but he challenges us with the context of the film to wake up and overcome it." (It is not clear from that final "it" whether what we are supposed to overcome is the modern world or the context of Godard's film. The antecedent, I suppose, is "conflicting impressions," which would require a plural pronoun, but the decencies of rational discourse are not for the Godardians.) Thomas seems to have in mind the scene in which the heroine, in a poolside café, flips through magazines containing erotic ads, illustrations, and stories, while two girls at the neighboring table exchange dating and sex talk. Now it must be conceded that *The Married Woman,* such as it is, is Godard's best film since *Breathless,* and that this particular scene, with its schizoid editing and incompletely overheard conversation, works well enough: One gets the feeling that these girls dabbling in sex, the sleazy stuff in the magazines, and the heroine's adulterous tergiversations are all somehow connected, and part of the moral *anomie* of our world. But we cannot "really see, really hear" more than a fragment of what is going on in that scene, which is probably what Godard intended and may be just right—only it remains unclear how this challenges us to overcome anything at all. In the "context of the film" the young woman's dilemma is seen as essentially pleasurable, and, except for a very few minor inconveniences, there is no evidence that her sexual ambidexterity is anything but a happy feast for her ego.

It will surely be objected that an artist is not obliged to take a stand, and that the mere presentation of existing problems is a sufficient task. True enough, provided that the presentation is incisive, suggestive, and provocative enough. But Godard's way, even in this more successful film, is merely to sketch in the ambience: sex in the magazines, sex on the posters, sex in the chitchat at the next table—immature, exaggerated, unevaluated sex. Very good; we get the point. But how does it affect the heroine; with what aspect of her personality, formed by what experiences, does it mesh? Exactly why can't she choose? What does the lover offer her that the husband does not, and vice versa? How does the society, if it is to blame, corrupt one in a profounder sense than by posters and periodicals? Godard does not really flesh out and develop the problem; he merely sketches in its context adroitly but without much urgency. And when the characters are to reveal themselves, he resorts to *cinéma-vérité* and has the actors (apparently) improvising at great, pretentious, vacuous, and boring length, while he holds their faces in assiduous frontal close-up. (Sometimes we are not far removed from the drivel of Andy Warhol.) Granted we do not look for answers from the artist, only for enlightenment on what the issues and possibilities are; but from Godard, we get either obfuscation or oversimplification.

Rather than inventiveness and multifariousness, I would call the hallmarks of Godard irresponsibility and overreliance on the accidental. The film-maker is running off after every whimsical, extraneous notion that occurs to his undisciplined mind, while being, at the same time, tied to the apron strings of chance, which, under the honorific "improvisation," is supposed to work wonders for him. I dare say one may call the mysterious process of creation with equal right by any name: inspiration, improvisation, or for all I care, indeterminacy principle. But there is a vast difference between the distances from the center artists allow their works to wander, between the widths to which authors open their arms to embrace the unforeseen. Godard's invention does not explore so much as it rambles; his camera does not merely welcome the occasional stroke of luck—rather, having had its lens cleaned with a lucky rabbit's foot, it assumes that whatever it stumbles on will perforce be genius. Unfortunately, where anything goes, almost nothing works.

The role of chance in artistic creation, and, more particularly, in the contemporary arts, could bear serious investigation, though what the proper tools for such a study would be, and how reliable the findings, remain open questions. With reference to Godard and the modern cinema—not excluding some applicability to other arts—a few words should be said here. It is undeniable that most works of art originate in a kind of biographical or autobiographical chance, that is, in something in life happening to strike their creators' fancy; but also, as a rule, there is need for much patient and hard work. The case of the painter whose hand slips is well known: quite by accident a line or smudge is created that proves, mysteriously, right. But wooing chance from beginning to end, as in most action painting, is something else again. We can distinguish, as it were, between "accidental chance" or "chance chance" and deliberately induced or "prefabricated chance." It seems to me that, as an unsolicited auxiliary, chance can be invaluable; as a steady collaborator, it is valueless. By the latter, I mean trying to make systematic use of chance, to exploit the irregular on a regular basis. That is sheer pataphysics, which Alfred Jarry defined as the "science of imaginary solutions" that examines "the laws governing exceptions."

In the cinema, chance is improvisation, or shooting at random, which may pay off under certain circumstances. In *Masculine Feminine,* when the hero interviews a Miss Nineteen, a silly teen-age beauty contest-winner, the stag-

gering ignorance and coy stupidity of the girl, and the
pitiful way in which she tries to minimize and cope with
them, constitute a genuine stroke of luck: an obtuseness
and frivolity emerge that are almost the equal of any artist's conception of them. Even so it may be questioned
whether such an obvious patch of *cinéma-vérité* blends
smoothly enough with the palpably contrived elements of
the plot. But in a film like *The Married Woman,* where a
bunch of actors is asked to improvise on metaphysical
subjects, or in *My Life to Live,* where a third-rate
philosopher and a tenth-rate actress are expected to produce an impromptu Platonic dialogue, the results are, as
they might be presumed to be, paltry.

Of course, Godard's courting of chance takes on more
basic forms than bits of interpolated *cinéma-vérité.* "The
ideal, for me," says Godard, "is to obtain right away what
will work—and without retouches. If they are necessary, it
falls short of the mark. The immediate is chance. At the
same time it is definitive. What I want is the definitive by
chance." And he adds: "If you know in advance exactly
what you're going to do, it's no longer worth the trouble of
doing it. If a spectacle is all written out, what's the point
of filming it? What's the point of cinema if it follows
literature?" That is the great dirty word: literature.
Against it we posit "the definitive by chance." But chance
is definitive only to the uncritical mind that accepts
whatever pops up; as Godard's Lemmy Caution says in
Alphaville, "I believe in the immediate inspirations of my
consciousness." (In Peter Whitehead's English translation
of the screenplay, the French *conscience* is rendered as
"conscience"—a possible meaning, but surely not the right
one here.)

What are these "immediate inspirations" of Godard's?
They are the wish fulfillments of a childish psyche, the
dreams of glory we know from Steig's cartoons, the games
played with toy pistols and machine guns in backyards
translated verbatim onto the screen, bang-bang by bang-
bang, and ending with a whimper. In *Pierrot le fou,* when
the hero enters the heroine's apartment, a bloody corpse is

lying in it in full view; this is accepted as the most natural of occurrences, with hardly a question asked. In *Band of Outsiders,* there is an inordinately long and indescribably preposterous gun duel, which, even though it is meant as a sort of black joke, is really understandable only in terms of cap pistols. So, too, the scene in *The Little Soldier,* where the hero follows his intended victim all over Geneva, his gun practically under the noses of various bystanders, including a batch of fellow-passengers on a small boat, and no one notices anything. So Lemmy Caution can walk in on the head scientist of Alphaville and, without any opposition from anyone, calmly shoot him. And so, in *My Life to Live,* rival gangs shoot it out without anyone being hit except the heroine, who is neither the intended target nor even in the line of fire. All this, apparently, stems from Truffaut's final scene in *Shoot the Piano Player,* not very convincing or funny either, but possible once, and not to be repeated.

Alphaville is, in fact, the perfect masturbatory fantasy, in which a brutish hero, but one with intellectual pretensions, triumphs over all opposition, but opposition so bumbling that one finds oneself taking its side out of sheer compassion. In his *Studies in Words,* C. S. Lewis has warned us that "when we try to define the badness of a work, we usually end by calling it bad on the strength of characteristics which we can find also in good work." And he gives this among other caveats: "The novel before you is bad—a transparent compensatory fantasy projected by a poor, plain woman, erotically starving. Yes, but so is *Jane Eyre.*" Well, I think there is a very clear difference between *Alphaville* and *Jane Eyre.* It lies, above all, in the nature of the needs. Charlotte Brontë was starving for love, for bare, essential human love, the very minimum and, if you will, maximum to which a normal, passionate, sentient and intelligent human being is entitled to. Godard's need is to compensate, or overcompensate, for puerile, irresponsible, indeed criminal, appetites; moreover, so infantile is his craving for instant gratification that he does not even bother to present the other side of a question or to give us a sense of the difficulties that have to be overcome, or to examine how the physical and intellectual prowess of his alter ego is evolved. Such matters are brushed aside, and Lemmy Caution proceeds with unthinking brutality to triumph over almost completely supine villains. In the end, the opposition's evil takes on an arbitrary, sporadic character, whereas that of Godard's alter ego is deepseated, convincing, and the more appalling for not being recognized as such.

Here now is Richard Roud, director of the London and New York film festivals, in his introduction to the printed scenario of *Alphaville*. In discussing the "pop art aspect" of the film, he writes: "Of course, Godard, like Marker and Resnais, has been intrigued by comic strips for many years before the term pop art existed. Comic strips seem to represent many things for Godard: first, a source book for the contemporary collective subconscious; secondly, a dramatic framework derived from modern myth—in much the same way as Joyce used the Ulysses myth; thirdly, a reaction against the subtleties of the psychological novel; finally, the attraction of comic strip narrative with its sudden shifting of scene, its freedom of narration, its economy."

To begin with, there is the bad English that distinguishes the good pop critic: You will have noticed Roud's use of "intrigued." But let us proceed to the argumentation, which is supposed to justify Godard's leaning on the comic strip. "A source book for the contemporary collective subconscious . . ." I should think that if the concept of a collective sub- or unconscious has any validity at all, and non-Jungians might well have their doubts, it would have to refer to something that is perennial rather than changing from generation to generation or season to season, so that the term "contemporary collective subconscious" seems to me of little significance or use. But, in any case, why should the comic strip be more of a source book than the fiction, poetry, or painting of the day? After all, the comic strip is no more a folk art than, say, the drama: It is created by an individual who signs his name to it; it does not have the primordial quality of myths, legends, or folk ballads on which many anonymous sensibilities have worked, even as many waves shape and polish the pebbles on a beach. Roud mistakes for the collective unconscious what is merely the lowest common denominator, if that.

Now, predictably, comes the reference to myth, the fashionable guarantee of profundity. But whereas we know that Oedipus or Theseus or Medea has mythic value, because history has proved it, we may entertain some dubiety as to the mythic value of Flash Gordon, Dick Tracy, and Pogo, though they might eventually achieve it. Obviously, though, it will take centuries of universal appeal and recurrence before one can start making comparisons to the myth of Ulysses and its significance for Joyce's novel. At that, the exact degree of usefulness of the Homeric archetype for the structure of Joyce's book seems to me an open question. What most certainly must be questioned is the implied comparison between Joyce and Godard, but this technique of "gilding by association" I have already warned against.

"A reaction against the subtleties of the psychological novel"—very well, one may get tired of Proustian analyses, but does that mean that the alternative is the complete rejection of psychology? In the novel, this has led to the disasters of the *nouveau roman*; in the theatre, however, men like Beckett, Genet, and Ionesco, for example, has been able to stand psychology on its head without committing the fatal error of pretending that it does not exist. In serious fiction, a Joyce or Kafka, who has taken significant liberties with psychology, has not had the unwisdom of modeling the novel on the comic strip (though Joyce was aware of Mutt and Jeff). Reaction may be desirable, but as with everything else, it is the *quality* of the reaction that counts.

Lastly, "sudden shifting of scene," "freedom of narration," and "economy"—but one can get these very things from Shakespeare as well as from Capp or Caniff. Indeed, what is less economic than the comic strip, which goes on

forever (even past the original author's dying or getting
fed up) and continues to exploit the childishness of
human desires *ad infinitum.* Sudden shifts of scene and
freedom of narration, moreover, can easily be overdone,
and it is good to remember the aphorism of the Austrian
poet-playwright Richard Beer-Hoffmann: "All 'form'
will forever be a 'truce' with 'chaos'—whether after a
victory or a defeat can scarcely be determined." In this
precarious state of affairs, form becomes desperately precious, but Godard has indeed no more sense of its value
than do the comic strips. Concepts of Form become meaningless: to Richard Roud, *Alphaville* and *Vivre sa Vie*
represents "classic perfection"!

In *Cinema Eye, Cinema Ear,* the British critic John
Russell Taylor states the difficulty with *Le petit Soldat*:
"Is it an acute, detached study of silly, pretentious people,
or a silly, pretentious film about people its author takes to
be intelligent?" I submit that this is the problem with all of
Godard's films, and that this is not a valid Socratic
aporia: When the possibility exists that idiots are being
idolized by the author—and even when this remains only
a possibility—things are not well. But it is depressing to
watch Taylor who, at least in the case of this film, inclines
toward the second alternative, nevertheless feel obliged to
come out for the defense. What our exegete finally falls
back on is this: "Even when Godard does not consistently
succeed in what he sets out to do . . . his work is still spectacularly worth watching; at least, whatever may be wrong
with it, it is 100 per cent cinema all the way." (One wonders just what 100 per cent cinema half the way might
be?) This is a rather unconvincing defense; one could as
well argue that Faith Baldwin's or Herman Wouk's work
is 100 per cent novelistic, which it is, but that does not
make it good. The horrible misconception underlying
Godard worship is the assumption that to take all the
liberties and perform all the tricks of which no other art is
capable makes a film automatically good. Actually it
makes it only film; unless one is prepared to argue that
film, just because it is not fiction, theatre, or basket weav-

ing, is a marvel, one had better avoid this tack. And Taylor gives the show away completely when he says of *Les Carabiniers* (which almost everybody, including many Godardians, hated) that "to the sympathetically disposed it offers a uniquely stimulating and unpredictable experience," which is to say that to those who are prepared to accept Godard uncritically it provides a series of jolts that can be enshrined as part of the mystique.

It is instructive to follow Taylor's argument in favor of his preferred Godard film, *A Woman Is a Woman,* in detail. He finds in it "a situation within which the personalities of the three stars . . . can flourish undisturbed and on to which can be grafted all sorts of odd devices and ideas that take the director's fancy." In other words, the "anything goes" principle I have already referred to: total self-indulgence resulting in chaos. This makes the film "irresistible" for Taylor; it "retains throughout the gaiety and *joie de vivre* of a private joke in which all can share . . ." Why, one wonders, is a private joke such a good thing; and how, one wonders even more, can a private joke also be for everyone? The joke, it seems, is "not least, that the resources of a 'big picture'—colour, cinemascope, important stars—are being used with the greatest casualness for the production of riotously irresponsible home movies." In the first place, color is no longer the prerogative of big pictures—even Brakhage and Kenneth Anger will use it for their minuscule maunderings; in the second place, since when are Anna Karina and Jean-Claude Brialy important stars? (Belmondo is another matter.) But, above all, there is the old cultist perversity: to make a virtue out of irresponsibility, out of using big, expensive things for private jokes, home movies—there speaks your camp mentality. And what does Taylor mean by that "not least"? If this is not the least part of the joke, I still want to know what the rest of it is. But we are not told.

We are, however, told that "for all its lack of pretension" (from the foregoing, we could as easily conclude the opposite), the film "is not about nothing; it is really, as a critic in *Les Cahiers du Cinéma* very acutely observed, a documentary about Anna Karina, lightly disguised as a fiction film." Now, I ask you, who needs a documentary about a silly nonentity and rotten actress whose only hallmarks are debatable good looks and indubitable narcissism? But such is Godard's infatuation with Karina, and arrogance in assuming that his marital problems with her are of universal interest, that a "documentary" we get. And once this magic word has been invoked, both Karina's incompetence as a performer and Godard's as a film-maker can be readily justified. "This is why," we read, "Godard so often uses the worst instead of the best takes in any given scene. The takes which come off, in which nothing gets in the way of the plot's requirements, may tell us most about the character; but the worst takes—those in which the actress forgets a line or unexpectedly trips over something—tell us most about her, and that is what Godard is after."

If this is true, Godard is performing the very opposite of what I consider the artist's function to be: Instead of shaping or reshaping reality, he allows, indeed exhorts, the most trivial realities to obtrude and have their way with him. But if what Taylor says is not true, it follows that Godard simply doesn't know any better, or just does not care, which, once again, makes him the quintessential antiartist. What respect can we have for someone who is more interested in his actress-wife than in his film; in his obsession and lust, than in his art? And even if Godard did for Karina what Taylor adduces as his supreme achievement, getting "virtually all spectators to agree with her husband's estimate of her charms," what on earth has this to do with the art of the film, or even with the art of the documentary?

That Godard is obsessive, I will not deny. The way his camera anatomizes Bardot's naked body in *Contempt* (in which, by the bye, he makes her look as much as possible like Karina) while going through an endless litany, "Do you find my feet pretty?—Yes, I find them pretty," and so on up for every part is certainly obsessive. (The conclusion of the scene, when the hero declares that he loves her "totally, tenderly, tragically," as if this itemized physical approbation were tantamount to love, let alone tragedy, is downright ridiculous.) Obsessive, too, is that parody of an English lesson in *Band of Outsiders,* in which an imbecile teacher in a language school dictates during an entire class a printed and easily available passage from a French Shakespeare translation, which the students are to translate back into English by way of homework! This feeble satirical conceit is, moreover, dragged out for minutes on end; the Godardians find it the height of the hilarious, but to me it is only another example of inane, mirthless obsession. And when the three kids in one bed in *Masculine Feminine* amuse themselves by rattling off endless synonyms for (is it?) "arse," what has this finally boring scatalogue to do with anything but obsession? To be sure, all true artists are apt to be, in some way, obsessed; unfortunately, however, all the truly obsessed are not necessarily artists.

If, indeed, Godard were an artist, could he wallow in dialogue so blatantly bathetic as this, from *Contempt,* "*Ce n'est pas toi qui me force, c'est la vie*"; or this, from *Masculine Feminine,* "*Etre fidèle, c'est faire comme si le temps n'existait pas*"? And here is Godard's celebrated verbal ingenuity, again from *Masculine Feminine:* "*Dans le mot 'masculin' il y a 'masque' et il y a 'cul.'—Et dans le mot 'féminin'?—Il n'y a rien.*" Very clever that, in the word "masculine" you can find "mask" and "arse," whereas in the world feminine" there is nothing—the only trouble is that the entire film is at great pains to demonstrate that it is *women* who play games (mask) and who are ultimately good only for screwing (arse), so where is the applicability?

The key to Godard's "creation" is—I cannot reiterate it often enough—giving in to every impulse, responding to every stimulus, recording everything in sight. And this is the very thing that gets him friends and worshipers. In an age when indiscriminate thrill-seeking is the *summum bonum,* Godard epitomizes the common man with his even more common cravings. But ask yourself which great

artist became great by reflecting faithfully the yearnings of
the little man, and nothing much else?

It is, therefore, saddening to find so alert a literary
critic as A. Alvarez generally is, lumping together, in a recent essay, Jean-Luc Godard and Laurence Sterne. "What
they have in common," Alvarez writes, "is a style and an
obsession. By style I mean something beyond their
elegance and wit and detachment. Instead, it is the ability
to maintain all those qualities whilst not leaving anything
out, whilst refusing a narrow, exclusive focus." By a
curious coincidence, the hortatory passage from C. S.
Lewis that I quoted earlier continues: "Another bad book
is amorphous; but so is *Tristram Shandy.*" Which merely
indicates that there are qualitative differences even in
amorphousness. Thus Sterne would never have conceived
of making a film such as Godard has been contemplating
". . . an immense film about France. Everything would be
in it. It would last two or three days. The film would be
in episodes and each episode would be screened for a week
or two. If one were to rent a theatre for a year, it would be
feasible. Anything is possible. To show everything has always been the temptation of novelists in their big books.
I'd show people going to the movies and you'd see the film
they see. You'd see an intellectual with the job of inter-
viewing people and you'd see the interviews. We could interview everyone from Sartre to the Minister of War,
including the peasants of Chantal or workers. We'd also
see sports, racing, etc. It would have to be organized in
principle and then go in all directions."

After that, you can see that Sterne's way of "not leaving
anything out" is very different from Godard's. And
"showing everything" may indeed have been the temptation of major novelists, but what made them major is that
they resisted it. They did show a great deal—sometimes in
a little, as in Constant's *Adolphe*; sometimes in a lot, as in
War and Peace—but they also knew what to leave out,
and where, and when. When Godard leaves out things,
they are almost without exception the essentials. In the
case of *Masculine Feminine,* for instance, several interest-

ing films could have been made out of what Godard merely grazes with his camera, or relegates to a spoken footnote. Only out of what he does show could nothing be made, though even that nothing Truffaut would have made better. As for the "elegance, wit and detachment" that Alvarez sees in Godard—well, I can see enormous detachment, so much of it that the film-maker succeeds in detaching himself from most of the basic human attributes; elegance, however, I find none in Godard, and as for wit, I'll grant him half.

But to go on with Alvarez's bracketing of Sterne and Godard: "Both are delinquent to the extent of, first, being unconcerned with any preordained moral order and, second, in their seemingly delighted assumption that, beneath all the elegance, their protagonists are interested only in gratifying their momentary impulses—though without unnecessary viciousness; the wit of both is essentially gentle. In their worlds everyone, elegantly, sadly, in one way or another, is on the make." In the first place, there is plenty of cruelty in any one of Godard's films, though it is sometimes psychological; when it is physical, it is often presented so childishly that it can be mistaken for mere play. Once again, I do not see where the elegance comes in among all these juvenile delinquents, punks, prostitutes, pop singers, bumpkins, loafers, strippers, and petty criminals. But about unconcern with moral order and everyone being on the make Alvarez is certainly right—as far as Godard is concerned, anyhow. Even more to the point is his stressing the delight in this amorality. Indeed, and this is most revealing, from the way Alvarez uses the word "delinquent" (the essay, printed in the Winter 1966-67 issue of *The Hudson Review,* is entitled "The Delinquent Aesthetic"), it emerges that it is, in fact, a term of praise. Praise of delinquency, that is what Godard's films are—moral as well as aesthetic delinquency, the putting together of the film being, on the whole, as untidy as its point of view. But if you feel, as I do, that the locus of art is the point of intersection of three lines of pursuit—the aesthetic, the intellectual, and, in the loosest sense of the word, the moral—you will find Godard's work far removed from that point, in short, quite beside the point.

There is, however, something even more dispiriting than man's lack of ethics, aesthetics, or thought that these films appeal to: his inability to see, his inability to use his senses, his stupidity. *"Etre sage, c'est voir, c'est vraiment voir,"* says Godard's mouthpiece in *Masculine Feminine,* and it is at least a valid half-truth. Modern youth is losing its ability to see and hear, let alone taste, smell, and touch. The basic sound is the roar of the discothèque, the basic sight is the vacant stare of the doped-up, transistorized television watcher. Consequently, the only way to see is not to look out into the world, but in, into TV, movies, happenings, psychedelic projections. One sees only what the movie-maker, for example, shows one. A tree in nature is of no interest; but let there be a tree in a Godard movie, and our youth is ecstatic, "Look! A tree!" It begins to appear as if only Godard could make a tree. Under the circumstances, because Godard puts so much brute sight and sound into his films, he gives the new blind, the new deaf their only seeing and hearing. And that, I submit, is truly dreadful.

There is a particularly preposterous gimmick in *Band of Outsiders* of the kind I have heard referred to as "intellectual games." And why not? Godard obviously considers himself an intellectual: You will have noticed how in that statement about his "immense film" he spoke of "an intellectual" going out to interview people, only to switch pronouns, very sneakily, in the next sentence: "We'd interview everyone . . ." We, you see: we intellectuals. Anyway, in *Band of Outsiders* there is a scene in which Franz, the intellectual hero named (naturally) after Kafka, says, "Since nobody has anything to say, we could perhaps have a minute of silence." And, promptly, there is a minute of silence and immobility. The idea is excellent: Since Godard's films have nothing to say, we could perhaps have ninety minutes of silence instead of each of them.

EIGHT

SPOTLIGHT ON THE NONWOMAN

The lines outside Jeanne Moreau's currently showing films give one pause—and not only literally, on the sidewalk, trying to get past them. For some time now, Miss Moreau has been seen only in poor or mediocre movies, but her popularity, as the pullulating magazine articles about her bear out, is enormous. Yet she is not what the public might consider a glamor girl, a sex goddess or kitten; she is not even in the prime of youth. But there is something very important that she has in abundance: femininity.

Unhappily, the image of femininity conveyed by American actresses is not feminine at all. Indeed, there is much in it to put a man off women altogether. Today's American actresses fall mainly into two categories, to be labeled (with slight exaggeration) freaks and sticks. In other words, those who in some way deflect, travesty, or blatantly overstate their womanliness and sensuality; and those who suppress it, or have nothing to suppress.

Hollywood has tended to specialize in the exaggerated female of the Mae West, Jane Russell, Jayne Mansfield variety—femininity grossly caricatured (Mae West) or simply inflated to the point of absurdity (Russell, Mans-

field). Of course, Hollywood is shrewd enough to use
such types generally not in their pure form, but more or
less toned down to emerge as Ava Gardner, Joan
Crawford, or Betty Grable; or, speaking more con-
temporaneously, as Carroll Baker, Ann-Margret, or
Elizabeth Taylor. Now the trouble with someone like Carroll Baker or Natalie Wood is that she does not possess
the physical endowments that she is obliged—or feels
obliged—to deliver, and that her sexual posturings are
belied by what is there (or, more precisely, isn't there), so
as to make for desperate overcompensation, giving the actress often a shrill, maniacal quality. With Miss Taylor, as
it was with Marilyn Monroe, the problem is different.
Here the physical voluptuousness is copiously present, but
there is a lack of acting ability or emotional maturity most
readily noticeable in the voice, which remains commonplace, childish, and distinguished only by its lack of
range and variety. The result is that, both consciously and
unconsciously, such an actress is forced to capitalize on
her looks and—as, for example, in *Cleopatra* or *Some
Like it Hot*—enhance them to the point of distortion and,
ultimately, ridiculousness.

However, when overdeveloped femininity is juxtaposed
with underdeveloped acting ability (and this is true of
most Hollywood actresses), an oppressive discrepancy appears. Overblown desirability is being waved at us without
the support of any real, rounded humanity, or the convincing enactment of it, so that this floating, unintegrated sexuality strikes us rather as would lipstick on a skull or a
padded bikini on a telegraph pole. For heightened sexuality and diminished personality do not go together:
They either cancel each other out or produce some kind of
travesty.

To be sure, attempts are always being made to invest
the sex goddesses with acting talents made out of whole
cloth—or very little cloth and much publicity. Thus
histrionic gifts have been attributed to Marilyn Monroe,
Elizabeth Taylor—even to Sue Lyon and Tuesday
Weld—which, under scrutiny, prove to be minimal at best.

With judicious casting and resourceful direction, such stars can be used effectively. But the danger is always great that the precarious balance will be upset, and the actress revealed in something worse than fleshly nudity: naked technical and spiritual poverty, on top of which all the most sumptuous erotic panoply can produce only an alienation effect of, alas, the undesirable sort.

More troubling, though, are the attempts to turn pubescence into an object of sexuality. In recent times Hollywood has come out with a slew of actresses like Ann-Margret, Sue Lyon, Tuesday Weld, Sandra Dee, Pamela Tiffin, Susan Strasberg, whose attraction lay in the fact that they were or seemed to be under age. Such a girl might have the body of a woman and the face of a child, or a wholly infantile quality punctured by random hints of nubility; in either case, she was meant to have the lure of the forbidden: to stimulate unholy curiosity about the debauched, or debauchable, child.

But surely the worst offense is the attempt to palm off total lack of femininity, to pass off anti- or nonsexuality as charming, healthy, and admirable. The classic example of this is Doris Day—or, at any rate, Miss Day's screen persona—which is meant to be a cross between the sweet young thing as incarnated some years ago by June Allyson and Jeanne Crain, and the tough, wisecracking dame as she used to be embodied in Eve Arden or Ann Sothern. It is noteworthy that the Allyson-Crain type was made only for chaste kisses on a porch in Indiana or on the campus of some papier-mâché college, whereas the Arden-Sothern type was basically too weather-beaten, disillusioned, and acerbic for any joyous sexuality. The one was presexual, the other postsexual; both were depressing.

The crossbreeding of the two types naturally yielded something even less inviting. It is the chaste wife whose chastity seems to fend off even her husband; the tailored girl whose quick wit gets her out of all physical encounters, which, apparently, she would find distasteful anyhow. It is, above all, the pleasingly but aseptically dressed-up doll, the manikin with the imperturbable cotton-candy coiffure, whose hair, clothes, and smugness stay unruffled by narrow escapes, until she ends up tastefully and sexlessly married to Mr. Right. He was, only a reel or two ago, the snarlingest of wolves, but is now cozily redeemed, or castrated, by our heroine. The horror of this is that Doris Day remains, year after year, the top box-office attraction—and if she were to be displaced, it would no doubt be by Audrey Hepburn—which suggests that any hope of raising the standard is perfectly idle.

Broadway, too, has contributed its types of the unwomanly actress. As might be expected, the distortion is apt to be of a subtler or more sophisticated sort than in Hollywood; in some cases, however, it is more daringly pronounced. There are the red-hot mamas and hypertrophic flappers of the Ethel Merman-Carol Channing ilk; the Bronx-Brooklyn viragos *à la* Anne Bancroft; the automata for dispensing of disingenuous, dehumanized warmth, like Mary Martin; the thoroughly mannish women, like Elaine Stritch; and the androgynous selfgratifiers, like Barbra Streisand; or the larger-than-life-size pastiches—nether divinities of "camp"—like Tallulah Bankhead.

But the original creation and proto-typical nonfemale of Broadway is the Actors Studio actress, very possibly the most discouraging, because the most influential, of the phenomena under discussion. This is the female counterpart of Marlon Brando, Paul Newman, and Ben Gazzara. But while these actors attempt to heighten their manliness, however misguidedly or even suspiciously, the Actors Studio actresses have systematically diminished and uprooted their womanliness. Though there are a good many egregious representatives of the type, such as Barbara Baxley, Shelley Winters, Joanne Woodward, and Maureen Stapleton, the prototype would be a composite of Julie Harris, Geraldine Page, and Kim Stanley. In all cases the strategy is in some way to sidestep attractive womanhood.

Thus Julie Harris refuses to grow up. Though old enough to portray youngish mothers, Miss Harris still plays adolescents or retarded young women with all their childish characteristics painstakingly preserved. Among her most recent roles are Ophelia, Baby June in *Marathon '33*, the infantile heroine of *Ready When You Are, C. B.!*, and, in summer stock, the young waif in *The Hostage*. Everything about Miss Harris, from her gawky movements to her voice strained through a lollipop, is an attempt to connect the first childhood seamlessly with the second.

Geraldine Page, on the other hand, has turned woman into one big flutter. She is the perennial Tennessee Williams heroine—an epicene figure, the self-portrait of the author as a not so young woman—even when she is not playing Williams: her speech trailing off into ghostly shreds and laughter, her arms bits of burlap in the wind, her movements either pained, shrinking, or hysterical overcompensation—overshooting or undershooting the feminine. When Miss Page recently attempted to play a simple, lively, droll woman in *P.S. I Love You,* the result was grotesque and pathetic.

Kim Stanley is to William Inge what Miss Page is to Williams—the typical heroine of another playwright who does not appreciate women as women. From auspicious beginnings, Miss Stanley has come to the point where her voice is a coyly adenoidal, pause-infested quaver, her gestures a ballet of tics, and her body a flaccid zeppelin quite unbecoming of a profession in which aesthetic standards matter. The image Miss Stanley has lately conveyed is of a woman who must make herself as uncouth as possible lest—heaven forfend—she is taken for a sexual object.

Thus we are confronted with a type of actress who strains to fall short and remain *this side* of womanhood, or deflect herself into something stagnant and wasted *alongside* womanhood, or spread into something bloated and garish *beyond* womanhood. It is disheartening to see how many younger actresses are ready to take over where the reigning trio leaves off—if it ever does. Barbara Cook, Sandy Dennis, Zohra Lampert, Shirley Knight, Elizabeth Ashley, Piper Laurie, Joan Hackett, Kathleen Widdoes,

Ellen Holly, and many others are standing by.

Yet it is not as if Broadway and Hollywood could not produce delightfully feminine actresses with genuine charm and grace, who have, in the last years, provided oases in one's theatre- and moviegoing. And one does not even have to count such welcome additions from abroad as Deborah Kerr, Vivien Leigh, or Sophia Loren. Consider Patricia Neal, Lee Grant, Janice Rule, Pat Stanley, Jane Fonda, Lee Remick, or, going back a little, Margaret Sullavan, Evelyn Keyes, Lynn Fontanne, Neva Patterson. Where is there today a star as shimmeringly many-faceted as Carole Lombard used to be, or as rousingly tomboyish as Katharine Hepburn was without ever becoming antisexual?

What has brought about the present state of affairs? The causes are so numerous and involved that I can do scarcely more than mention some of them. On Broadway, the problem is, chiefly, the enshrinement of neurosis. As Method acting has capitalized on quirks, tics, inchoate sounds, and sundry dredgings of the subconscious, what was meant to be a quest for primeval humanity has led to the emphasizing and hallowing of that which in the balanced personality has been sublimated or controlled: what is suited to derangement or moments of stress was gradually enthroned as the norm. As a result, women (and men) with emotional disturbances have become the pattern for Broadway, and actresses must either possess aberrancies, or develop them, to succeed. But there are also the conditions of Broadway: the cutthroat competition in a theatre that does not properly train and screen people, where the supply of qualified, semiqualified, and unqualified actors is inordinate, repertory almost nonexistent, ephemeral plays disappear overnight and the toast of today is jobless for months, perhaps years, to come.

Since training is inadequate, and for the kind of plays usually produced not even desirable, employment depends, maddeningly, not on technical expertise, but on type-casting or on being a "new face." New faces, however, are rapidly superseded by newer faces, and even dependable types, in a restlessly shifting society, soon become obsolete. Such insecure conditions are just what it takes to bring out the latent hysteria in woman.

In Hollywood the problem is different. Here the need is to compete with the avalanche of completely womanly and often very talented European and Oriental actresses while still adhering to certain atavistic concepts of what constitutes a "star"; the difficulty, in short, of creating a woman out of the corporate notions of womanhood harbored by producers, directors, talent scouts, press agents, the box office, and whatever other cooks join in to spoil the broth. Just as the Hollywood films produced on a corporate basis end up as artistic failures; so the film "personalities" concocted according to formulas by corporate enterprise turn into exaggerations, grotesques or clichés. A Jeanne Moreau would not be possible in Hollywood. In her American-made pictures she is incomparably less fetching and profound than in her European movies. The same is true of any other vitally feminine European actress, from Danielle Darrieux to Ingrid Thulin, from Anna Magnani to Sophia Loren.

The matter is of considerable importance. For it is on our actresses that young women model themselves to a large extent, and the sexual health of our society could benefit appreciably from saner models. Of course, a sociologist or psychologist could examine the problem in terms of what has happened to the American woman in general, which in turn might lead to the question of what has happened to the American man. I do not feel qualified to indulge in this tracking down of what the American female has made of the American male, or vice versa—which comes first, the chicken or the rooster?—to grapple, in other words, with the psychic or sexual difficulties of America. But a way must be found to hire some talented yet feminine young women, to interfere with them only to the extent of teaching them diction, deportment, and other basic disciplines, and to enable them to act in decent plays and films. It might catch on—if for no other reason, for its very novelty.

INDEX